IBM Rational Team Concert 2 Essentials

Improve team productivity with Integrated Processes, Planning, and Collaboration using Team Concert Enterprise Edition

Suresh Krishna

TC Fenstermaker

BIRMINGHAM - MUMBAI

IBM Rational Team Concert 2 Essentials

First published: February 2011

Production Reference: 1020211

Published by Packt Publishing Ltd.
32 Lincoln Road
Olton
Birmingham, B27 6PA, UK.

ISBN 978-1-849681-60-5

www.packtpub.com

Cover Image by Fillipo (filosarti@tiscali.it)

Credits

About the Authors

Suresh Krishna is a Software Engineer with over 11 years of experience in building SDKs, IDEs, and RCP applications. He has extensive experience in applying object-oriented concepts to solve industry problems. He has led several projects as a software developer, technology manager, and as an architect. He has worked in the Automotive, Internet, and Utility industries helping customers to bridge the gap between technology and business domains.

Suresh is an avid blogger on technology and life. He contributes several tutorials on latest technologies, products, Agile methodologies, and product management. In his free time, he captures the fine moments of nature with his photography. He has a Computer Science degree from CUSAT, India and is currently pursuing an MBA in Entrepreneurship from the University of California, Davis.

You can find his website at `http://sureshkrishna.com`.

Acknowledgement

This book would not have seen the light without constant encouragement of my parents, sisters, wife, and daughter. A very special thanks to my wife Vidya and daughter Saahithi for their boundless patience and support. In spite of many instances that I was not available to them for many household duties, they provided all the encouragement that they could.

Over many years, many people have indirectly contributed to the content of this book. Martin Lunt, Peter Kirschner, Sri Guha V, and Jyothi G S from Robert Bosch were my mentors for several years. I would not be the same person as I am now without these wonderful and sweet personalities. My sincere thanks to Amey Kanse, Susmita Panda, and Vishal Bodwani from Packt Publishing, who successfully guided me and my co-author during writing of this book. For a first-time author, all of them gave a huge support and hand-holding when needed.

Erich Gamma, Christophe Elek, Seth Packham, and many others from IBM and Jazz team who have provided timely help on many topics when needed. As a reviewer, Thomas Starz did a fantastic job of asking tough questions and making sure that the content is valuable for the reader. Finally, Trebor, my co-author has been very supportive and helpful when I was juggling with time and personal priorities.

TC Fenstermaker is a Software Engineer with over 20 years of experience building n-tiered OLTP applications for a variety of business and government endeavors. He has experience with various Java technologies, relational databases, and software engineering practices. He is the co-author of several IBM developerWorks articles, including *Using Eclipse Ganymede to develop for the desktop, Web and mobile devices*, which he wrote with Suresh.

My sincere thanks to the team at Packt Publishing for this opportunity to experience co-authoring a technical book with a talented and enthusiastic software engineer like Suresh; and of course my thanks to Suresh for his extensive efforts in researching, drafting, and putting together this work, in which I merely assisted.

About the Reviewers

Thomas Starz has more than 25 years of experience as a software developer, technical writer, team leader, and Agile coach with IBM Software Group in Böeblingen, Germany. Thomas was among the early adopters of Agile methods in his organization. He is a Certified Scrum Master and an enthusiastic user of Rational Team Concert. While working as a mentor and coach, he has also helped several teams get started with Rational Team Concert.

Geetu Garg Berry has a total experience of five years in IT. She has come across excellent opportunities and projects, which helped her gain extensive technical knowledge.

Her experience involves working mainly with Java, J2EE technologies, and related tools.

She also has various certifications to her credit, including Sun Certified Java Programmer (1.4), Sun Certified Mobile Application Developer (SCMAD), IBM Certified Associate Developer, and IBM Certified SOA Associate.

At present, she is working on extending the Rational Team Concert tool and customizing it for business clients.

> I would like to thank my current employer for encouraging me to pursue this book review as my personal interest.

www.PacktPub.com

Support files, eBooks, discount offers and more

You might want to visit www.PacktPub.com for support files and downloads related to your book.

Did you know that Packt offers eBook versions of every book published, with PDF and ePub files available? You can upgrade to the eBook version at www.PacktPub.com and as a print book customer, you are entitled to a discount on the eBook copy. Get in touch with us at service@packtpub.com for more details.

At www.PacktPub.com, you can also read a collection of free technical articles, sign up for a range of free newsletters and receive exclusive discounts and offers on Packt books and eBooks.

http://PacktLib.PacktPub.com

Do you need instant solutions to your IT questions? PacktLib is Packt's online digital book library. Here, you can access, read and search across Packt's entire library of books.

Why Subscribe?

- Fully searchable across every book published by Packt
- Copy & paste, print and bookmark content
- On demand and accessible via web browser

Free Access for Packt account holders

If you have an account with Packt at www.PacktPub.com, you can use this to access PacktLib today and view nine entirely free books. Simply use your login credentials for immediate access.

Instant Updates on New Packt Books

Get notified! Find out when new books are published by following @PacktEnterprise on Twitter, or the *Packt Enterprise* Facebook page.

Table of Contents

Preface

Software development is a collaborative effort needing active and timely input and response from all its members. Every day, project managers face ever-increasing pressures to produce high-quality software with increasing constraints. With IBM's Rational Team Concert collaborative software delivery environment, you can tremendously improve the productivity of your entire team through a web-based user interface, continuous builds, a customizable process with work support, team support, integration, and many more features.

What this book covers

Chapter 1, Beginning with IBM RTC, introduces you to several software development challenges such as technology advances, distributed teams, collaboration, and software processes. You will also have a bird's-eye view of the Rational Team Concert and Jazz platform.

Chapter 2, Installing RTC and WebSphere, looks at various offerings from Rational Team Concert. We will download the Rational Team Concert Enterprise Edition and configure it on the WebSphere application server. This chapter also gives a basic introduction to using the Eclipse Client as well as navigate through the JUnit Example from Sandbox.

Chapter 3, Setting up the Project, introduces the Book Manager Application that will be used throughout this book. We will also get an in-depth knowledge of the architecture and functionality of the application as well as import, set up, build, and run the Book Manager Application in Rational Team Concert.

In *Chapter 4, Team and Source Control,* we will see how Rational Team Concert enhances the source control management experience by giving the power to the development team. We will also explore different concepts in the Team Source Control and then move on to see how to work with the Rational Team Source Control.

Chapter 5, Team Collaboration and Work Items, introduces how Rational Team Concert takes care of some important collaboration challenges. We get an in-depth working knowledge on Mail Configuration, Instant Messaging, and Feeds in the Collaboration space. Using the Book Manager Application, we will explore several important aspects of Work Items and Dashboards.

In *Chapter 6, Development Process and Release Planning,* we will explore various aspects of software development process and release planning and management. For the software development process, we will be introduced to the software process templates, configuring the templates, and team roles and from Release Planning, we will get an overview of iterations, sprints, backlogs, and tracking releases.

In *Chapter 7, Build Management,* we will see an overview of the build engine, build toolkit, how to define the build, and track the progress from the Eclipse and Web client. In the process, we will set up the build engine and track the Book Manager Project's builds from the perspective of a developer and build user.

In *Chapter 8, Extending RTC,* we will see the Jazz extension architecture and explore various ways to extend Rational Team Concert. We will set up the SDK for extension development and then take a quick peek into the client and server extensions.

In *Appendix A, Quick Reference,* we will see several frequently used terms in the context of Jazz and Rational Team Concert.

In *Appendix B, Installing the Express-C Edition with the Tomcat Server,* we will install the Express-C edition on the Tomcat server. We will also start the server and configure the Jazz server.

In *Appendix C, The BookManager Application Architecture,* we will see the BookManager technical architecture that uses JEE technologies such as JSPs, servlets, Struts, and Hibernate. We will also look into the BookManager Application's functionality.

In *Appendix D, What's New in RTC v3.0,* we will see an overview of new features in the latest release of Rational Team Concert. A JUnit project example will be used to explore the various new features.

What you need for this book

The following software products are needed for this book:

- Windows XP/Vista/ 7
- RTC Express-C Installation 2.2.0.2 (for Chapter 8 and Appendix B) and RTC Enterprise Installation 2.2.0.2 (for chapters 2 to 7)
  - ° `https://jazz.net/downloads/rational-team-concert/`
    `releases/2.0.0.2iFix3`
- WebSphere Installation
  - ° `http://www-01.ibm.com/software/webservers/appserv/`
    `was/`
- Tomcat Server (to test the BookManager Application)

Who this book is for

If you are a Project Manager or Team Member who would like to find an integrated approach to deal with modern software development challenges, this book is for you. Or, if you are someone who likes to stay one step ahead in team management, then this Essentials Guide is also for you.

Conventions

In this book, you will find a number of styles of text that distinguish between different kinds of information. Here are some examples of these styles, and an explanation of their meaning.

Code words in text are shown as follows: "This file is available in the `<jazzWSRoot>\ conf\jazz` directory."

A block of code is set as follows:

```
<oslc_cm:cmServiceProviders
  rdf:resource="
  https://localhost:9443/jazz/oslc/workitems/catalog"/>
```

Any command-line input or output is written as follows:

```
>jbe -createPasswordFile buildPass.txt
```

New terms and **important words** are shown in bold. Words that you see on the screen, in menus or dialog boxes for example, appear in the text like this: "Click **Apply** to save the configuration".

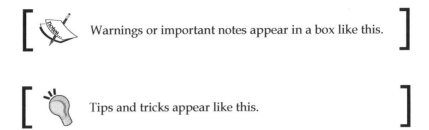

Warnings or important notes appear in a box like this.

Tips and tricks appear like this.

Reader feedback

Feedback from our readers is always welcome. Let us know what you think about this book—what you liked or may have disliked. Reader feedback is important for us to develop titles that you really get the most out of.

To send us general feedback, simply send an e-mail to feedback@packtpub.com, and mention the book title via the subject of your message.

If there is a book that you need and would like to see us publish, please send us a note in the **SUGGEST A TITLE** form on www.packtpub.com or e-mail suggest@packtpub.com.

If there is a topic that you have expertise in and you are interested in either writing or contributing to a book, see our author guide on www.packtpub.com/authors.

Customer support

Now that you are the proud owner of a Packt book, we have a number of things to help you to get the most from your purchase.

Downloading the example code for this book

You can download the example code files for all Packt books you have purchased from your account at http://www.PacktPub.com. If you purchased this book elsewhere, you can visit http://www.PacktPub.com/support and register to have the files e-mailed directly to you.

Errata

Although we have taken every care to ensure the accuracy of our content, mistakes do happen. If you find a mistake in one of our books—maybe a mistake in the text or the code—we would be grateful if you would report this to us. By doing so, you can save other readers from frustration and help us improve subsequent versions of this book. If you find any errata, please report them by visiting http://www.packtpub.com/support, selecting your book, clicking on the **errata submission form** link, and entering the details of your errata. Once your errata are verified, your submission will be accepted and the errata will be uploaded on our website, or added to any list of existing errata, under the Errata section of that title. Any existing errata can be viewed by selecting your title from http://www.packtpub.com/support.

Piracy

Piracy of copyright material on the Internet is an ongoing problem across all media. At Packt, we take the protection of our copyright and licenses very seriously. If you come across any illegal copies of our works, in any form, on the Internet, please provide us with the location address or website name immediately so that we can pursue a remedy.

Please contact us at copyright@packtpub.com with a link to the suspected pirated material.

We appreciate your help in protecting our authors, and our ability to bring you valuable content.

Questions

You can contact us at questions@packtpub.com if you are having a problem with any aspect of the book, and we will do our best to address it.

1
Beginning with IBM RTC

Software development is technical activity conducted by human beings

- Niklaus Wirth

This chapter introduces you to the bird eye view of IBM's Jazz platform and **Rational Team Concert (RTC)**.

First, we will look at some different challenges in modern software development such as technology advances, distributed teams, collaboration, and software processes. These challenges will help us understand the nature of the complexity and set the context for the need of the Jazz platform and Rational Team Concert.

Later part of the chapter gives an introduction to the Jazz platform and Rational Team Concert. **Jazz** is the software development platform that brings the phases of software development together. The Jazz platform focuses on the collaboration, productivity, and transparency in the team.

Finally, you will be introduced to Rational Team Concert and an overview of various features such as process awareness, team awareness, work items, source control, agile planning, continuous builds, project health, and project administration. We will briefly look at other Jazz-based products and their functionality.

In this chapter, we will look at the following:

- A discussion on software development challenges
- Why is Rational Team Concert built on Eclipse?
- Introduction to Jazz platform and Architecture
- Bird's eye view of Rational Team Concert
- An overview of other Jazz-based products

Software development challenges

With decades of software engineering and software development advances, we have learned techniques and methods to improve the software productivity and customer satisfaction. However, every day we push the bar to a new limit and software development organizations are faced with the challenge of catching up with the ever increasing expectations from customers.

The hardware costs are steadily declining and the software is growing in complexity day-by-day. Yet, customers are baffled by the fact that the software is slow even on faster machines. With the increasing restrictions on costs, resources, and time, software vendors identify the improvement areas. Thereby, software vendors want to increase the productivity by filling the gaps and adopting efficient processes, methods, and tools. Therefore, the next important question is "What are the crucial software development challenges"?

Today, several software development projects are faced with similar challenges, primarily focused on the distributed teams and collaboration. Major categories of the challenges include but are not limited to the following:

- Teams are **globally** spread out
- **Cultural** differences make it difficult to **communicate** effectively
- Difficulty in **coordination** with Global Teams
- Fast paced **technology** paradigms
- Customized **development practices** in teams

In the following sections, we will see the distributed teams, collaboration, and team management aspects of software development in detail.

Distributed teams

Increasing globalization has brought a few changes in the software development industry. One of them is "off shoring" either part of the system or whole modules. Off shoring is chosen for obvious reasons such as business cost effectiveness, availability of talent pool, and other strategic reasons. Off shoring has led to global software development teams with members from at least two geographical regions collaborating on the same project.

Software Professionals must adapt to the new reality of offshore outsourcing.

-- Bertrand Meyer, ETH Zurich

A team based on the same culture often has many common things to share and communicate informally compared to the teams spanning multiple cultures. Time zone difference, geographical distance, language, and cultural barriers create more information and psychological gaps in the project.

The co-located teams have the advantage that they have a line of sight, which helps them have informal discussions and thereby understand each other well. In the case of the geographically distributed teams, there is a possibility of misunderstanding created by communication. The tone of the language, and the choice of the words used in written or verbal communication, largely depend on the culture that one belongs to.

In practice, team members get information necessary to perform their tasks largely from peers, as opposed to formal, documented sources. To be able to tap this social resource, team members need to build social capital, meaning that they need to establish trust relationships with their peers.

This process of building trust does not occur so readily in a globally distributed team, sometimes leading to problems in the collaboration process. Informal collaboration tools, coupled with appropriate management practices, are an important part of the solution.

Collaboration

The act of working jointly in a co-operative manner to achieve a piece of a task is **collaboration** and it can happen in a formal or informal way. In the formal way of collaboration, typically the project manager or team leader assigns a "contact person" for any kind of questions or issues to answer. In the informal way of collaboration, team members work together at lunch or over a cup of coffee.

> *No matter what the problem is, it's always a people problem.*
>
> *- Gerald M. Weinberg*

The proliferation of several technological advancements such as Web 2.0, Service Oriented Architecture, Mashups, Software as a Service, Cloud Computing, and many others made teams depend on each other for expertise and carry out the knowledge management in a collaborative manner.

Due to the nature of the cultures and backgrounds, formal or/and the informal way of communication is preferred one over the other. Convergence of the collaboration tools into the software development tool was needed to solve the collaboration problems. Collaboration tools offer much more than the basic communication channels provided by e-mail and telephones. These tools can make team members aware of each other. After team members are aware of each other, they are then able to communicate and work together to achieve common goals.

Collaboration is supported through tools that allow communication, knowledge sharing, and analysis. Tools such as blogs, Wikis, bulletin boards, and instant messaging clients are a few collaborative tools used now. An interesting side effect of informal knowledge sharing tools, such as blogs and Wikis, is that they increase awareness. When people read blogs, they can learn more about the authors and their interests. In this way, even if two people are in a totally different geographical area, they may know a lot of each other from the social collaboration and communication tools.

Project management

With the global teams in place, pressure to achieve higher team productivity makes team management even more challenging.

Team addition

When a member joins the team, he should be introduced to the project technology, development environments, given proper access rights to the tools, and so on. The team member is forced to learn several tools, processes, and techniques in a fast paced environment unless he comes from a similar environment.

Task assignment and scheduling

Once the project is broken in to smaller chunks, they should be scheduled to meet the release schedule. The team manager should be sensitive about the geographically distributed teams with different vacation times, holiday times, or anything that affects schedule. In such situation, the communication between the team manager and team member becomes the bottleneck for the success of the project.

The team manager should have efficient tools for task assignment and task scheduling. The challenge is multidimensional where a single module's team is spread across the geography. In such case, the team within should co-ordinate to achieve their tasks and must find an efficient way to communicate.

Task assignment and scheduling includes the following:

- Tasks dependency analysis
- Determining the amount of slack
- Dealing with uncertainties
- Tolerances in estimation

Project tracking

Defining the requirements, designing smaller chunks of tasks, and scheduling the tasks does not yield the project success without tracking the project. Project tracking should make it visible about who is doing what, tasks in progress, whether there's any slack, whether there are any problems, whether anyone needs help, and team-member efficiency. A burn-down chart will also help to get an idea of the work left to do versus time. In Agile development, a burn-down chart is a graphical representation of work left to do versus time.

Build, test, and release

Once requirements are coded for the functionality, they must be integrated to verify and validate. Any issues in the build should be immediately notified to the team and corrective action should be taken. In the modern software development, it is not uncommon to track the software stability with nightly builds.

Many projects follow the practice of writing unit tests and sometimes automated tests are embedded during the build process. Considering that developers covered all the functionality with the unit test cases, a build gives a considerable confidence about the product. Then, the **Quality Assurance** (**QA**) team can do the functional testing.

Depending on the project and team, one may have different release time frames. Some projects have relatively shorter release cycles (for example, 2-4 weeks) and some have longer release cycles (every six months or even longer than one year). In either case, it is important to communicate the importance of the releases and schedule to the entire team.

Transparency

In the global or distributed team setting, it is very easy to misunderstand and misrepresent the communication. Project updates not happening on an open platform leads to team members feeling insecure and mistrusted. Or even worse when you come to know about something after the fact.

Transparency increases the team member's confidence and trust.

Choosing the tools in a way to make the requirements, task estimates, task schedule, work progress, project tracking, project health, build results, release schedule, and project announcements transparent is crucial to gain the trust and confidence of the team. Each one contributes to the complexity of the software being developed.

The following table summarizes the challenges in the software development with respect to each stakeholder:

Software development challenges	
Team member	<ul><li>What tools should I use?</li><li>How should I get the access rights?</li><li>Who should I approach for the project plan?</li><li>Who are my colleagues and what are they responsible for?</li><li>What's happening in my team?</li><li>Should I get the code reviewed by someone? If yes, who is it?</li><li>The process documents are too large. I don't have time to read those documents.</li><li>I need to back up my current changes as I have to work on a higher priority task. Context switching is complex.</li><li>I want to know which team members are online and discuss things with them.</li><li>I can plan better if I know the release schedule. I always have to ask my project manager for the release schedule as it's not published.</li><li>If a build failure is due to my code changes, I would like to know first and fix it.</li><li>I want to know my pending tasks and completed tasks.</li><li>Something went wrong in the build. How can I know all the change sets from past one week?</li><li>I have a customer bug. Can I trace between the code and issue and vice versa?</li></ul>

Software development challenges	
Project manager	• Global or distributed team's availability should be known.
	• Scheduling and assignment of tasks must consider the global work days.
	• Work in progress for all the team members should be available.
	• Not sure if we will be able to meet the schedule. An indicated risk is valuable.
	• Depending on the team's load, the tasks should be assigned or reassigned. Therefore, I should know each member's work load.
	• Unit tests and successful build gives confidence on the existing functionality.
	• It is necessary to know the changes between last and current build in an integrated way with requirements and test cases.
	• Project updates should be propagated to the whole team, even if they are in different time zone.
	• Making updates to the project plan is tedious and cost me a lot of time.
	• I need to do a high level presentation to my manager. How can I get the project overview?
	• All the design discussions should be tracked and recorded. Is there a simple way to do it?
	• I want to know whenever a high severity task is raised on this project categorized by the QA team or external customer.
	• This process is very specialized and customized. How can I help the new team member to follow the process effortlessly?
	• My team should concentrate on the productivity rather than spending time on issues tracking, documenting, communicating, and building the software.
	• Can I give role-based access to the development and QA team?
	• It is very crucial to know the time taken to resolve the external issues. I want to categorize the bugs and track them.
QA team	• Is there a way to know the release schedule?
	• Is there a way to know the build schedule?
	• If there is a problem with a module, who should I contact?
	• I want to know the stability of the code. Is there a way to check this?
	• Even if I am not given all the access rights, I need to at least have the overview of the project progress.
External stakeholder	• I need to get an overview of the project progress.
	• I want to see special reports (such as burn-down chart) based on the current state.

Depending on the organization, geographical location, and technology area, the challenges could be multidimensional. Two projects may not have the same situations and constraints. However, they may have very similar challenges of collaboration and distributed teams in project management. All the mentioned problems in the table can be summarized as follows:

- A team member inception must be easy
- Team members do not want to deal with the process overheads
- Team members need process transparency
- Version control systems must know and understand issues
- Task switching must be easy
- Management needs a crisp overview of project available 24/7
- Tracking of requirements and tasks must be easy
- Replanning must be lightweight and easy
- Team communication must be easy — without overheads
- Development, QA, and management teams must have access to project status
- QA must have access to release schedules and any impediments
- Stakeholders must have a controlled access to the project status reports

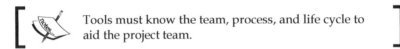 Tools must know the team, process, and life cycle to aid the project team.

Going the Eclipse way

Why should we discuss the "Eclipse way" in the chapter serving as an introduction to Jazz and Rational Team Concert.

Eclipse is a software development environment comprising an **Integrated Development Environment** (**IDE**) and an extensible plug-in system. Initially it was perceived as a Java IDE, a **Rich Client Platform** (**RCP**), and a Tool Integration Platform. However, in time Eclipse transformed as an eco-system of platform, application frameworks, tools, and runtimes.

 Eclipse is a universal tool platform— an open, extensible IDE for anything and everything, but nothing in particular.

The Eclipse team always worked on small, stable, and extensible features, and delivered the quality software on time. The team developed, used, and improved the Eclipse by constantly reviewing and listening to the feedback from the community. They incorporated the best practices from **eXtreme Programming (XP)**, Scrum, and **(Rational Unified Process) RUP**.

The Eclipse team took the best practices and modified or adapted them when necessary. The team followed the incremental, iterative, collaborative, transparent, and customizable practices, which enabled them to scale-up in time.

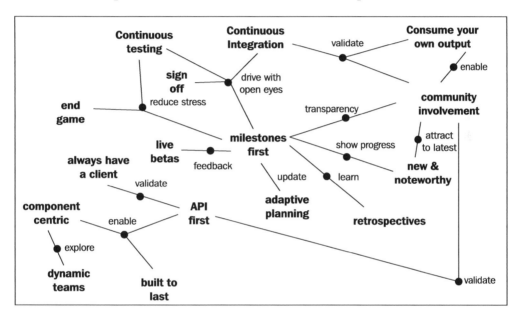

The Eclipse way is very often described by the set of practices (in the previous figure) that made Eclipse an extensible, robust, intuitive, and high quality platform. Very importantly, having the community involvement, consuming our own output, always having a customer, and adaptive planning are the key success factors. This ultimately reduces stress on the team and thereby leads to higher productivity.

Along with the focus on coding, the team also puts in place the release plans, iteration plans, and test plans. Planning gives the team certainty, predictability, and a sense of general direction. With Eclipse, it was possible to improve the individual coding productivity. It gave the developers all the tools necessary to deal with the common and boring tasks such as stub generation, renaming, importing and extracting code, file search, and others. As a developer you want to concentrate on the challenging stuff rather than boring tasks.

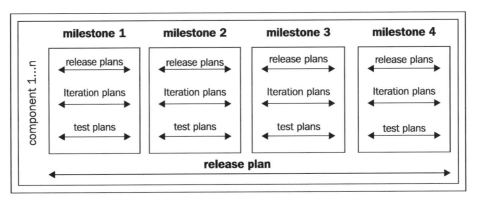

The team took the Eclipse's experiences and best practices to build the Jazz platform and Rational Team Concert. These best practices—often called the Eclipse way—helped the Jazz team to concentrate on to the team productivity, collaboration, and process awareness.

Jazz platform

Software is best developed by a team of people, reacting and responding to each other in order to achieve the best outcome. – Jazz

Jazz is an open, extensible, and scalable platform by IBM that is built to keep team, collaboration and productivity at the forefront of software development. The Jazz platform integrates the various phases in the software development life cycle and helps the team to increase productivity and reduce human errors. Tool vendors can build powerful tools on the Jazz platform by using the frameworks and APIs.

Introduction

With conventional software development, you spend a lot of effort setting up the development environment, setting up source code repository, getting the role-based access rights, and other infrastructure-related tasks. You typically connect to a requirements and/or issue management tool so that you can view assigned tasks and requirements to fulfill. In the worst case scenario, teams maintain a shared spreadsheet where they could see the assigned tasks on a weekly or monthly basis. Collaboration is typically done through casual discussions or e-mails. Source code management and requirements are often disconnected and it's difficult to connect or trace the requirements, source code, versions, and builds. Continuous integration builds are achieved with disparate systems, which might prove difficult to integrate into the development environment.

With Eclipse's success using the best practices tailored and adapted from various agile methodologies, the focus moved from individual productivity to team productivity. The central idea, *"Build process into the tools and make tools aware of the team"*, gave the team the power to collectively collaborate and focus on the real job.

Vision

The Jazz platform got its name from the inspiration of a team of artists playing Jazz on a brightly lit platform. The Jazz orchestra team is visible to everyone and the audience knows who is doing what. Each member of the team has a complete understanding of one's own responsibility and that of the other team members. They work in a co-ordinated way to generate great music.

The Jazz platform has team collaboration, process awareness, transparency, and customization as its fundamental building blocks. Traditionally, software development tools were designed in a way that the focus is on development process or on coding productivity. In either case, focusing more on one aspect and ignoring another is not desirable. Instead, Jazz takes the approach to integrate the process into the tools and make the tools aware of the team. By embedding the collaboration tools of the choice, you have the integrated experience where each feature knows the context of the other tool.

Instead of considering the process as monolithic documentation and a set of training slides, the team process is truly integrated into the tools. This helps us concentrate on true innovation and focus on the tasks rather than worrying about the process implementation. It is not uncommon to imagine that the process implementation takes a considerable amount of time to learn and implement in traditional methods.

The amount of time spent by managers to pull the data from numerous sources to put together the status reports and project health charts can be huge. Each time, a report is needed for the higher management, and the manual data collection and report generation can become tricky and erroneous. The Jazz platform tries to solve these problems by unifying and automating the data collection and report process. This enables every one on the team to look at the same data and report at any time. Managers can also leverage the role-based access system so that they can hide the confidential data from certain team members.

 Jazz is not a product. It is an application life cycle integration platform that provides APIs and open services to be used by the other participating tools.

To summarize, the Jazz platform takes the integrated approach to focus on collaboration, transparency, and automation. The Jazz initiative is composed of the following key components:

- **Jazz Integration Architecture**: Customers can develop their own delivery environment from their preferred tools and practices. Jazz follows an evolutionary process so that companies can adapt the tools as the need arises using the open APIs. It also incorporates the specification provided by the open services for life cycle collaboration project.

- **Product Portfolio**: Jazz stands as an open, extensible platform whereas several tools are developed on it. Tools such as Rational Team Concert, Rational Quality Manager, and Rational Requirements Composer are some examples for the tools built on the Jazz platform.

- **Community**: This is one of the crucial aspects of Eclipse's success. A community is an eco system in which the members help each other and improve with the help of a constant feedback. Members have an interest to improve and care for the eco-system so that they collectively grow with it. The Jazz community and stakeholders can drive the product features and provide a constant feedback to improve the product.

Architecture

The Jazz platform follows some key aspects of architecture to differentiate itself from the others. The noticeable aspects of the architecture are as follows:

- Separates the tool implementation with the data representation and definition. That means, tools does not have to care about the closed data representation, which helps the other tools to participate easily.

- Jazz consolidates the data from different databases over the internet protocol and does not assume data at a single location. This makes it possible for a large organization to scale up as it grows in an evolutionary manner.

- Any language that understands the Internet can be used to program a tool for Jazz. No language restriction was made on the tool implementation. This helps when organizations have a varied skill set and tools need to be developed on the available skill set without forcing them to use a specific technology.

- Finally, Jazz has the single point of access to all data. This reduces the unnecessary time consuming data manipulation and data cleansing processes among various tools.

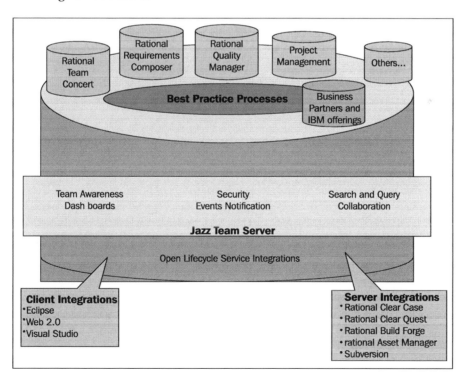

Jazz Team Server (JTS) provides the foundation services or APIs that provide the access to the team, dashboards, security, event notification, search, and collaboration aspects. The JTS is built on the **Open Life cycle Service Collaboration (OLSC)** platform so that any tool that conform to the OSLC can be easily plugged in. For this, one needs to develop the server integrations on the OLSC layer and all the client integrations are done on the JTS, as shown in the following figure.

Jazz allows the community to develop different tools on the JTS by providing the language-specific libraries for accessing the Jazz APIs with Eclipse, Visual Studio, and Web 2.0 client integrations. This has the advantage that an organization can build the tools of their choice in their choice of technology.

JTS provides open APIs, helping groups of tools to work together. The foundation APIs enable the tools to access the work items, issues, build plans, release plans, and other project artifacts. The beauty of the JTS is to have the multiple physical JTS servers, but still consider it as one logical server, as shown in the next figure:

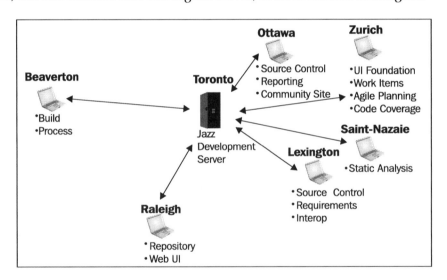

The Jazz technology platform is developed at `jazz.net`, where you can register to participate. You can open enhancement requests, projects reports, track schedules, participate in discussion forums, download and play with the Rational Team Concert, and other Jazz-based products.

Openness and transparency is the vision of Jazz team and is put into practice at `jazz.net`.

Rational Team Concert

In today's software development, we spend a considerable time in configuring, managing, and updating several tools. These tools aid us to manage the software lifecycle and yet they are disparate and complex. We spend more time in learning about tools and less time in focusing on the core job. Traditionally time is spent in educating the tools about the way we want to work, which made the software development less intuitive and a painful process.

What if we have a tool that understands the source/version control system, source code editing, issues, work items, team members, team process, schedules, builds, releases, and does reporting for us? It is not too difficult to imagine how easy it would be to focus on the actual business value and core functionality than to worry about the tools.

Overview

Rational Team Concert is the first commercial product offering based on the Jazz technology platform. The Rational Team Concert 2.0 is the recent publicly available stable release that offered both Web and Client versions. The Client interface is based on the Eclipse platform and another flavor on Microsoft's Visual Studio. The Web client has a Web 2.0 style interface for the fast access of dashboards and reports.

Team collaboration and productivity is the focus of the Rational Team Concert. This means that the product offers an integration of all the aspects of our daily work, such as coding, plans, tasks, revision control, build management, and reports.

Rational Team Concert integrates with several other products, including IBM and third-party tools. Some of the current offerings are as follows:

- IBM Rational ClearCase
- IBM Rational ClearQuest
- IBM Rational Quality Manager
- IBM Rational Build Forge
- Subversion
- JIRA
- Hudson

- Cruise Control
- Maven

Any organization using a variety of tools can adapt the Rational Team Concert and have the infrastructure and functionality provided by the Jazz technology platform and Rational Team Concert. As the third-party offerings increase, we will have more flexibility to use different tools along with Rational Team Concert.

> You don't have to give up your existing tools to use Rational Team Concert. However, you would integrate them into Rational Team Concert by writing the server and client adapters (as shown in the previous figure).

What's in RTC?

Rational Team Concert gives you the power to collaborate in real-time, direct control of the project plans, build plans, and finally real-time project status reports. Development is a lot more about communication than writing code. It's critical that everyone understand the goals, timelines, and what is expected of them. Developers can update plans, start builds, and configure the team's process. Project managers can see the code, work items, and what is being delivered. Testers can see what is planned in the milestone.

> Rational Team Concert supports accessibility features to aid users who have physical disability, such as restricted by mobility or limited vision, to use the software successfully.

In the following sections, you will see an introduction to the Rational Team Concert features and how they ease your daily tasks.

Administration

Rational Team Concert provides an easy-to-use, web-based admin utility to set up, configure, and tune the JTS. The server utility allows you to configure the database, e-mail, user management, and LDAP.

The web-based admin UI provides a way to see the server status, accessed users, and license settings. If you need to configure users in a large organization, you can use "import LDAP users" to ease the admin task.

Built-ins

Rational Team Concert has integrated the products such as Rational Quality Manager, Rational Requirements Composer, Rational ClearQuest, and Rational ClearCase. These built-ins are achieved with the help of importer and connector components.

With the built-ins, you can take full advantage of already existing infrastructure—ClearQuest, ClearCase, Requirements Composer, and others—in your organization. You can link the work items from Rational Team Concert to Requirements Composer and then trace them to the test cases and test plans in the Quality Manager. In this way, you get a seamless integration of existing tools with Rational Team Concert.

Several third-party integrations are available to give a total flexibility to you so that you decide what to use and integrate. Some of the current offerings include but do not limit to Hudson, Cruise Control, Subversion, CVS, JIRA, HP Quality Center, Google Talk, and Skype.

Agile management

Agile project management can get tricky with large and distributed teams. Without the use of proper tools and integrated methods, project management can get complex. Rational Team Concert provides you a set of tools that would allow you to create plans for individual development tasks, sprints, releases, and builds. All the planning activities are connected back to the version control and issue management software. You can see the work load of an individual developer, current tasks that a developer is working on, track the release progress, and see the project health from the nightly builds.

A very interesting feature is that the Rational Team Concert provides a graphical planning feature that shows the tasks that are in progress, done, and to be done. This can be used to run daily scrum meetings without any extra effort. As a manager, you could get the overview of the sprint's risk from the project dashboard and take corrective action early in the phase.

Continuous builds

Continuous integration and nightly builds are becoming rather necessary tasks in any software development projects. Rational Team Concert not only integrates the continuous builds but also does more than the basic features of a "build".

Rational Team Concert supports the Ant, Maven, and command line build systems out of the box. That means you can re-use existing Ant and Maven scripts from your projects and get the additional benefits of integrated build tracking, traceability, build reproducibility, build compare, and build health.

Process awareness

Traditionally, you spend a lot of time and effort to write process documents, train the project team to use the process, and finally to enforce the process rules into the system. While implementing the process, there is always an extra overhead introduced due to the manual errors and also you are left with team members who are unhappy as they need to follow the boring process and spend considerable time on process implementation.

Rational Team Concert takes the approach of "teaching your tools about the process". All your best practices can be directly configured into the Rational Team Concert, which will help you know the process violations on the fly. This makes it possible for you to concentrate on the real business problem and let the Rational Team Concert take care of the process implementation.

The great value of the process awareness in Rational Team Concert is the ability for you to choose from out of the box processes such as Scrum, Eclipse Way, and OpenUp. If your organization defines its own process, then you can define it as a new process and save it as a template for future uses. The Organizational process template used with your team's customization is a powerful way to leverage the process awareness.

Team awareness

Rational Team Concert understands the human aspects of who is in your team, who is who, and the technical aspects of team artifacts. You can get an overview of the team builds, team members, different release plans, and work items. Configure the team members that you want to see and track their work item's progress.

Setting up a new team and adding the team members to the team are very intuitive and at the end of team set up, the individual team members would be notified through e-mails. As a team member you would receive an e-mail with all the necessary details of how to join the team and immediately you can start working on then work items of the project.

Collaboration is enabled through context-sensitive communication—chat and team feeds. As soon as a user becomes online, you can chat and exchange files directly in the context of Rational Team Concert. This means, you can directly start chatting with your colleague to talk about a defect number and the chat client would turn it into links that your colleague can open and work with. Team feed is a great way to get informed about the work items, builds, and team events.

Work items

Work items are the building blocks in Rational Team Concert that enables you to track and co-ordinate the tasks and workflows. Work items are used to connect the Rational Team Concert's sprint planning, change sets, and builds.

Eclipse IDE, Visual Studio, and the web-based interface allow you to create, modify, and query the work items. You could also share the frequent queries with the team. You can add specific approval process to critical work items and have it marked with different status Ids such as pending, approved, or verified.

You can create the work items or import the items from the built-in adapters. Currently you can import the work items from Bugzilla, Rational ClearQuest, and CSV. All the importers allow you to define an XML file that contains the mappings from source formats to work item's attributes.

Source control

Rational Team Concert has a component-based source control system that supports geographically distributed teams. The source control system supports a highly integrated collaborative development environment, integration with defect tracking, and integration with builds. The storage model is entirely based on change set, which provide atomic changes to sets of files. Change sets are the base currency and can be shared (through work items), suspended, discarded, and reverted.

The source control provides a full tracking of file moves and renames. You can quickly suspend the task at hand and start a high priority task. Once that task is finished, you can resume the suspended task.

Project dashboards

Rational Team Concert provides project dashboards and reports that give an overview of the project's health. You can get several reports based on the task priority, team member, burn-down charts, and many more. The project dashboards are a great way for the management and external stake holders to get the overview of the project's progress. Rational Team Concert provides more than 50 reporting templates and all of them are configurable depending on then process.

You can export the reports from a project in the forms of PDF, PostScript, Excel, Word, and PowerPoint, and present them to the higher management as status reports. You could get a variety of the project activity reports such as the work item report, source control reports, and build reports.

Jazz-based products

While Rational Team Concert is the first matured product built on the Jazz platform, there are other products from `jazz.net` in the beta and development stages. In this book, we will not go into the details of these other products. However, the following is an overview of the various products on Jazz. You can participate and download these products from the IBM website to get an in-depth understanding.

Rational Quality Manager

The increasing complexity of the software requires ensuring the quality product by extensive test plans and test coverage. Rational Quality Manager provides a collaborative environment to create test plans and execute them. The product offers the tracking and traceability of requirements to test cases and metric analysis. As a manager, you can get the impact analysis of how the project is affected by project decisions.

Rational Requirements Composer

In modern day software development, you can imagine that the requirements are coming from multiple stakeholders and in different formats. It is always challenging for you to integrate these silos of information in a meaningful manner.

Rational Requirements Composer gives you the power to capture the requirements from different stakeholders and transforms the spreadsheets, Word documents, presentations, whiteboard discussions, and online conferences to manageable requirements.

You can leverage the rich editors to create use cases, user stories, user interface mock-ups, process diagrams, and many more. The real value comes when you combine different requirement sources from stakeholders through hyperlinks, tags, and attributes.

Rational Project Conductor

Very often you have the project management and program management software disconnected from the team, tasks, and development environments. Rational Project Conductor enables you to plan, schedule, and have a work break down structure. You can attach various artifact types when a work item is being created and the project calendar can be fully customized to reflect the team and location.

Rational Project Conductor allows you to schedule work, assign work items, and view timesheets of the team members. It allows you to import the project plan from the Microsoft project.

Rational Insight

For the management, measuring of the progress, identifying the potential problems, and development risks could be daunting. Rational Insight gives you the ability to find the blind spots in the development and mitigate the risks. You can enforce the governance in a globally changing environment.

Rational Build Forge

Rational Build Forge is an integrated approach for the automated builds and release management. You can utilize the existing project infrastructures such as scripts, tools, and development languages to achieve the automation and scheduling.

Rational Asset Manager

Maintaining your teams' software, hardware, and business assets in simple spreadsheets or disconnected systems could be very daunting and error prone. Rational Asset Manager lets you manage, define a reuse strategy, and track the asset usage for business and software assets across the enterprise.

Summary

In this chapter, you have seen how the advancements in modern software development lead to new challenges of integrated systems and collaboration among team members. As the software complexity and customer expectations increases, the project management is looking "*to do more in less time with high quality*". You have seen how the best practices made the Eclipse platform robust, extensible, high in quality, and ensure on-time deliveries.

Next, you have seen that Jazz has collaboration, team productivity, and transparency at the forefront in its Vision. The Jazz platform architecture allows several tool vendors to plug in their functionality by writing server and client adapter components. In this way an organization can still use the tools of its choice yet take the advantage of the Jazz platform.

You have seen that Rational Team Concert is built on the Jazz platform and takes the complete advantage of the Jazz capabilities such as team awareness and process awareness. Finally, you saw an overview of the other Jazz-based product offerings.

2

Installing RTC and WebSphere

Simplicity is prerequisite for reliability

--Edsger W.Dijkstra

In this chapter, we will see different download offerings from Rational Team Concert and the features that distinguish them. Once you are familiar with these offerings, we will download the Enterprise edition and install the server and client parts.

Afterwards, we will do an initial setup and check the basic functionality. We will install WebSphere and do a basic configuration so that the Rational Team Concert server runs in the WebSphere environment. Jazz provides a sandbox mechanism that allows users to play with the full featured projects. From the Eclipse client we will connect to the Jazz sandbox and play with JUnit Project. This will give us an opportunity to set up the example and get introduced to different aspects of the system.

In this chapter, we will look at the following:

- Rational Team Concert Enterprise Edition Installation
- WebSphere Application Server configuration
- Setting up the Jazz Team Server
- Setting up the Eclipse Client
- Play with the JUnit Project from Sandbox

Installing Rational Team Concert

Before we install, let's first, explore the different editions available as of this book's publication. Currently there are four versions offered for a variety of operating systems including Windows, Linux, and Solaris as well as other IBM operating systems such as AIX, IBM i, z/OS, and Linux on System z. These differences between these editions is shown in the following feature matrix:

How can I install Jazz?

Jazz is a technology platform and not a product. Therefore, whichever edition of Rational Team Concert, you get Jazz with it as a server component. No separate installation is necessary (unless you choose to install each component individually).

Understanding RTC editions

IBM RTC is available in four editions, as follows. Each of the editions offer different features, and receive varying levels of support from IBM .The following link helps you get a better understanding:

```
https://jazz.net/downloads/rational-team-concert/
releases/2.0.0.2iFix2
```

- **Express-C edition**: If you are a small team of 10 users or less , Express-C edition is the right one for you. A Tomcat application server and a Derby database are embedded by default. This is available as an all-in-one package with the server, client, and build system and is very easy to install.

- **Express edition**: The basic feature set in Express edition is similar to Express-C. However, Express edition has licenses for 50 clients and a limitation on the number of Derby users. Unlike Express-C, which is available only as a ZIP, Express-C can also be installed from the IBM Installation Manager. In both the editions—Express C and Express—some advanced features such as work item customization, LDAP Imports, ClearCase, and ClearQuest bridges are not available.

- **Standard edition**: This edition supports 250 users. In addition to Derby, DB2 or Oracle can be used for the Jazz repository.

- **Enterprise edition**: This edition supports unlimited users on the server and has many more configuration features, including a mechanism for configuring a second copy of the server to support failover mode.

In this book, we will use the *Enterprise* edition of Rational Team Concert running with the following configuration:

- Derby database
- WebSphere Application Server
- Eclipse as IDE (client)

Note that this book uses the examples and screenshots from a PC on a Windows XP 32-bit version of Rational Team Concert. The ideal hardware configuration suggested by IBM is the following:

- Intel Pentium Xeon (32 or 64 bits)
- 1024 x 786 screen resolution
- 2 GB RAM
- 1 GB disk space

Installing Enterprise edition

You can get the *Enterprise* version of Rational Team Concert from either the IBM or Jazz websites. There are different ways to download the required pieces; choose the method suitable for your download speed and required flexibility:

- IBM Installation Manager lets you download only the selected components from the web. It manages future updates and gives you the flexibility to manage when you want to download.
- You can also download the individual server, client, and build system components as ZIP files or with the help of the IBM Installation Manager Local that downloads all the components before install.

We will download the individual ZIP file for the client (client for Eclipse IDE), server, and build system toolkit components for the Windows x86 architecture. Once downloaded, you can expand the contents into a single directory to maintain consistency. If you want to connect the ClearCase and ClearQuest applications to Rational Team Concert, you must also download the individual connectors for each.

 The installation directory for Rational Team Concert is now referred to as <root>.

Unless you choose to expand the ZIP files into different locations, the contents typically have the build system, client, repository tools, **Source Control Management (SCM)** tools, and server components. Let's see a quick overview of what each of these modules does.

Name	Size	Type ▲	Date Modified
buildsystem		File Folder	6/10/2010 10:09 PM
client		File Folder	6/10/2010 10:05 PM
repotools		File Folder	6/10/2010 9:59 PM
scmtools		File Folder	6/10/2010 10:07 PM
server		File Folder	6/10/2010 9:59 PM
help.css	13 KB	Cascading Style Sh...	6/2/2010 12:35 PM
ibmidwb.css	7 KB	Cascading Style Sh...	6/2/2010 12:35 PM
install_client_zip.html	35 KB	HTML Document	6/2/2010 12:35 PM
install_client_zip_cs.html	42 KB	HTML Document	6/2/2010 12:35 PM
install_client_zip_de.html	41 KB	HTML Document	6/2/2010 12:35 PM

Build system

Build system is responsible for the build integration in Rational Team Concert, providing the link between the builds, work items, and change sets. It provides the "build engine" and "build tools" modules. Build engine processes build requests from Jazz and executes build scripts; build tools are a set of utilities that communicate the build progress to Jazz repository.

Client

Rational Team Concert client is based on Eclipse. This client module is the window for the developer to work on the project sources, create work items and source code management, and much more. From Rational Team Concert's client, you can work on the build, reports, source code management, collaboration tools, and work items.

 Rational Team Concert offers MS Visual Studio client too. However, this book does not use the Visual Studio client.

SCM tools

The Source Control System is accessible through Web UI and client modules. While these modules concentrate on the rich user interface experience for you, the SCM tools provide the command line access to the repository. This is extremely helpful when you want to provide an automation and scripting environment.

You can perform the command line tasks such as listing the various types of files in repository, loading contents of workspace, checking the changes, delivering a change, and creating workspaces.

Repository tools

Rational Team Concert provides the tools to migrate repository from one version of the Jazz server to another one. Also, the repository tools aid you when moving from one database provider to other, either within the same version of Jazz server or across Jazz server versions.

Repository tools help you export the repository data to a TAR file format and import the TAR format file into another Jazz repository. TAR stores the data in an independent format and the importers would take care of how to import that data to a specific database.

Server

This is the heart of Rational Team Concert. The Server component provides all the infrastructure and APIs for the repository management, work item management, deliveries, release management, and build management. It manages the repository and the artifacts in it.

Now that we have the Enterprise edition of Rational Team Concert downloaded and installed, let's take a look at IBM WebSphere configuration.

What if I want to upgrade from older versions of RTC?
The installation folder of the Enterprise version of RTC has a "help" with instructions on how to upgrade. This help file will give you all the information you need to successfully migrate to a new version.

Configuring WebSphere

IBM WebSphere Application Server is an integrated platform that contains an application server, web development tools, a web server, and additional supporting software and documentation.

In this book IBM WebSphere server is installed on a single machine and a standalone application server profile is created. The standalone application server profile has a `server1` application server process. This is the simplest configuration on which WebSphere can be installed.

We also assume no major custom configuration is done for WebSphere server.

Before you start

Before we move to configure WebSphere to work with the Rational Team Concert server, we need to make a few configuration tweaks, as follows. Without these configuration changes, the RTC server on WebSphere may fail.

- We installed the RTC server as a standalone and it has all the files to run completely independent in Tomcat. However, we need only a subset of the files to make it run on WebSphere. Copy the following files and folders to a directory (now called as `<jazzWSRoot>`) ready to be used by WebSphere Application Server:
    - The file `<root>/server/tomcat/webapps/jazz.war`
    - The directory `<root>/server/update-site`
    - The directory `<root>/server/conf`
    - The default repository database in `<root>/repositoryDB`
    - The repository tools in `<root>/repotools`
    - The directory `<root>/server/license-update-site`
    - The directory `<root>/server/nl1-update-site`
    - The directory `<root>/server/nl2-update-site`
- We use the Derby database; therefore, make sure that the `teamserver.properties` file points to the correct database properties. This file is available in the `<jazzWSRoot>\conf\jazz` directory.

WebSphere version

At the time of writing this book, the latest version of WebSphere is 7.0.0.9. If you want to install previous versions of the WebSphere, then you need to make sure that you install the WebSphere Application Server Fixes and JVM updates and bring the Application Server version to a minimum of 7.0.0.7.

JVM custom properties

Rational Team Concert needs JVM configuration changes that will help Jazz to know its configuration files and other related settings, as shown in the following screenshot:

1. Navigate to **Servers | WebSphere Application Servers** and select the server instance **server1**.

2. In the **Server Infrastructure** section navigate to **Administration | Custom Properties.**

3. Click on **New**, which would display the **Name**, **Value**, and **Description** details, as follows:

   ○ Name: **java.awt.headless** Value: **true**

   ○ Name: **org.eclipse.emf.ecore.plugin.EcorePlugin. doNotLoadResourcesPlugin** Value: **true**

   ○ Name: **JAZZ_HOME** Value: `file:///<jazzWSRoot>/server/conf`

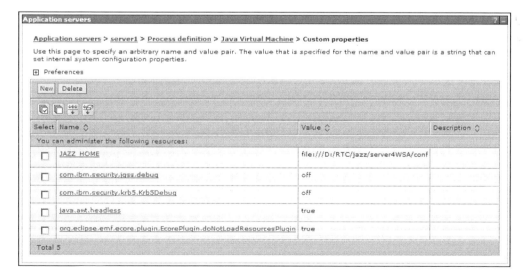

Heap size settings

A typical configuration change would be to increase the memory allocation for the server instance of the Rational Team Server. WebSphere comes with the Derby database drivers by default. In case, you want to use different database drivers, then the path to the driver needs to be specified.

The WebSphere Application Server's default memory settings may not be enough for production applications to run. Set the server's initial and maximum virtual memory size from the Integrated Solution Console.

1. Navigate to **Servers | WebSphere Application Servers** and select the server instance **server1.**

2. From **Server Infrastructure** section navigate to **Java and Process Management | Process Definition.**

3. From the **Additional Properties** navigate to **Java Virtual Machine.**

4. Set the **Initial Heap Size** to **100.**

5. Set the **Maximum Heap Size** to **1000.**

6. Click on **Apply.**

Depending on the software choice and team size, the actual configurations on your production server might change. Remember that the configuration is primarily a function of database, team size, network connectivity, and server memory. The current configuration targets a Derby database, a team size of 10, and the server machine with 3 GB RAM. Except for the WebSphere Application Server and Rational Team Server, no other major application is running on this machine.

 By default the initial memory is set around 50 MB and maximum memory is set to 256 MB. Setting the values more than the default could greatly increase the system startup time.

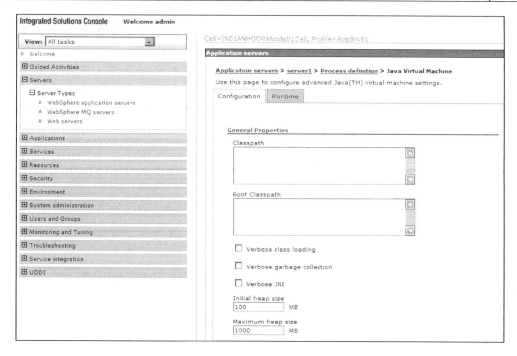

Changing log details

Rational Team Server uses the BIRT engine for report generation; the default settings produce a lot of verbose information. To prevent this, we need to perform the following:

1. Navigate to **Servers | WebSphere Application Servers** and select the server instance **server1**.

2. From the **Troubleshooting** section navigate to **Change Log Detail Levels**.

3. Under the **Configuration** section add `org.eclipse.birt.*=severe`.

4. Click **Apply** to save the configuration.

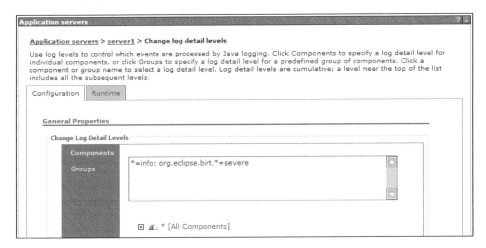

Security Settings

Security settings are a crucial part of the configuration and must be set carefully. The following settings specify how Jazz authenticates and authorizes users:

1. Navigate to **Security | Global Security** from the **Integrated Solution Console.**
2. Check the **Enable administrative security** option.
3. Check the **Enable the application security** option.
4. Check the disable the Java 2 security option.

Finally, make sure that the WebSphere security setting **Use available authentication data when an unprotected URI is accessed** is checked. This can be done from **Security | Global security | Web and SIP Security | General Settings**.

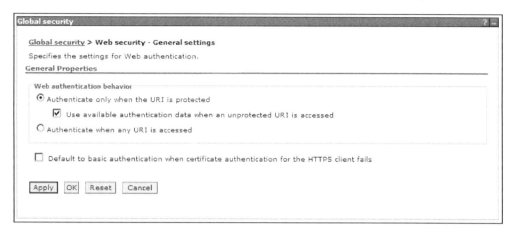

With this, we have done all the necessary configuration changes and are ready to restart the server.

Deploying Jazz Team Server on WebSphere

Now that we've configured WebSphere and restarted, we will install the Jazz Team Server on to WebSphere Application Server `server1`.

From the **Integrated Solutions Manager**, navigate to **Applications | New Applications**. Click on the **New Enterprise Application**.

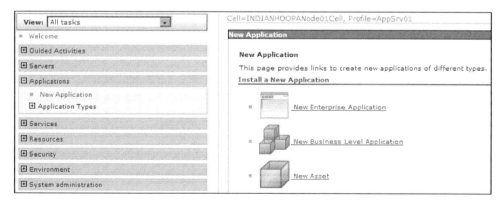

You will be asked to enter a local or a remote file system path. Enter the `jazz.war` path from the directory that you previously copied to, for example, `D:\RTC\jazz\server4WSA\jazz.war` referred to as `<jazzWSRoot>/jazz.war`.

Click **Next**. In the next step, you can choose either the **Fast Path** or **Detailed** installation option. The Fast Path installation assumes several default values and you are asked for an input only when required. In this case, we will set up the WAR file with the Detailed installation option. In the latest version of the WebSphere application server there are 10 steps in the Detailed installation option.

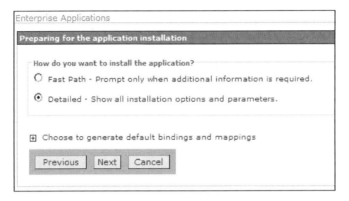

In the first step you can optionally change the name of the Application from `jazz_war` (set by default) to any meaningful name that you like. This is the application name that WebSphere knows our JTS by. You can continue the steps from 1 to7 without any modifications. In step 7, select the `jazz.war` web module to map the web module to a contained virtual host.

In the next step (step 8) change the context root for the web module `jazz.war` from "/" to "**/jazz**". Click **Next** (step 9) to set up the Security roles to users and groups. Remember that all roles defined by a Rational Team Server application must map to users or groups defined by the WebSphere domain registry. You may have already imported the LDAP users and groups, or created users and groups in WebSphere Application Server. Select each of the user roles and map them to appropriate groups or users.

The final step (step 10) gives an overview of the configuration and click **Finish** to deploy the application. Integrated Solutions Console shows a high level deployment log on the screen. Once the deployment is finished successfully save the changes directly to master configuration by clicking **Save directly to master configuration**.

From the main menu, navigate to **Applications | WebShpere enterprise applications**. Select the name of the application you configured for Jazz and start the server. It will take couple of seconds to start the application and a green arrow is displayed next to the server for a successful startup.

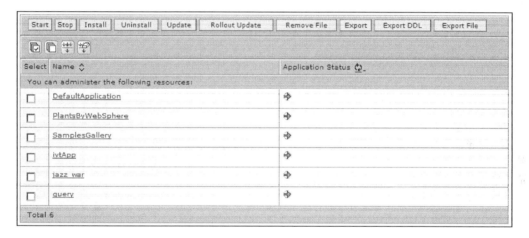

Testing the installation

Once the **Rational Team Server** (also called the **Jazz Server**) successfully starts, we should be able to access the Team Server URL `https://localhost:9443/jazz/setup` for the initial setup steps. If you would like to test it from another machine you should be able to substitute the localhost with the machine name or IP address to access the application.

In most cases, the installation should be successful and the application should start without any issues. In case you experience problems, check if prerequisites are missing. Typical problems are as follows:

- **Error 404: ProxyServlet: /jazz/setup**
- A blank screen appears with message as **Loading**
- **You are not authorized to access the Jazz Team Server Admin UI**

In each of the previous scenarios, we really want to make sure that the following points are carefully checked and verified. Sometimes, uninstalling and reinstalling of the Jazz application may be required.

1. Check if the relative path of the database is replaced with the absolute path in the `<jazzWSRoot>/server/conf/jazz/teamserver.properties` file.
2. Make sure that the `JAZZ_HOME` property is set to `file:///<jazzWSRoot>/server/conf` without spaces in the path and the physical files exist.
3. Make sure that the Security settings are done exactly as described.
    - Enable administrative security
    - Enable application security
    - Disable all Java 2 options
4. Make sure that you enable the **Use available authentication data when an unprotected URI is accessed** option from **Global Security Settings**.
5. In step 7 of the application war installation, ensure you selected the **Web module mapping**.
6. In step 8, check if you have the application context as "`/jazz`".
7. Finally, check if the application roles have been mapped to the domain user groups or users in step 9.

This check list can also be used before the final installation of the Rational Team Server application. Make sure that you can access the application and log into it. In the next section, we will set up the Team Server.

Setting up the server

Use the default user name and password (ADMIN/ADMIN) for the initial login to the application. For security, it is recommended you create your own admin user during the initial setup and delete the default ADMIN user (or at least change its password). If you choose to use the LDAP directory, use the **User ID** and **Password** defined in LDAP directory, as shown in the following screenshot:

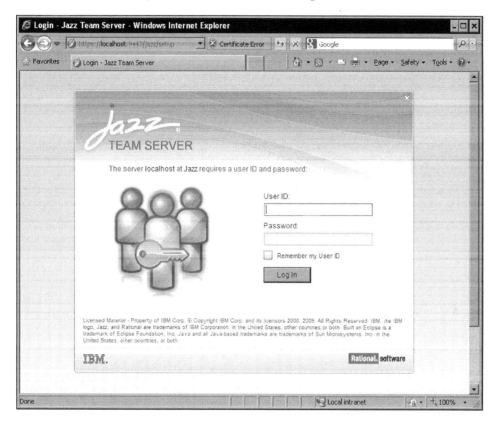

Once logged in, the "startup" steps appear. The first step asks you to decide whether you need a **Fast Path Setup** or **Custom Setup**. If you want to quickly launch the application with default values, then Fast Path is preferred; otherwise use Custom Setup to change e-mail and database configurations. Click **Custom Setup** as shown next:

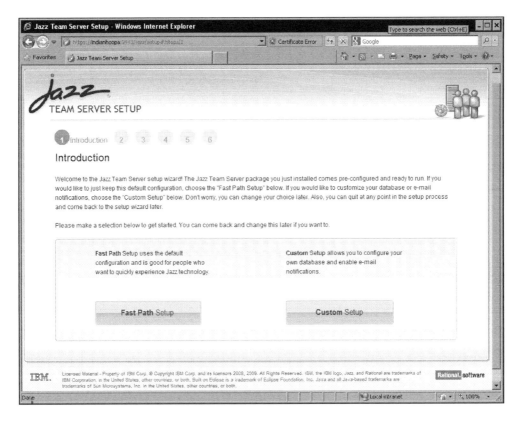

Rational Team Concert has the Derby database and JDBC driver set up for you by default. In this step you can configure the database vendor and the connection properties. You can change the settings if you like and test them right away for the connection, as shown next:

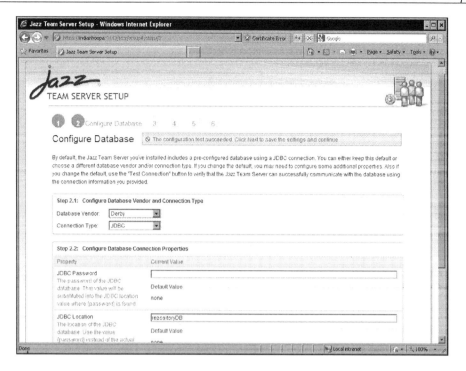

Collaboration is the key component of Rational Team Concert and it uses e-mail to communicate with team members. You can set up the **SMTP Server**, **SMTP Username**, **SMTP Password**, **From Address**, **Reply Address**, and test the connection, as shown in the screenshot:

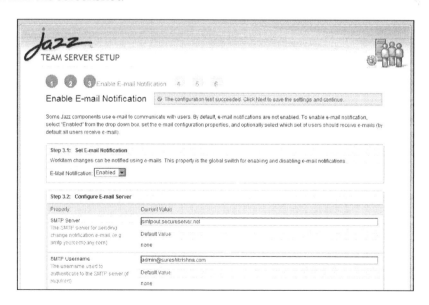

All the resources used in the communications, e-mails, and other context sensitive operations are assigned a URL to be able to uniquely identify them. However, when you want to share the resources and URLs outside the organization or across the proxy, you need to create public URLs. In this next step, you can enter any public URL root:

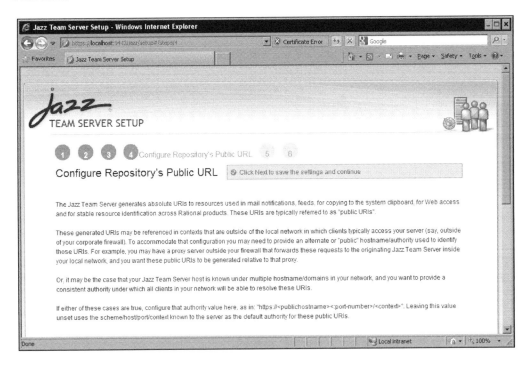

With the *Enterprise* installation you have several options to manage users. You could use the already configured **Tomcat User Database** or **LDAP** or **Non-LDAP External Registry**. Rational Team Server uses this user registry to provide the application and web server authentication.

 During this step you could create a new administrator account and delete the ADMIN user account, which you used to login. If you want to have the ADMIN user account, you should at least have the password changed.

Remember that we set Jazz to configure with the WebSphere application server, and hence we cannot use the Tomcat user registry. If your organization uses the LDAP registry, you could use LDAP groups mapped to the Jazz roles. Or, use the Non-LDAP External Registry and define the users in WebSphere and also in the Jazz application. The following screenshot shows these options. Note that you will not be able to view and modify the roles of the users from the Jazz application.

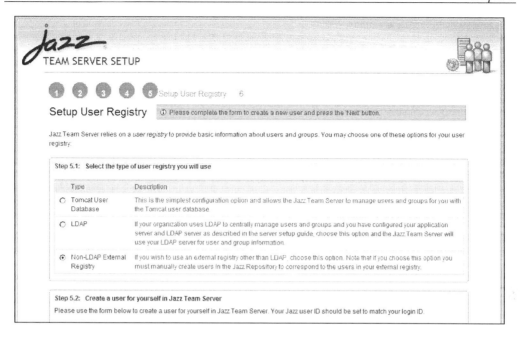

The final step shows an overview of the configured options for the database, e-mail, and user registry. Here you have the option of creating the Rational Team Server users and creating projects for your team, as shown next. Finally, you can complete the setup by clicking **Finish**. This will directly take you to the **Administrator page**.

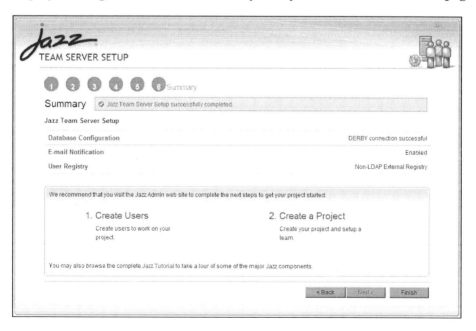

Introduction

Once the server is successfully started and the basic configuration is done, you will be automatically taken to the `https://localhost:9443/jazz/admin` page. Rational Team Server's admin module provides a dashboard showing **Server Status**, **Active Services**, **Configuration**, and **licensing information**, as shown next:

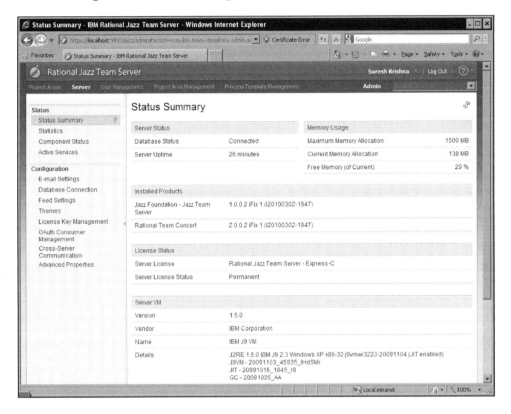

The Admin module of the Rational Team Server has several smaller modules that you can manage and configure. As a project administrator, you will now see the functionality of these different modules:

- Project areas
- Server
- User management
- Project area management
- Process template management

Project areas

The project area is the system's representation of a software project. It defines the project deliverables, team structure, process, and schedule. Also, it references project artifacts and stores the relationships between these artifacts. All this is stored as a top-level or root item in a repository. Access to a project area and its artifacts is controlled by permissions.

When you, as administrator, enter Rational Team Server you can see a list of all the team servers. Selecting one would show you the burn-down charts, project events, release plans, and other artifacts related to a specific project.

Server

Rational Team Server's user interface provides all the information needed by an administrator. The **Status Summary** page gives an overview of the database status, server uptime, memory information, installed products (such as Rational Team Server and Rational Team Concert) and license information.

Email Settings, **Database Connection**, and **Feed Settings**, are a few important configurations shown in the server UI. The following screenshot shows the **License Key Management** screen, displaying the current license and user type:

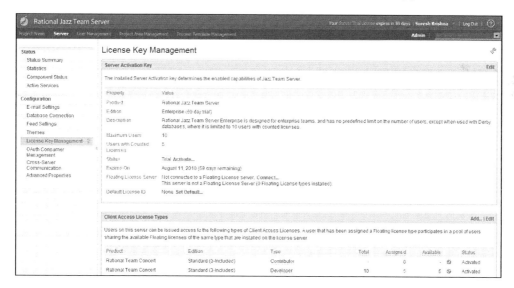

User management

The user management UI shows the list of all the users and provides the ability to add new ones. You could also modify a user's role to be a contributor, developer, build system, or ClearCase contributor. This complements the users found in the user registry configuration setup. The following screenshot shows the **Active Users** pane:

Project area management

Project area management lets you create and manage the project areas, including team members, process, permission, access control, and roles. Note that once you've created a project area, it can never be deleted; only archived.

Process template management

Process template management is one of the great aspects of Rational Team Concert to integrate the process into tools. This module allows you to deploy the predefined process templates, or import an existing one. Once Rational Team Server has the templates, you can easily associate the process templates to any existing project area. The first time you access the module, the process templates are yet to be deployed or imported, as shown next:

Any existing templates you have can be deployed by clicking the **Deploy Predefined Templates** button, as shown in the following screenshot:

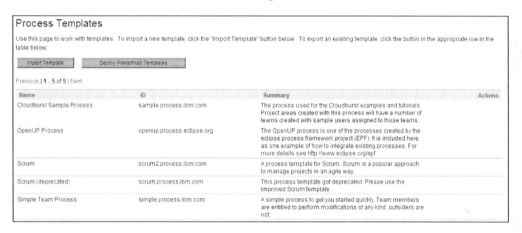

Setting up the client

You have seen the Rational Team Server basic and administrative setup. Now, you will see the Rational Team Concert client features and how to set it up. Rational Team Concert 2.0.2's client is based on Eclipse 3.4.2 and allows you to do variety of tasks:

- Accept a team invitation
- Connect to a project area
- Create a project area
- Create project plans
- Create work items
- Define process templates

- Import the source code from SVN, ClearCase
- Create team builds

In the *Enterprise* installation, the client is installed as one of the components and is supplied with its own JDK to run out of the box. You can start the Rational Team Concert client from `<root>\jazz\client\eclipse\eclipse.exe`:

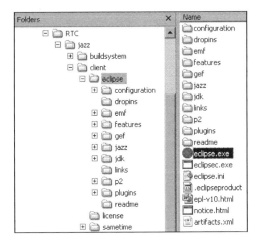

Rational Team Concert client asks for the location of the workspace. This is the workspace location where any new project is created and/or imported, as shown in the following screenshot:

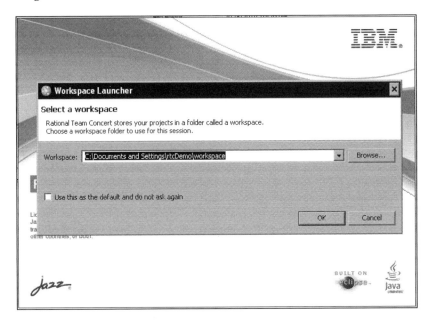

Once the workspace is selected, Rational Team Concert's client is started and the **Welcome** screen appears, as follows:

 Welcome screen:
The Welcome screen has several useful tips, tutorials, and introductory material on Rational Team Concert and Jazz. You get a wealth of information from the Welcome screen.

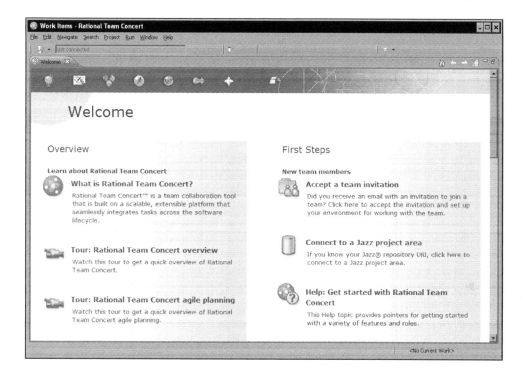

After you minimize the Welcome screen, the "work items" perspective is opened. At this time the work items perspective contains the empty views and editors:

By now, you may be wondering how you would start exploring Rational Team Concert. On the client's Welcome screen, you may have noticed the JUnit Project example. Setting up the JUnit Project would give you an overview of the several features in Rational Team Concert's client and gives you a platform to experiment.

In Rational Team Concert version 2.0.0.2, the JUnit Project example runs only when you set up Rational Team Server to run on Tomcat. Installing this example application creates user entries and updates the repository, which can be done only within the context of the Tomcat environment. Therefore, we cannot simply import this project into our repository as we use the WebSphere for the application server.

In the next section, we will see how to import the JUnit Project example into the Rational Team Concert client and use it to explore different features.

JUnit project example

The JUnit example project is based on a realistic software development project whose goal is to deliver JUnit Version 4.4. The JUnit Project team uses Rational Team Concert to plan, track, collaborate, and deliver the release. The project is set up in such a way that the Team Artifacts view gives you a feeling that the project is already started with many releases, builds, and work items.

Working with Sandbox

Rational Team Concert lets you play with and explore the complete product from a hosted installation called **Sandbox**. This is a very convenient way for many who want to explore Rational Team Concert without worrying about installing and configuring.

Access the Sandbox at `https://jazz.net/sandbox` and login with your `jazz.net` credentials. You can get to Sandbox through any standard web browser and then use it to create your own project and start working. A single project area can be created per Sandbox per user. Once you have the `jazz.net` user credentials, it just takes few minutes to set up a project; or you could explore one of the two provided read-only examples—Junit and Call Center.

The Sandbox is for evaluation and testing only and is not to be used for production data. The data is not backed up and will be periodically scrubbed. We will however do our best to keep the Sandbox running as we understand that many of you are using it to give demos and run evaluations—`jazz.net`.

When working with the Sandbox, you do not have to install any extra software on your machines. If you wish to play with either the Eclipse or Visual Studio clients, you could download them separately and connect to the Rational Team Server on the Web.

Connecting to Sandbox from the client:
Once you download the client, you can connect to Rational Team Concert's Sandbox with the repository URL `https://jazz.net/Sandbox/rtc`. Use your `jazz.net` credentials for the Sandbox connections.

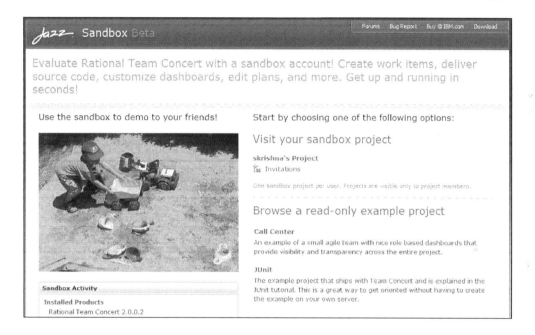

After creating a project area, you can send project invitations to any registered Jazz user and play with different roles. You can also explore several Rational Team Concert features right from the Sandbox account, as follows:

1. You can create and customize the dashboards. Here you can add several viewlets to help you better understand the project and your role.

2. Project areas show you a list of the projects. In Sandbox, you can see your own project and other projects from Jazz registrants.

3. Once you define the project area, you can create work items and create queries on the work items.

4. You can explore the project's release, sprint, and backlog plans and see the plan progress.

5. Explore the source code, repository workspaces, and modules from the **Source Control** section of the Sandbox.

6. **Build Definitions**, **Build Engines**, and **Build Queue** can be explored from the **Builds** section.

Walking through a working example is a great way to learn Rational Team Concert. The JUnit Project gives us an opportunity to effortlessly set up the project and explore the features. In this section, you will set up the project and explore a bit of client and Sandbox application. The idea is to get familiar with the Rational Team Concert client's features on the project area, views, and perspectives and know how to administer the project with Rational Team Concert's web application.

> If you are using Rational Team Concert on Tomcat, it is very easy to import the JUnit Project and start exploring the project artifacts. Refer to *Appendix B, Installing the Express-C Edition with the Tomcat Server*, to get complete step-by-step instructions on how to do the import.

When using the Eclipse client for the first time, we need to connect to the Server Repository and the wizard asks for details, such as the Jazz Repository Connection URL, username, and password. Connect to `https://jazz.net/Sandbox/rtc` for the Sandbox experience as shown next:

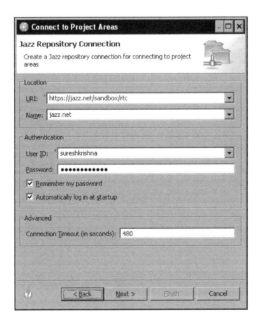

The next page displays a set of example projects from the Jazz Sandbox.

Select the example project as **JUnit Project** and click **Finish**. The JUnit Project is imported into the client and you can now explore the Team Artifacts, Team Organization, Process Templates, and other views.

Switching from the work items perspective to Jazz Administration perspective lets you do a variety of admin tasks such as:

- Create a project areas
- Administer the project users
- Invite project team members
- Deploy the process templates to repository

In the following section, we will be introduced to work items and Jazz Administration perspectives and their respective views. This will give us a brief overview of the Rational Team Concert's perspectives and views.

Work items perspective

If you are a team member, you can open the "work items" perspective and start exploring the views. From here you have a complete overview of your current tasks, project events, and the project build health. This is, in fact, the most used perspective for a team member.

Work items perspective includes several views such as Team Artifacts, My Work, and Team Central views that help you as a team member.

Team Artifacts view

Rational Team Concert installs the necessary code, templates, team members, and roles and gives you an out-of-the-box project. The Team Artifacts view contains a very important collection of project items.

Repository Connections gives you a list of currently connected repositories. You can get server information such as Server name, edition, build ID, and license type. Other information such as username, password, and URL for the team server is available. Client access license is also mentioned in the Repository Connections. In general, this section gives you an overview of the server connection, client license, and login credentials.

The **Project** Section contains the defined **Builds**, **Plans**, **Source Control**, and **Work items** related to that specific project. You can request new builds, view the old builds, define the build definitions, and build engines. Sprint and release planning is an integral part of the Team Artifacts. You can get a complete picture of the open and completed tasks.

The **Source Control** section in Team Artifacts has all components of the project and the association of the components to several streams.

A stream is a repository object that includes one or more components. Streams are typically used to integrate the work done in workspaces. Team members deliver their own changes to the stream and accept other team members' changes from the stream into their repository workspaces.

In any traditional project considerable time is spent in work planning and issue management by team leads and team members. It could be bugs, enhancements, or new features, but without an integrated solution with the development environment, you spend time on referring the disconnected systems of the development environment and issue/bug management tools. You can take advantage of the pre-defined work item queries and use the shared queries from your project team. Depending on the process template you use, Rational Team Concert knows a variety of work item types such as bugs, enhancements, tasks, and user stories.

 A work item is a way of keeping track of the tasks and issues that your team needs to address during the development cycle. The status and number of work items are indicators of the health of your project.

The next thing we want to do is to create the Repository Workspace and import the code into the Rational Team Concert client. Go to **JUnit Project | Project Area | Source Control | JUnit**, right click and select **New | Repository Workspace**.

 We can also create the Repository Workspace from the **My Repository Workspace** within the **Team Artifacts**. All the Repository Workspaces that you create will appear in the "My Repository Workspaces".

Enter the name you desire and description of the project in the dialog and click **Next**.

Select the workspace visibility depending on your project needs and click **Next**.

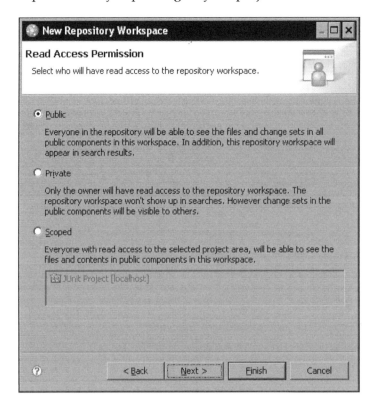

In the next step, select the available components of the project that interests you (as shown next). By default, the **Load repository workspace after creation** is checked. This means once the Repository Workspace is added, the code for the respective components will also be loaded. In this case, you can see the imported code in the project explorer of Rational Team Concert's client.

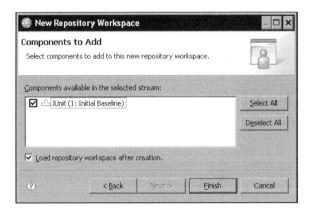

Once the Workspace Repository is created, various components are loaded. There are different options to load the Repository Workspace; for now select the **Find and load Eclipse projects** to add the projects to the client, as seen next.

The "load" action invokes a wizard that gives you a choice to select how to load the projects. The root component has three Eclipse projects that we can load by selecting **Find and load Eclipse projects** from the wizard.

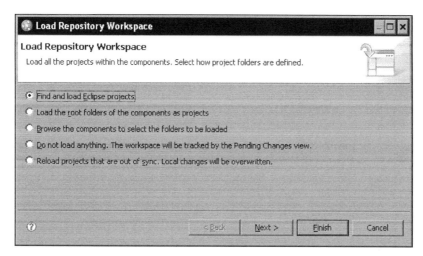

In the next page, select the projects that you want to import. Optionally select the directory location of the source code to be imported, as shown next:

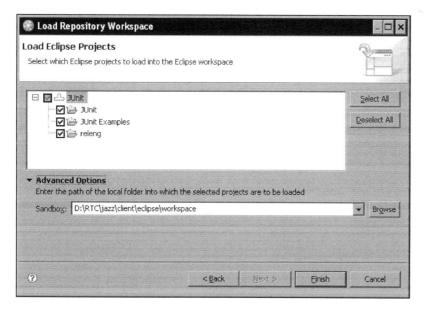

You can browse the source code from package explorer of Rational Team Concert's client, as in the following screenshot:

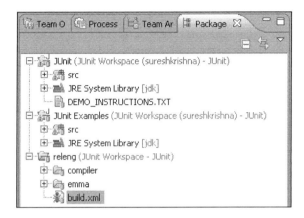

Now we can explore the JUnit Project plans. From the team artifacts view, go to various Sprint and Release plans. Sprint backlog shows a list of all tasks for each team member, along with each task's status (open versus completed). A Release backlog shows all the sprints for that release and a high-level view of the task status:

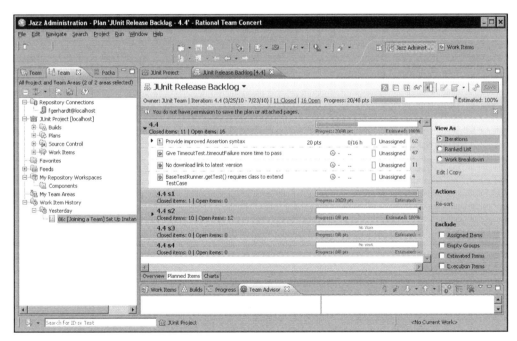

Team Collaboration being perhaps the most important feature of Rational Team Concert, the client provides a way to see and subscribe to the news feeds that let you know everything happening in your project. The news feeds gives you a good platform to understand who is doing what, on a regular basis. All the information regarding the team changes, builds, and plans are tracked and stored for future reference. These feeds can be added to your favorites, and you use the URL of the feed to publish and follow from other websites.

My Work view

The My Work view is the most commonly used view for a team member. This view shows work items that are assigned to you in several categories. Inbox section has the work items that are recently assigned to you. These work items must be processed to keep them either in the **Current Work** or **Future Work** section. The **Current Work** section contains work items that belong to current iteration. These items must be arranged and planned in the order of completion. Future Work section includes all open, closed, and unplanned work items for the future iterations, as shown next:

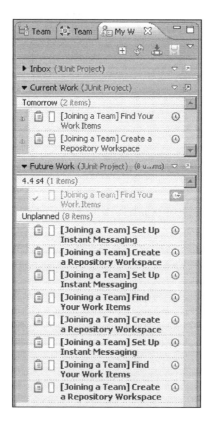

Team Central view

The Team Central view includes multiple sections that help you as a team member to have a transparency over the project development. This view has news feeds, build updates, open items in graphical representation, new unassigned work items, and team load. You get a real time view of the project load on various team members as seen in the following screenshot:

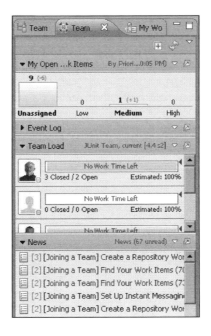

Jazz Administration perspective

The Jazz Administration perspective provides several views and editors to assist the project administrator. As an administrator, you can use these views to manage users, process templates, and to manage the team artifacts. Jazz Administration perspective includes process template, team organization, and team artifacts view. Team artifacts view caters the same functionality described in the work item's perspective.

Process Template view

You normally attach a process template when a project area is created. Process template is a guide and compass for the process followed in the project. Rational Team Concert provides set of templates for common processes such as Scrum, OpenUP, Cloudburst, and SimpleTeam process. Process Template view contains set of templates deployed in that Jazz repository as shown next:

Team Organization view

Rational Team Concert integrates the team into the project and development environment. The Eclipse client enables you to view and manage the users for a project. Along with assigning the users, you can also assign the roles for each user in that project. Remember that each user can have one or more project roles, such as team member, stakeholder, Scrum master, and product owner. The project roles very much depend on the process template that we choose. In our case, these roles result from the Scrum template.

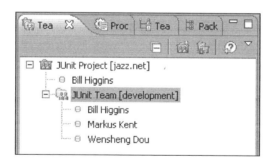

Ideally, you can add another team member for development team and assign role. From the **Team Organization** view, select the **Team Area** and open it. In the Team Area editor, you can add a team member and assign appropriate roles. However, because this JUnit Project is a read-only demo, we cannot save any newly added members to the repository. The following screenshot shows the members' feature:

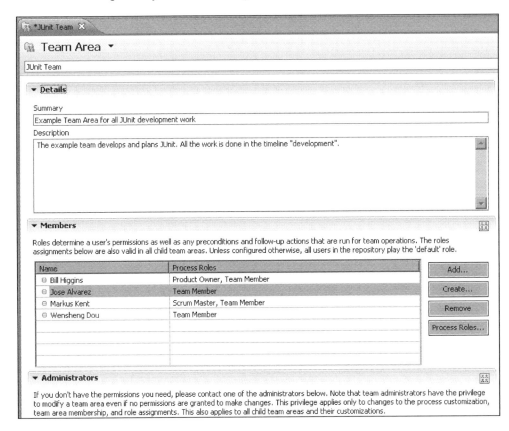

When you add a new user, Rational Team Concert will automatically ask whether or not you'd like to send a project invitation. This contains all the information the user needs to join the project and start working, including the team repository name, the user ID, and the project area name, as shown next:

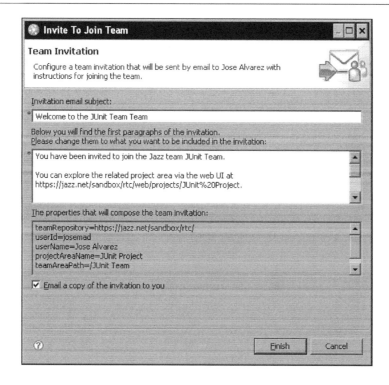

JUnit Project on the Web Interface

Many features available on the client are also available on the Web Interface for team server. A team member, stakeholder, or manager can log into the online application and get an overview of the project. In fact, the complete project management can be done from the online application too. Information on the dashboards, project areas, work items, plans, source control, and builds can be obtained from the online team server application.

The online application dashboards are the most useful ones to get a quick overview of the project. The dashboard has a customizable interface and user can add, delete, or modify the existing views. The following is a screenshot of the dashboard for the JUnit Project:

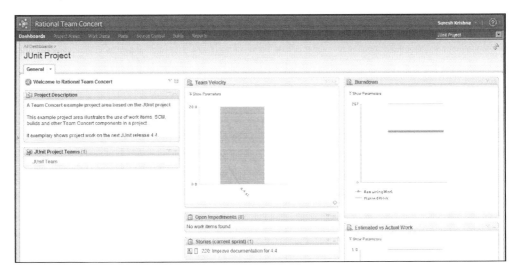

In general, the dashboard gives an overview of all the plans, tasks that have been recently opened or closed, and any blocking items. The project manager can connect to the team server and get the project status at the click of a button. Along with the work items, you will also see the Sprint and Release backlog and the percentage of the work completion. As a manager, you could get a real time graphs for the burn-down, actual work versus estimated tasks, and many others.

Team Advisor

Every operation in Rational Team Concert enforces a set of pre-conditions and post-conditions. When an operation needs to be executed and pre-conditions are not met, the error and reasons are communicated to the user with the help of the Team Advisor view. This view shows the list of all the operations that violated the pre-conditions and the reasons. Team Advisor increases the confidence of the team members as it describes the reasons why an operation did not work.

As an example, open the **JUnit Team Area** and add a user as a project member. Rational Team Concert provides a convenient way to add users to the Team Area by providing a lots of registered users with the Jazz Team Repository; an administrator can select the users and add to the project. As soon as the user is successfully added to the Team Area, the administrator can send the team an invitation e-mail:

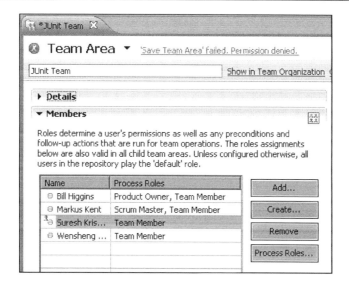

Remember that the JUnit Project is a read-only project from the Jazz Sandbox and any modifications are not permitted. In our case, the Team Advisor shows that the save operation could not be completed as the user does not have sufficient privileges. As you can see from the view, the Team Advisor shows you the complete description of violation and how it must be rectified.

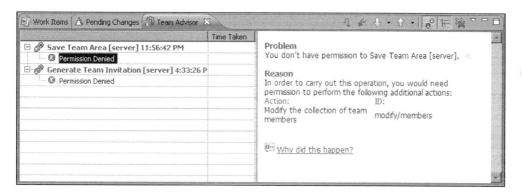

The JUnit Project gives a starting platform to explore several features of both Rational Team Concert's client and server. In this section, you have imported the JUnit example project, explored the team artifacts with work items, builds, plans, source code, and other components of the project.

You have seen how easy it is to connect to a repository, add a new team member to the project, create the Repository Workspace, and start working on the project right away. Finally, you explored the JUnit Project on Rational Team Concert web application. This project is intended to give you familiarity with several Eclipse clients' views and other functional areas.

Summary

In this chapter you have seen the different available versions of Rational Team Concert, and installed the Enterprise version's client and server. We have configured Rational Team Concert to work with the WebSphere application server.

After we set up the server, we played with the JUnit Project from the Jazz Sandbox. This gave us an overview on how to import the Project, create the Workspace Repository, and explore several other features of Rational Team Concert from the client.

In the next chapter, you will see how to import source code form the subversion dump file and start working on an example project. This example demo project will be used throughout this book for illustrating Rational Team Concert's features.

3

Setting up the Project

Tell me and I forget. Teach me and I remember. Involve me and I learn.

– Benjamin Franklin

In the previous chapter, we set up the Rational Team Concert team server and client, and configured it for WebSphere. Assume that a small team is developing a non-trivial project, which is called the **BookManager Application** on the Subversion configuration management system. In this chapter, we will perform the following:

- Importing the subversion dump of this project into the Rational Team Server
- Setting up the users
- Loading the source code
- Building and running the war from a Tomcat environment

Introduction

Until now, we have been using the JUnit example application provided by Rational Team Concert. Going forward, we will use a custom JEE demo application called "BookManager" to demonstrate Rational Team Concert's functionality.

Our goal is to create a simple application that will allow us to demonstrate the techniques of this book. The BookManager Application by design is a real working system, however, it is not so complex that we must invest a lot of time in trying to understand the application itself. Details of its architecture can be found in *Appendix C, The BookManager Application Architecture*.

In this chapter, we will review how to import the source code from subversion to Rational Team Server. In the next chapters, we'll enhance this application using Rational Team Server and Client.

Setting up the project

As we've seen in previous chapters, Rational Team Concert represents a software project as a **Project Area**. The project area defines the project deliverables, team structure, process, schedule, and more. A project area is stored as a top-level or root item in a repository and references project artifacts and stores the relationships between these artifacts. Access to a project area and its artifacts is controlled by permissions.

Similar to what we did when importing the JUnit sample project in the previous chapter, we are going to create a project area, only this time for the BookManager Application. Log in to the Rational Team Server as administrator. This can be done either from the Team Server web application or from the Rational Team Concert client. In the web application, go to **Project Area Management** from the main toolbar and create a new project area by clicking **Create Project Area**. Remember that a project area cannot be deleted from the repository; however, it can be archived, which places it in an inactive state.

At the time of creating the project area, we would need to enter some important attributes of the project, as follows:

- **Project Name**: This is the name key that will be used throughout the system.
- **Process Template**: Select the process template that our team uses.
- **Members**: Select the team members of the team for this project. We can select the users from the global list provided by the Rational Team Server.

- **Administrator**: Remember to add an administrator to the project, which enables the administrator to add permissions, roles, and so on.

Once we click on the **Save** button, it takes a few minutes for the team server to create the project area. As an administrator, we can also tweak into the timelines, roles, permissions, and access control.

Once the project area is created, the Rational Team Server prompts us if we would like to send the project invitations to the new users as shown in the next screenshot:

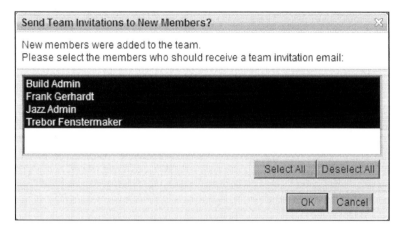

Once we select the users and confirm to send the invitations, we will be prompted to review the team invitation that is generated by the Rational Team Server.

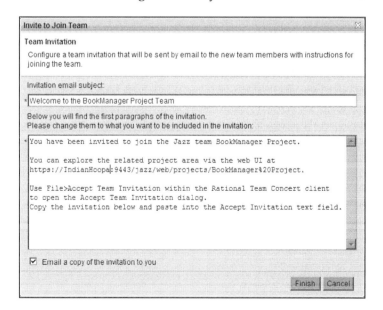

With this, the process of setting up the **BookManager Project** team area is complete. Now go to the Rational Team Concert's client, navigate to **Team Artifacts** view, and right-click to add a new project area as shown in the following screenshot:

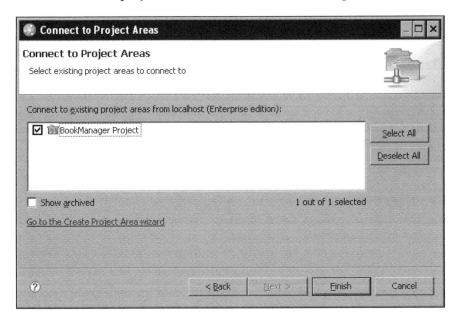

In the next step, we will import the SVN dump file into the Rational Team Concert.

Importing the subversion dump

In this section, we will see different steps to import the source code from the subversion to the Rational Team Server. Assume that the code is being developed and versioned in subversion. It is assumed that the administrator has already created the subversion dump file and it is available for use. We can download the project dump file and other source code from the Packt Publishing website.

In the first phase, we specify the subversion dump file and destination, which is a component in a repository workspace. In the second phase, the importer opens the dump file and displays the folders that can be selected for import and a list of subversion user names that we can map to Rational Team Server users.

Importing the subversion dump file is done from the Rational Team Concert client. From the client, open **File | Import**, as shown in the following screenshot:

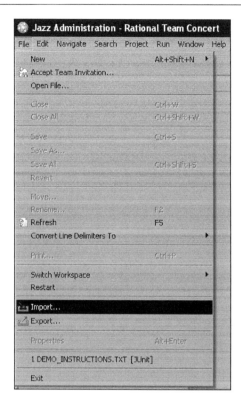

In the **Import** dialog, select the **Jazz Source Control | SVN Dump File** and click on **Next**. Notice that we could also import the **Change Set Archive** and **ClearCase Stream or Branch** into the Rational Team Server repository, as shown next:

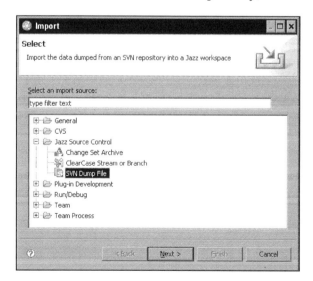

Select the dump file by navigating and selecting the appropriate file through the **Browse** button. Optionally, to save a compressed dump file, select **Save a compressed version of the dump file for additional imports**, as shown next:

[We cannot enter a ZIP file that contains the SVN dump file. Make sure that the SVN dump (`<filename>.dump`) file is extracted from the ZIP file.]

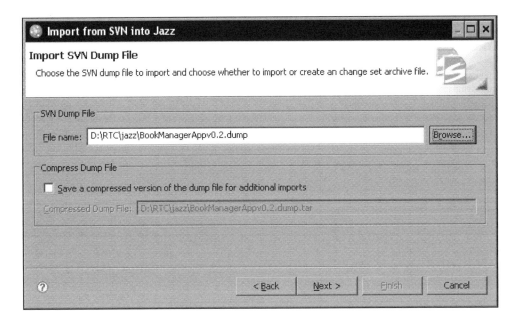

Create a new repository workspace and new component by selecting **Create a new repository workspace named:** and type a name for the new workspace. The import creates a new workspace and component. The component has the same name as the workspace, as shown next:

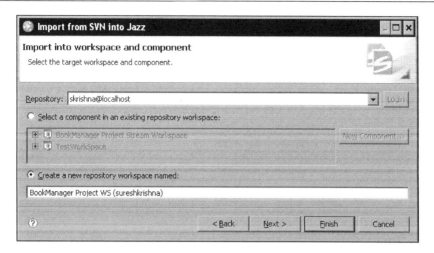

To specify a baseline name in the **Post Import Baseline Name** field, type a new baseline name. To generate baselines for branch and tag points, select **Create baselines for branch and tag points**. To specify a text file encoding in the text file encoding pane, select **Other** in the drop-down list, select an encoding type. To reconcile existing and imported files, select **Reconcile any overlap between existing imported files and folders**. To specify a revision range to import, in the **Revisions to import pane**, select **Import all revisions within the specified range**; in the **Start Revision** and **End Revision** fields, specify the revision range as shown next:

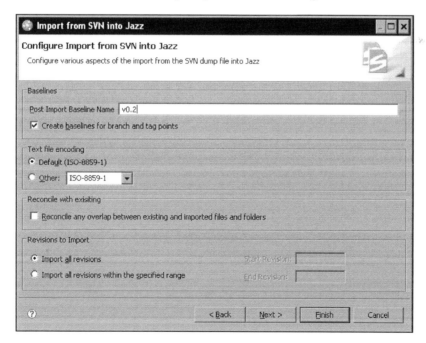

The following screenshot lets us map the SVN users to Jazz Users. Rational Team Concert allows us to choose how we want to map the users, as follows:

- **Prompt for Jazz users once the SVN user IDs are discovered**: When we want to defer the mapping of usernames until the SVN usernames are discovered.

- **Do not map SVN users to Jazz users**: When we do not want any relation between SVN users to Rational Team Server users.

- **Automatically map SVN users to Jazz users with the same id and create any missing users**: When we want automatic discovery of the usernames and we want Rational Team Server to create any missing usernames automatically.

- **Use the mappings entered below**: When we know exactly which SVN usernames map to Rational Team Server users.

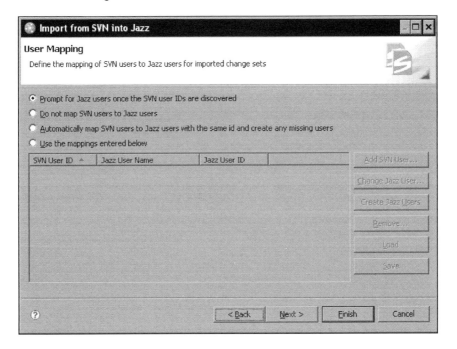

- If we are not sure of the structure of the subversion repository, select **Prompt to determine what folders to import when the SVN repository folder structure is known**.

- To import a path as a top-level folder in the target component, select **Import the paths specified below as top-level folders in the target component**. To add a path, click on **Add Path,** and in the **Add Path** dialog box, type the path name in the **Path** field and click on **OK**. To load a set of paths saved to a file, click on **Load** and navigate to the file. To save the file to a specified location, click on **Save**.

- To import a path as a component root, select **Import the path specified below as the root of the component**. To edit a path, select it and then click on **Edit**. In the **Path** field of the **Edit** dialog, change the path and click on **OK**.

We have the complete project directly under the SVN trunk, so choose to **Import the path specified below as the root of the component**, as shown in the following screenshot:

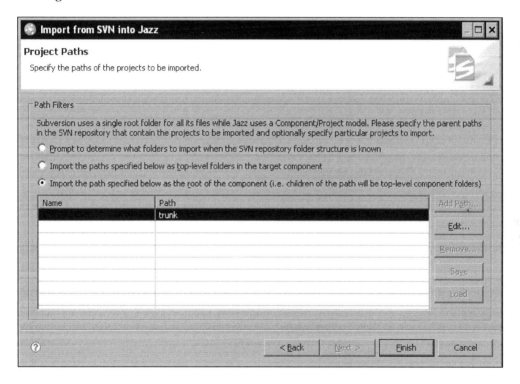

Rational Team Concert reads the complete SVN dump file, discovers the users, and asks us which source folders to import. As we have the complete project under the top-level, click on **Add Projects**, as shown next:

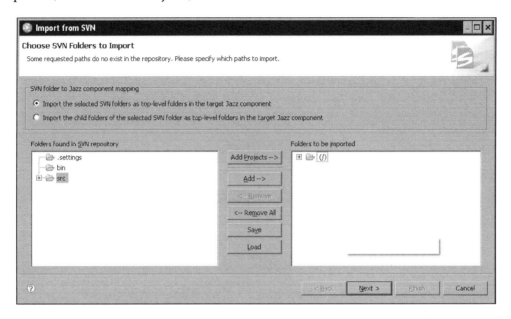

Now, the user IDs from the SVN dump file are discovered and Rational Team Concert displays the users. Notice that there are two user IDs, and one SVN user ID is already mapped to a Jazz user ID, as shown next:

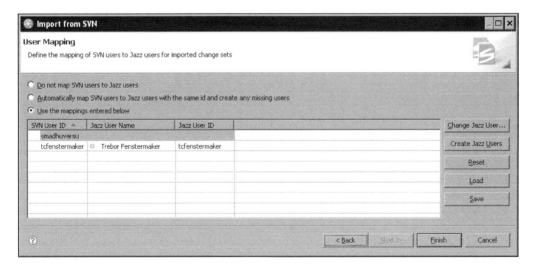

For the other SVN user ID (smadhuvarsu), which does not have the corresponding Jazz user ID, select the respective Jazz user ID and click on **Finish**. This completes the SVN dump import.

 Mapping the users between the SVN system and Jazz Team Server is a very important feature for administrators. It is not uncommon that the usernames are different across an organization's systems.

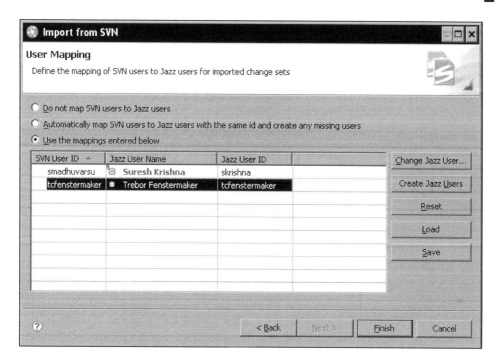

Rational Team Concert's team has imported the complete SVN dump (read the usernames) and read the source code and revisions. This provides a seamless experience when working with team server source control. The Team Artifacts view shows an overview of the project as shown in the next screenshot. However, we need to do a few things first to be able to work with it, which are as follows:

1. The BookManager project component is added to the Components under the **My Repository Workspaces**.

2. The BookManager project repository is added to the **My Repository Workspaces**.

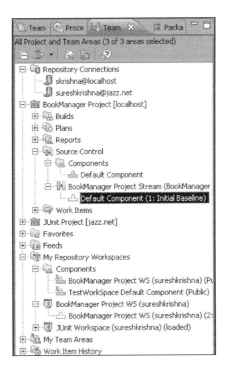

Once the project area, repository, and components are set up, it's time to load the source code and work on it. We import the source code by selecting the component from Repository Workspace, right-clicking, and selecting **Load…**.

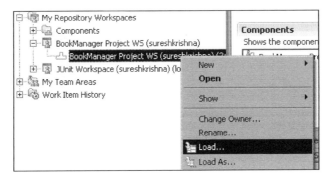

The **Load…** action invokes a wizard that gives us a choice of how we would like to load the projects. As we have an Eclipse project, select **Find and load Eclipse projects**. Components, that are not developed as Eclipse projects can be imported and set up from the root folders as shown next:

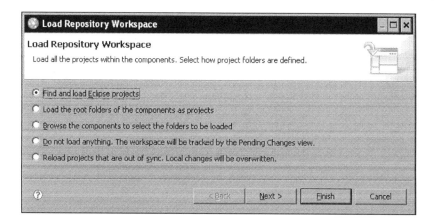

The wizard lists all the available projects from the `root` directory of the repository. We can select the appropriate project and optionally select where the source code should be imported.

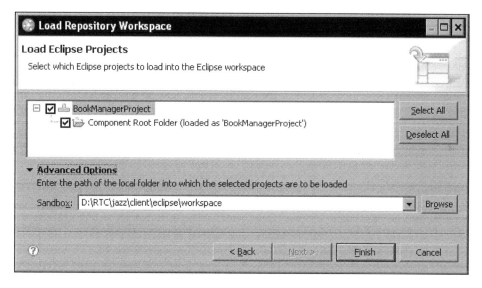

Once the import source code is finished, the component is loaded and the source code is visible in the **Package Explorer**.

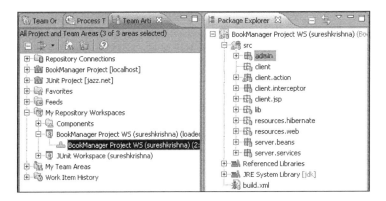

Project source code

Now that we have the code from the BookManager project, let's look at how the source code is organized. This section serves to give an introduction and overview of the application and the technologies used.

The BookManager source is comprised of servlets and JSPs, as well as some Java beans for persistence. These operate in the Apache Struts and Hibernate frameworks; therefore, we also have the libraries needed for these along with the configuration files that tell these components how to work together. The building and packaging is done using ANT, a popular, robust open source build system available from the Apache Project. The `build.xml` file controls this build process.

These sources in turn are organized in packages, as shown in the following screenshot of the Package Explorer in Rational Team Client:

Each package is represented by a directory under **src** and contains the following:

- **admin**: A command-line administrative utility that allows one to create user accounts (both administrative and non-administrative), as well as the full Derby database schema, populated with demo data.

- **client.action**: It has the `Struts ActionServlet` classes containing the required `execute()` method, that perform the business logic for each user-generated action.

- **client.interceptor**: It has the interceptor classes for log in and log out. It always validates for an authenticated session.

- **client.jsp**: It has all the JSP pages responsible for the UI representation on the client.

- **lib**: It has the library files necessary for all the third-party utilities we use, including Derby, Hibernate, and Struts.

- **resources.hibernate**: It has the `Hibernate config` file for the database connection and also the `domain mapping` file for the `Book` entity.

- **resources.web**: It has the resources such as `web.xml`, `struts.xml`, and `style.css` that are needed to deploy as a web application.

- **server.beans**: It has the domain objects, implemented as simple Java beans with the required getters and setters.

- **server.services**: It has the Hibernate persistence utilities that handle the connections, CRUD functions, and so on.

Building and running the application

Now that we've imported the source, we're ready to build, deploy, and execute the finished application.

From the Rational Team Concert client, go to **External Tools | External Tools Configuration** and create a new **Ant Build** configuration. Remember to use the same build file defined on the project (called, by convention, `build.xml`). The build file is available on the project root of the client.

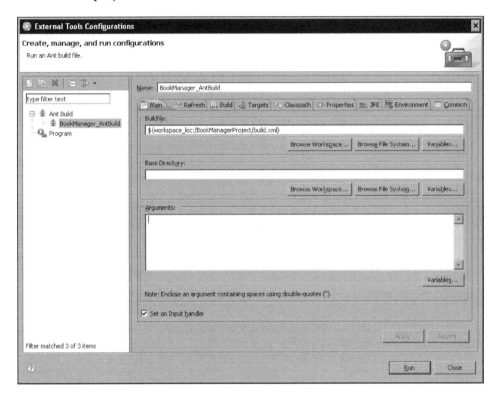

Once the Ant Build configuration is set up, add the configuration to the External Tools' **Favorite** menu, and run the **BookManager_AntBuild** configuration, which compiles the sources and creates both the standalone `admin.jar` (for the command-line administrative utility) and an application WAR file that can be deployed to any standard servlet container.

Admin utility

The `bookmanager-admin.jar` file is an executable JAR that provides a simple command-line administrative interface for managing the database and users for the BookManager application. There are options to create and list users, and assign them administrative roles. It can also be used to populate the database schema with sample data from the **comma-separated value (csv)** file created during the build.

Before we run the web-based application, let's use the `bookmanager-admin.jar` to create some administrative and non-administrative users, and populate the database with sample data. Copy the `bookmanager-admin.jar` and `samplebooks.csv` files created from the BookManager build to the `<tomcatHome>/bin` directory. Open a command prompt and go to `<tomcatHome>/bin`. We assume that the java path is already set and we can run java from the command line. To create a user, enter the following command line:

```
java -jar bookmanager-admin.jar adduser <username> <password> <usertype>
```

Select the username of our choice, and a password that will be SHA encrypted. If we wish to make this user an administrator, enter "admin" for the **usertype**; otherwise enter "user."

If the BookManager database doesn't already exist, `bookmanager-admin.jar` will first create the necessary Derby files and schema, before adding the user.

We can use this utility to add as many administrative and non-administrative users as we like.

```
C:\WINDOWS\system32\cmd.exe                                          _ □ ×

D:\RTC\1605_RTC-Essentials\apache-tomcat-6.0.26\bin>java -jar bookmanager-admin.
jar adduser skrishna tempPass1 user
Hibernate: select book0_.book_id as book1_0_, book0_.catalog as catalog0_, book0
_.title as title0_, book0_.author as author0_, book0_.copyright as copyright0_,
book0_.binding as binding0_ from book book0_
Hibernate: select max(user_id) from booklookuser
Hibernate: insert into booklookuser (username, password, usertype, user_id) valu
es (?, ?, ?, ?)

D:\RTC\1605_RTC-Essentials\apache-tomcat-6.0.26\bin>
```

To see a list of existing users, along with their SHA encrypted password and their role, enter `java -jar bookmanager-admin.jar listusers` as shown next:

```
C:\WINDOWS\system32\cmd.exe                                          _ □ ×

D:\RTC\1605_RTC-Essentials\apache-tomcat-6.0.26\bin>java -jar bookmanager-admin.
jar listusers
Hibernate: select book0_.book_id as book1_0_, book0_.catalog as catalog0_, book0
_.title as title0_, book0_.author as author0_, book0_.copyright as copyright0_,
book0_.binding as binding0_ from book book0_
Hibernate: select booklookus0_.user_id as user1_1_, booklookus0_.username as use
rname1_, booklookus0_.password as password1_, booklookus0_.usertype as usertype1
_ from booklookuser booklookus0_
Current users:
admin d033e22ae348aeb566fc214aec3585c4da997 admin
skrishna e4199c3b23f8762d28462a6a3e64030df706a6c admin
user 12dea96fec20593566ab75692c9949596833adc9 user
```

To populate the database with sample data, enter the following:

```
java -jar bookmanager-admin.jar popdb ./samplebooks.csv.
```

```
C:\WINDOWS\system32\cmd.exe                                          _ □ ×

D:\RTC\1605_RTC-Essentials\apache-tomcat-6.0.26\bin>java -jar bookmanager-admin.
jar popdb ./samplebooks.csv
Hibernate: select book0_.book_id as book1_0_, book0_.catalog as catalog0_, book0
_.title as title0_, book0_.author as author0_, book0_.copyright as copyright0_,
book0_.binding as binding0_ from book book0_
Hibernate: select max(book_id) from book
Hibernate: insert into book (catalog, title, author, copyright, binding, book_id
) values (?, ?, ?, ?, ?, ?)
Hibernate: insert into book (catalog, title, author, copyright, binding, book_id
) values (?, ?, ?, ?, ?, ?)
Hibernate: insert into book (catalog, title, author, copyright, binding, book_id
) values (?, ?, ?, ?, ?, ?)
Hibernate: insert into book (catalog, title, author, copyright, binding, book_id
) values (?, ?, ?, ?, ?, ?)
Hibernate: insert into book (catalog, title, author, copyright, binding, book_id
) values (?, ?, ?, ?, ?, ?)
```

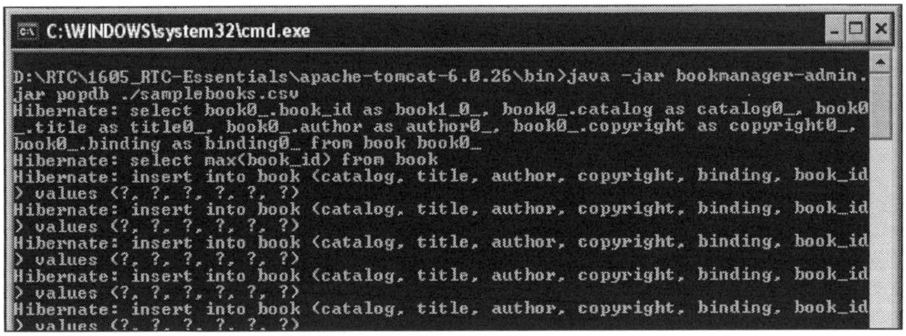

BookManager application

We're now ready to deploy the generated WAR file to any standard servlet container. In our case, we will use Apache Tomcat.

1. Start the Tomcat server using the appropriate Tomcat utility. Make sure that this is a separate instance from the Rational Team Server, listening on a different port.

2. Go to **Management** console. If we deployed Tomcat on 8080, browse to `http://localhost:8080/manager/html`.

3. Select the WAR file generated by the build and click on **Deploy**.

4. Once the application is deployed, we can access the application by browsing to `http://localhost:8080/BookManager/welcome.jsp`.

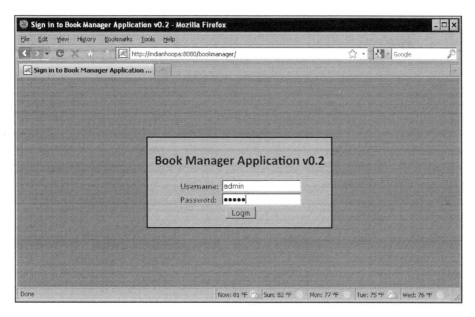

If we log in as an **admin** user, the **Welcome** screen enables us to add, modify, delete, and list the books. Each time we add a new book, the application automatically redirects us to the List View action. Every screen in the application displays the current username and a logout facility.

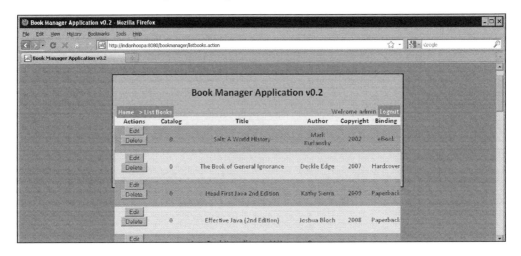

All the actions in the application are represented by the breadcrumb widget, and as a user, we know exactly how to get to the **Home** screen. Try using the Add Books action to put more books in the database; we will see a simple web form with basic information about the book. Clicking **Add** will execute the appropriate Struts action, and save our new book in the Derby database, Hibernate. It should then appear on the list of books.

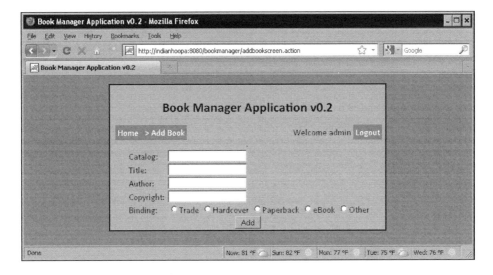

In the next chapters of this book, we will test the BookManager application and enhance it using Rational Team Concert client and server. In particular, we will get introduced in depth to various aspects of team server, collaboration, work items, planning, builds, and release management.

Summary

In this chapter, we revisited importing a subversion dump into Rational Team Concert, only this time using the sample application that we will use through the rest of this book—BookManager. We created the team area for our new project, and added the Repository Workspace where we loaded the components of the project. We took a quick look at the BookManager's functionality, and learned how to use Rational Team Client to build it into a distributable application. Finally, we ran both the command-line administrative utility for BookManager, to create the database and add users, and deployed and ran the WAR file that comprises the user functions of BookManager.

In the next chapter, we will see in-depth aspects of team and source control in Rational Team Client and Server. We will see items such as team roles, permissions, configuring teams, change sets, submitting the change sets, streams, and more.

4

Team and Source Control

Change in all things is sweet.

--Aristotle

Source control is a fundamental aspect of modern software development. The source control system helps us to store, version, and control the requirement documents, design documents, architecture blueprints, test documents, and of course, our source code.

The following is a quote about SCM from Roger Pressman's book *Software Engineering: A Practitioner's Approach*:

> *Source Control Management (SCM) is a set of activities designed to control change by identifying the work products that are likely to change, establishing relationships among them, defining mechanisms for managing different versions of these work products, controlling the changes imposed, and auditing and reporting on the changes made*

With the increasing complexity of software development, we must consider the following:

- Integration of source control with team processes
- Seamless integration of source control system into coding environment
- Traceability of the issues/bugs/enhancements to the source code and vice versa
- Ability to suspend the current work in favor of another task
- Creating branches that allow for parallel development and merge there after
- Ability to resolve conflicts from other team members changes on the same source code

Introduction

In this chapter, we will see:

- How Rational Team Concert enhances the source control management experience giving greater control to the development team
- Different concepts in the source control
- How to work with the Rational Team Source Control

The source control component of Rational Team Concert manages the change flow of the source code, documents, and other artifacts generated by each team member. Rational Team Concert's source control organizes files and folders into components and streams, and provides workspaces where we can view and modify file and folder contents. The repository objects represent the configuration of the system being developed and allow any configuration to be retrieved, shared, or built.

Rational Team Concert's source control is integrated into the other parts of the life cycle as follows; this enables the developer to focus on the real domain problems and worry less about the tools that they use:

- The Ration Team Concert's Build Engine is integrated in such a way that it can pull the snapshot of the files from source control and reproduce the exact source build.
- Work items and Change sets can be linked together providing traceability of changes to the reasons for a change.
- Process management uses source control as an integrated mechanism. For example, we can set up the process in such a way that new hires in our team must get their change sets reviewed by the project leader before submitting.

Rational Team Concert lets us benefit from SCM's ability to track and version our changes, whether or not we are ready to share those changes with our team. As a user we have our own private repository workspace that stores the changes we've made, independent of everyone else's changes. When we load our repository workspace, the files and folders in it are transferred from the repository on the server to our Eclipse workspace on our computer. To push a change from our Eclipse workspace to the repository workspace we check in the change.

In the next sections, we will look at some examples using the team invitation and team source control system.

Team invitation

In the first chapter, we have seen several things to consider when joining a new team, such as getting the project details, source control login information, repository access, and so on. Rational Team Concert tackles these issues by letting the administrator log in to the server or client and adds the new team member to the project. The system will immediately send an e-mail to the new team member with all the details he needs to start working. This reduces the probability of mistakes when providing the information because all team members receive uniform information.

In this section, we will see how to accept a team invitation for a team member with user ID `fgerhardt` and set up the complete project to start working on. As a team member, the Team Artifacts view lets us to accept the team invitation, as shown next:

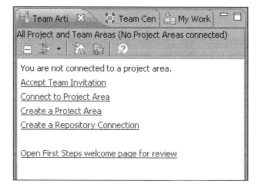

The **Accept Team Invitation** action needs us to enter the e-mail content in the message area. Enter the invitation e-mail content and click on **Finish**.

The following screenshot shows the content of an e-mail sent to a team member when an administrator invites him to join a project. It contains the link to access the web UI and the details of how to log in to the client. The first time when we, as a new team member, log in to the client, we have a variety of actions to do such as **Accept Team Invitation**, **Connect to Project Area**, and so on. **Accept a Team Invitation** will do everything necessary for us to start working on the project.

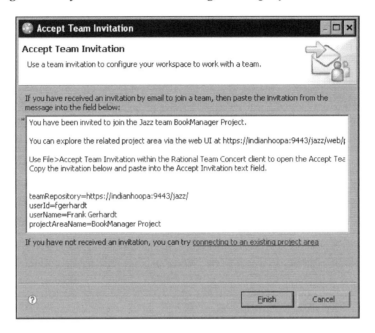

The Rational Team Concert client sets up the complete project for us. We could see that the project area and streams are set up and components are displayed. The Team Artifacts view gives us a high-level view of the project. We can browse the work items assigned to us and create a local repository workspace to start working on these. When we join the project for the first time, we may not have any project-related work items.

Another major chunk of information is in the project area editor (see the following screenshot). The editor has all the information we need to know about the project, including the following:

- List of team members and their e-mail addresses
- Administrator of the project and their e-mail address
- Development timelines for sprints and releases (depends on the process template)
- Complete transparency on the process from the **Project Description** section

- List of previous releases of the project
- Access control
- Links to builds, iteration plans, work items, and source control

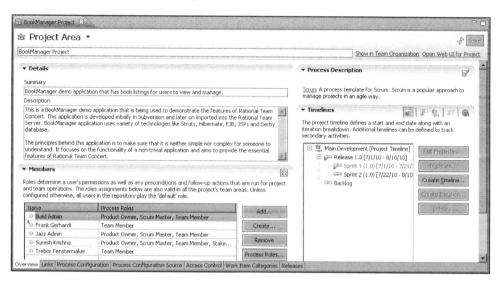

In this section, we have seen how to accept team invitation in no time and set up the complete project to work on. In the next section, we will see in-depth details on the team source control and how a team member can leverage its powerful features.

The next section assumes that we are logged in as an admin user and all the steps are done using the admin user.

Streams and components

A **Stream** is a repository object that includes one or more components. Streams are typically used to integrate the work done in repository workspaces. As a team member, we would deliver changes from our repository workspace into the stream and accept other team members' changes from the stream into our repository workspace.

A **Component** is a collection of artifacts (analogous to a module in conventional software development). We can make any component in the repository as a part of a stream. Typically, the components in a stream are related functionally so that they are grouped together. After we have created a stream, we can use the stream editor to manage components.

We can create a stream to hold several components with different versions that represent an important configuration of a system. A milestone release or development version of the BookManager project is an example of such a configuration. When we deliver change sets from our workspace to a stream and accept other team members' change sets from the stream, the stream represents the current state of the team's development effort.

Imagine the stream as a concept similar to "branch" in other version control systems, but with many more capabilities. A component is a collection of source files, documents, or other artifacts; and a stream contains a set of versioned components. By using multiple streams, we can start working on different components with different versions. This is an extremely helpful scenario when we want to do tasks such as the following:

- Developing the next major version on a new stream
- Making a project release ready by working on a release branch
- Maintaining older versions of components on a maintenance branch
- For large projects, document components can be in a single document branch

An example may look like the following diagram:

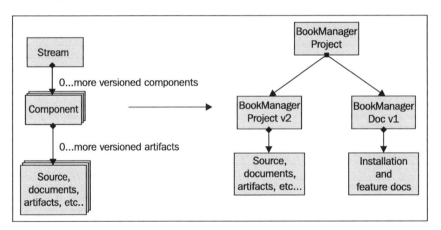

We can imagine several other possibilities to organize the code into components and components into different streams. In the previous diagram, we can see how the BookManager project is organized into components, namely *BookManager Project v2* and *BookManager Doc v1*. In a similar way, we can imagine that the BookManager project also has another stream called **BookManager-Release-v0.1** that deals with all the versioned components used for a specific release.

In the previous chapter, we imported the source code from the Subversion version management dump file and set up the BookManager repository and component. Now, we will create the bare bones of a BookManager Doc component (as shown in the following screenshot) and add it to the team source control, then add this new component to the BookManager Project (dev) stream.

We already set up the component BookManager Doc as an Eclipse project, and in the next step, we will add the component to the team source control and share it with the entire team. In this component, there are two folders: **design-doc**, to contain the architecture and design documents; and **install-doc**, to contain application installation documents.

To share the BookManager Doc project into the team source control, select the **BookManager Doc** project, right-click, and select **Team | Share Project** as shown next:

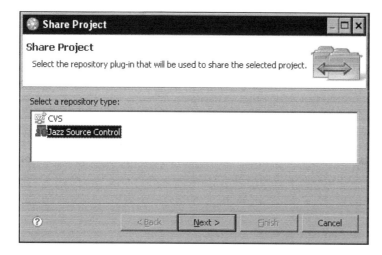

As seen in the previous screenshot, from the **Share Project** dialog, select **Jazz Source Control** and click on **Next** to select further details. We can either select an existing workspace or create a new one. For now, we will use the existing repository **BookManager Project** and click on **New Component**. Enter the name of the component and click on **OK**, as shown next:

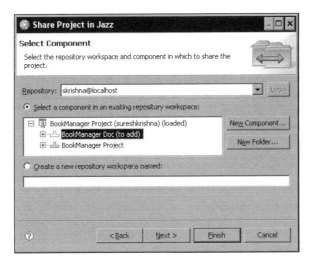

In the next dialog (refer to the following screenshot), we can see all the resources that need to be added to the team repository and a set of resource ignore patterns. The dialog provides a good interface to manage the ignore patterns of the resources. When we are not sure of the resources to add, check the **Show all resources** option, then selectively choose which resource to ignore.

Once we've specified the resources to ignore, click on **Finish** and Rational Team Concert will add the needed artifacts to the repository and make a change list for us. The change list shows the files and folders that are affected by this change. We can accept the change and deliver it to the stream from the context menu of the **Pending Changelists** view, as shown next:

Once the component is delivered, we can see that the repository workspace added the BookManager Doc component. The component has the baseline information attached to the view. In our case the baseline says **1: Initial Baseline**.

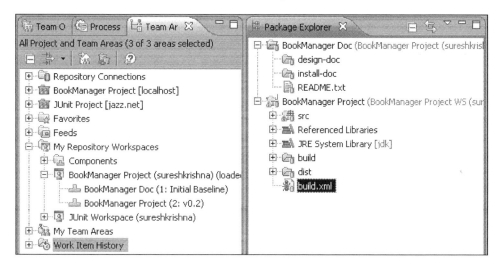

Here we have seen how to share the code from client to team source control and create a new BookManager Doc component. Now this component is available for any team member to view and work on. When a user who is authorized to see the project sources, for example, fgerhardt (see the setup at the beginning of the chapter), logs in to the client and loads the BookManager project, he can see the BookManager Doc component as shown next. This user can load the components into the local repository and start working on them when needed.

Repository workspace

A **repository workspace** is a mirror of the repository artifacts available on the local machine from the server repository (as shown in the following screenshot). We can create a repository workspace and add or create new components that contain project artifacts. We can deliver the project artifacts to make sure that the client's local workspace and repository workspace are in sync.

As a team member, we create a repository workspace to be able to work with the components. If a component already exists, we can import and load it. Otherwise, we can share a new component through our repository workspace. We create the local repository workspace either from a source control stream or from **My Repository Workspaces** section, which is available from the Team Artifacts view. Once we create a new repository workspace, add the required components and then load them. **Load** is the act of synchronizing the code or artifacts from the server repository to the local repository.

Flow target

Flow target is the target area where the delivered changes flow into. The flow target for repository workspaces can be a stream or another workspace. Flow target can be modified from the repository workspace editor.

Once we load the code, we can start working on the code changes and can submit the change lists back to the flow targets. Check-in copies work from our local workspace to our repository workspace. Our changes or work items remain private and local to the workspace until we decide to deliver it to a team flow target such as a shared stream. We can also replace the contents of the components with other repository workspace components or different baselines of that component.

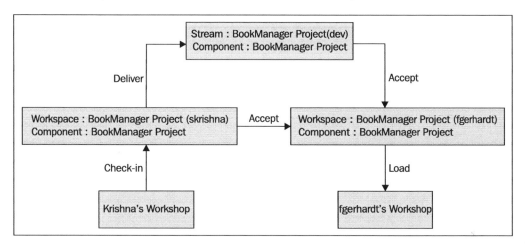

The previous picture gives an overview of the complete process from check-in to load steps. Let us see a scenario where the user `skrishna` checks-in and another user `fgerhardt` loads the changes.

1. The user `skrishna` made changes to the component's source code and checks-in. Remember that these changes are applied only to the repository workspace.

2. From the repository workspace, we need to deliver the change list to the stream. This step makes the source code available to the rest of the team.

3. Now, the user `fgerhardt` sees the changes done on the same component that he is working on and accepts the changes. However, the changes are made only to his local repository workspace.

4. Finally, the user `fgerhardt` loads the component explicitly by calling out the **Load** action on the component.

Repository workspace without flow target

When we want to experiment with modules locally, we can create a repository workspace without a flow target. When we use the repository workspace wizard, on the **Select a Stream** page, select **Just back up my work. Don't flow changes to a stream yet**. This will create a repository workspace without a flow target.

At times, we want to work on a piece of functionality and do not want to deliver the changes to a stream. This could be because we are experimenting with a piece of functionality or this is a quick customer demo. In such cases, we can create a new repository workspace where the artifact changes in the component will not flow to any target.

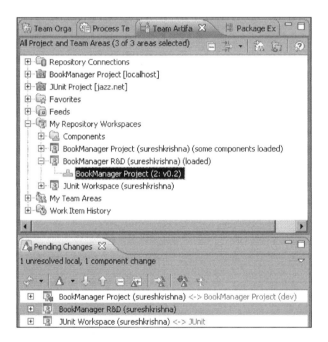

A repository workspace without a flow target can be identified with the help of visual clues as seen in the previous screenshot. In the **Pending Changes** view, we would notice that while other repositories have the flow targets represented by "<->", the repository without a follow target misses this representation.

Remember that when the repository workspace does not have a flow target, we could still do the changes on the component and check in. However, we do not have the option to deliver the changes as there is no associated stream as a flow target. Thus, we can take full advantage of the source control features except that we cannot flow to a target.

Repository ownership

Whether or not the repository workspace has a flow target, every repository has an owner who manages the repository visibility, components, and flow targets. It is a rather natural scenario in software development that a piece of work is created by one team member and later edited by another. In this case, the Rational Team Concert client enables us to change the ownership of the repository workspace so that other team members can continue the work as an owner.

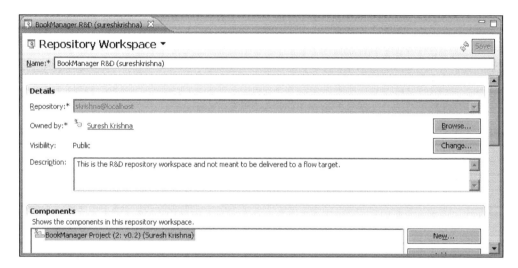

As an administrator, we want to know the number of repository workspaces for a project or average repository workspaces for a team member. As a team member, we want to search for one of many workspaces that we own. Rational Team Concert's client provides an easy way to search for the available workspace repositories and ownerships. On the Team Artifacts view, select **My Repository Workspaces** and select **Search for Repository Workspaces** on the context menu. This will show a complete list of the available workspace repositories and the associated owner.

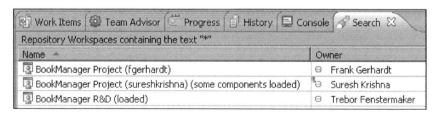

Workspace snapshots

A **snapshot** is a repository object that includes exactly one baseline for each component in a repository workspace. (A **baseline** is a repository object that records the state of a component at a specific time. Every component has at least one baseline, which was created when the component was created.) Snapshots are useful for capturing the state of a workspace, and are typically used to record important workspace configurations so that they can be recreated. A workspace snapshot gives a collection of component baselines at an exact point in time.

A snapshot is created on a repository workspace with all the available components and, if needed, the snapshot can be promoted onto a stream. When we create a snapshot, the process will automatically create a baseline for the components that do not have one. Snapshots are also created by the Rational Build Engine so that we exactly know which snapshot is used to do a build. The snapshot and baselines created by the build are private to the build workspace. If we want to make them official, we can promote them to a stream.

We can create a snapshot by selecting the appropriate repository workspace and on the context menu select **New | Snapshot**. Enter the required information and select the list of components that participate in the snapshot. Finally, click on **OK** to create a new snapshot as shown next:

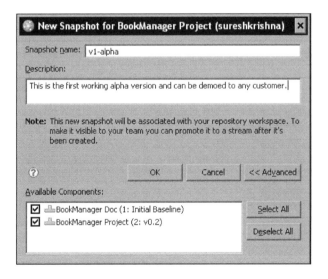

The creation of a snapshot also creates a new baseline for the available components in the workspace. In the repository workspace of the BookManager project, we can notice that the component version numbers increase by one. Also, in the **Pending Changes** view, the new versions of the components are ready to be delivered to the stream as shown in the following screenshot:

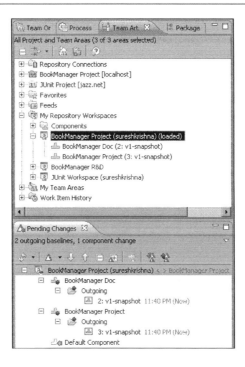

It is a common scenario that once software is released, we want to work on a specific baseline or snapshot of the component to fix issues or bugs. Without a baseline, it could become very painful to find the exact code base and then discard or back up the current changes manually. With Rational Team Concert, we can easily replace the repository workspace contents with components from another baseline.

Ignoring resources

Many times projects generate files that do not need to be under the source control. In such cases, Rational Team Concert's client provides the capability to identify and make the files ignored by the source control. Ignored resources are not checked in by the source control.

Why does RTC have its own ignore list?

Rational Team Concert provides a way to ignore the files that fall under some patterns defined by the user. Eclipse too has the file ignore mechanism. However, Eclipse does not provide a way to distribute and share the ignore file list. Thus, Rational Team Concert gives the power to the user by providing a way to share with the team.

The list of resources to be ignored by Rational Team Concert source control is kept in a file named .jazzignore. There is typically a .jazzignore file in the project root folder. Files and folders whose names appear in .jazzignore will not be checked in, and therefore, cannot become part of a change set. While ignoring a resource, we can choose to ignore them project-wide or in a specific folder. By default, Rational Team Concert source control ignores two types of files—resources ending with a .class extension, and the bin directory of an Eclipse workspace. To add additional resources to the ignore list, follow the next steps:

1. In the **Eclipse Package Explorer** view, right-click the resource and click on **Team | Add to ignore list**. Files added to the ignore list are immediately removed from open change sets or the Unresolved folder, and the modified .jazzignore file becomes part of the current change set.

2. To remove a resource from the ignore list so that we can add it to a change set, right-click the resource, and click on **Team | Remove from ignore list**.

3. We can edit any .jazzignore file to manage patterns and file names. To specify names and patterns to be ignored in all folders of a project, add the names and patterns to the value of the core.global.ignore property in the .jazzignore file at the project root. For example, to ignore all files in a project that have suffixes .htm, .html, and .cat, set the value of core.global.ignore as: core.global.ignore= *.htm *.html *.cat.

A .jazzignore file is treated like any other file under Rational Team Concert source control. When we modify it and want other team members to take advantage of this, we must check it to copy it to our repository workspace.

The following is a sample .jazzignore file that specifies the .class files as a pattern to ignore for the BookManager project component:

```
### Jazz Ignore 0
# Default value for core.ignore.recursive is *.class
#  Changing this value changes check-in behavior for the entire
project.
#
# Default value for core.ignore is bin
#  Changing this value changes check-in behavior for the local
                                              directory.
#
# Ignore properties should contain a space separated list of
                                       filename patterns.
# Each pattern is case sensitive and surrounded by braces
                                          ('{' and '}').
# "*" matches zero or more characters, and "?" matches single
                                              characters.
```

```
#
#   e.g: {*.sh} {\.*}     ignores shell scripts and hidden files

# NOTE: modifying ignore files will not change the ignore status
                                                    of derived
# resources.

core.ignore.recursive= \
  {*.class}

core.ignore= \
  {bin} \
  {build} \
  {dist}
```

This component has a build file that generates the class files, compiles, and makes it distributable in local directories. Therefore, the different files `bin`, `build`, and `dist` are added as patterns so that the build-generated directories are ignored. This is an extremely useful feature for the team that everyone uses a single configuration and reduces the erroneous check-ins.

Explicit resource locks

Rational Team Concert provides an efficient way to "lock" and "unlock" the project artifacts depending on a project's need. Many times, it is necessary to lock the resource till the change is done and delivered to the stream. In instances when we are fixing a critical customer bug or a document file that is difficult to merge, we need an explicit lock. This ensures that our version of change is always delivered without conflicts from other team members.

To lock a resource from the Rational Team Concert client, select the resource, and from the context menu, select **Team | Lock**.

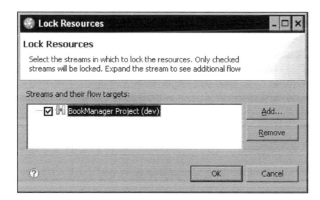

Before a resource is locked, we are asked to select the streams that this resource will remain locked till the change set is delivered as shown in the previous screenshot. Depending on the requirement, one can select multiple streams to lock the resource while not locking the same resource in some other streams.

Soon after locking a resource, all the users will be able to see that this resource is locked by a specific user on a stream. The Rational Team Concert client UI indicates the lock by a visible marker that reads like **Locked by <USERNAME> in <STREAM>**.

Change sets

A **change set** is a collection of changed resources in a single component, which can be either checked-in and delivered or suspended till a later time. Change sets flow between a repository workspace and its flow targets. Workspaces usually have at least one flow target and many have more than one.

Change sets are classified as outgoing when they are present in a local workspace but not in its flow target. In a similar way, change sets are classified as incoming when they are present in a flow target but not in the local workspace itself. Flow targets specify the sources and destinations of incoming and outgoing change sets. Streams have flow targets only if they are part of a stream hierarchy.

Once team members change project artifacts, the changes need to be applied to the streams so that the entire team can see the changes. Of course, in this case, the other team members need to accept the incoming change sets. In general, we refer to "change flow" to define the flow of the changes from the repository workspace to the flow targets. These flow targets can be one or more streams.

Let's see a simple scenario of making a change in the BookManager Doc component, then contribute it to the associated flow target:

1. Make a change to the `README.txt` file in the BookManager Doc component and save the file from the Eclipse client.

2. The Rational Team source control knows the file change and adds this change to the **Pending Changes** view as an unresolved change.

3. You can now check-in and deliver the change set. In our case, we create a new change set from the context menu of the unresolved change set by selecting **Check-in | New Change Set**.

4. Once the change set is created, we can edit the comment, as well as choose from several other options, as follows:

   ◦ Open the change set in the **Change Explorer** to view all the affected files.

   ◦ Deliver the change set to the flow target so that the changes are applied to the stream and is visible to the entire team.

   ◦ Suspend a change set to remove it from the repository workspace and unload it from the local workspace. However, the code is preserved in the repository so that it can be restored when we want to resume work on it.

   ◦ Discard a change set, when we think that the change set is invalid or could cause a problem to the source code. We can discard either an outgoing change set or an accepted change set.

   ◦ Reverse a change set to remove the captured changes. The reverse operation on a change set creates a patch. If we want to undo the delivery of a change set, we can create a new change set that reverses all the changes in it and then deliver the reversed change set.

   ◦ **Deliver and resolve work item** action will deliver the change set to the flow target and, at the same time, associate the change set to the work item.

   ◦ **Submit for review** action sends a message to the assigned reviewer for the module. To submit the change set for review, we must associate the work item to a change set.

   ◦ **Complete** action marks the Change set as complete. Remember that the change set is in "working" state until it is explicitly marked as complete.

   ◦ Associate work items to the change set to have a traceability of changes.

5. Select the change set and deliver it to the following target. Now the rest of the team members will be able to see the delivered change set.

These steps complete the roundtrip between changing a resource and finally making it available to the team through flow targets.

Source control from the RTC Web UI

Until now we have seen how different elements of source control are managed from the Rational Team Concert Eclipse client. The client provides a powerful way to create and manage different aspects of source control and project artifacts. Rational Team Concert also provides a way to access and navigate through the project artifacts from the Web UI. This helps team leaders, managers, scrum masters, and many other stakeholders to get an overview of the streams, components, and other artifacts.

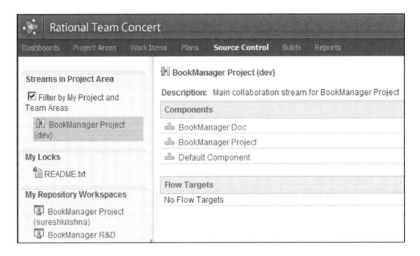

As seen in the previous screenshot, the **Source Control** view of the Rational Team Concert's Web UI shows a complete overview of available streams in the project, a list of resources locked by us, and our repository workspaces. The stream also lists its components and any flow targets it has.

Notice that Rational Team Concert's Eclipse client allows us to browse through the project or component artifacts from the stream. The Web UI also allows multiple operations to be done on an artifact such as lock, unlock, download, upload, and delete. However, it may be more convenient to work and operate from the Rational Team's Eclipse client. Therefore, it is easy to make source code changes and other build operations.

As we have seen, many operations can be done from the Rational Team Concert's Web UI. This provides a lightweight access to the source repository and a quick access without the Eclipse client.

Summary

In this chapter, we have seen how to accept a team invitation and set up the project in the Rational Team Concert Eclipse client.

Later, we saw the relationship between streams, components, and project artifacts, and how to create and maintain them. We created a new component BookManager Doc, shared it in source control, and added it to the default stream. Next, we took a deep dive into repository workspace concepts such as flow targets, repository ownership, workspace snapshots, ignoring resources, and explicit resource locks.

We have seen how to create and manipulate change sets so that changes are checked-in to the resource repository and delivered to the stream. Several operations that are possible on change sets are also discussed.

Finally, the Rational Team Concert Web UI is explored to see its support for the source control artifacts. We can navigate through the components and repository workspace to see artifacts and do some limited operations, along with a full history view.

In the next chapter, we will have an in-depth view of team collaboration and work items. One of the essential parts of the Rational Team Concert is the way team collaboration is made easy. We will see different user interface elements in the client where the collaboration aspects are embedded, and how to make use of this wonderful feature to communicate with team members effectively. Work item is an important aspect of the traceability of the change sets to the actual issues, bugs, features, and enhancements. From the change sets concept gained from the current chapter, we will add the work items to take it further. We will use the work items to capture the details of the work, effort, design, and many other things.

5

Team Collaboration and Work Items

The poor workman hates his tools; the good workman hates poor tools.

-Gerald M. Weinberg

Software development involves people, knowledge, technique, tools, methodologies, and more. Managers, software architects, developers, and quality assurance teams have many challenges to deal with, particularly with the increasing geographic dispersion of software services teams across the entire globe. A lot of focus in the software industry has been on improving the productivity of these global teams, with particular emphasis in recent years on giving teams a seamless experience in collaboration.

Consider some of the problems we normally encounter when we communicate and collaborate with colleagues on a software development effort:

- When you need to see if a colleague has arrived at work, you actually go to their desk and see if they're there.

- When you want to talk to a colleague about an issue, you meet in person or make a telephone call to discuss.

- Information on an employee's absence, such as when he is on vacation, is often stored in a shared spreadsheet, which may not be properly kept updated and may not be integrated with the project plan.

- Because you don't know everyone's vacation schedule, you may be waiting for a response from a colleague, only to learn afterwards he is out of the office.

- Likewise, part-time consultants may have irregular schedules that change, making it difficult to know when they are available for work.

- Regular updates to the team on the project's progress requires status meetings, which may require gathering everyone into one place, and take time.

Software development tools are designed to help some aspects of managing a team, but they also introduce some challenges:

- Tools designed to facilitate tasking, such as issue trackers and requirements management tools, are separate from the coding environment, causing a disconnect between the coding change and the impetus for the change.

- Instant messaging such as Google IM is very effective for communication. However, they too are disconnected from the coding environment, meaning context is lost when messages are sent about bugs and requirements. Likewise, they are one-on-one communication, so there is no sense of communicating with a team this way.

- E-mail is of course a great way to communicate with both, whole teams and individuals, but the same problems persists—no context between the mention of a bug ticket and the code the developer will change as a result.

- Neither e-mails nor IM integrate with the bug trackers, and discussion on these items between developers, managers, and end users can be lost or misfiled, or stored in a decentralized manner, in the inboxes of those who participated in the discussion but are not visible to the entire team.

All of these add up to one main problem—it is not elegant to see all the team activity on a project. On one extreme, there are too many disconnected tools; on the other, too many manual processes—both lead to reductions in team productivity. They are all challenges related to collaboration. The following is the Wikipedia definition of collaboration:

> *Collaboration is a recursive process where two or more people or organizations work together in an intersection of common goals. For example, an intellectual endeavor that is creative in nature, by sharing knowledge, learning, and building consensus.*

In this chapter, we will see how Rational Team Concert takes care of these collaboration challenges. Rational Team Concert integrates many useful tasks into the client, giving a seamless tool integration experience.

A focus of software development is to manage the requirements and bugs of a project. Sometimes, developers spend time manually associating code changes with the tracked bugs, introducing a myriad of problems to deal with.

There are many benefits to integrating the issues and bug management into the development environment. Any software system's health and quality can be quickly accessed by looking at the bugs and issues. When the issue and bug management system is integrated into the development environment, issues can be linked with the source code and other related artifacts. By providing an integrated view, you can efficiently keep track of all the work your team needs to complete, which makes it easier to decide on the health of your process.

In this chapter, we will also see an overview of the **Work Items**, which is a way of keeping track of the tasks and issues that your team needs to address during the development cycle.

Team Collaboration allows us to exchange information with other team members in the context of the work being done. When you talk about a bug, you can make sure that everyone sees the same bug description and preserve the discussion summary on the bug for any future reference. In the coming sections we will see specific topics that improve your daily experience as a software developer, manager, architect, QA engineer, or a project stakeholder.

Collaboration can be seen as an ingredient in the global software development context. In such a case, the interaction of a developer in setting up a project, working in the source code editor, work items, plans, and releases become a part of the collaboration. In this book, we focus on the specific tools of the collaboration that help and facilitate improving the productivity of teams.

Work Environment

In the global workforce scenario, the challenge is to use various information attributes such as the location and time zone of the team member, the capacity of a team member to work on a project, and the work schedule. We would like to know if a team member in a different time zone has arrived to work or if he is on vacation. **Work Environment** is a collaboration aspect of the Rational Team Concert that helps you specify several information attributes in a convenient user interface. Team members and managers can make use of this information for planning and scheduling purposes.

Rational Team Concert gives you the ability to enter the schedule information in the client as well as web UI. From the Eclipse client, you can open the complete overview of a user from Team Organization view, right-click on the user, and select **Open**. From this interface you can configure the **Work Environment**, **Scheduled Absences**, and **Mail Configuration** as shown in the following screenshot:

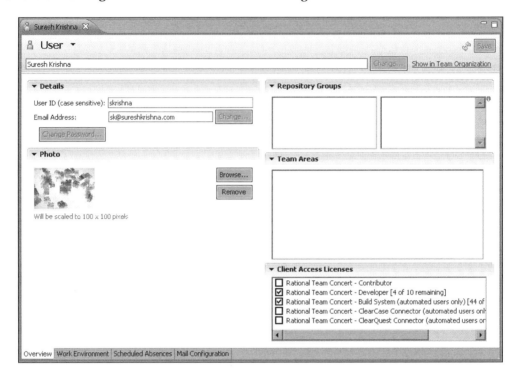

In the **Overview** tab of the editor, you can view and modify the important information about the user such as the username, e-mail address, team areas he belongs to, workdays and hours he normally works, and scheduled absences. Repository permissions are allocated to users using group designations in **Repository Groups**. Remember that at this time, you will not see the repository groups as we initially configured the users to be in the *External Non-LDAP User Registry*.

If you are using a WebSphere application server, users are assigned to repository groups at the time of user creation by your administrator. Unless users are configured to be on Tomcat or on LDAP, repository groups are not visible in the Rational Team Concert client or web UI.

In the **Work Environment** tab, you can enter your **Work Location** and **Work Days**, which will help other team members to know the availability of a team member to plan and schedule meetings. You can also edit your work days and number of hours of work that you would put in. This information on the work week and hours of work is used in scheduling, planning, and burn down charts. This also gives you the opportunity to adjust the percentage effort dedicated to each team or project in case you are assigned to multiple projects, as shown in the following screenshot:

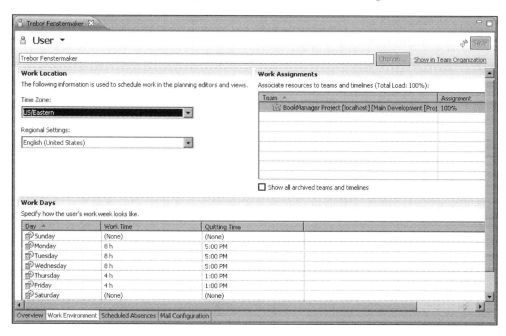

In the above example, the user Trebor (`tfenstermaker`) edited the details relevant for him. He changed the **Time Zone** to **US/Eastern** and changed his time of availability and work hours using this editor. Notice that this user has changed the work hours from 40 hours a week to 32 hours a week. This information is extremely useful for the project manager or project administrator who wants to schedule work, or who wants to know the availability of team members for meetings or to get a quick response via instant messaging.

> Throughout this chapter, unless otherwise stated, we use the admin user account in Rational Team Concert.

Scheduled Absences

In many projects, team members use versioned or shared spreadsheets to store their vacation schedules. Project managers often have to remind people to keep these updated, and team members may or may not do so. The manager must find these spreadsheets, hope they're correct, and compile the information from them manually to determine the available work hours and properly schedule work.

Rational Team Concert has the ability to capture all the team member related vacation time so that it can be used for planning, reporting, and other tasks. The **Scheduled Absences** tab lets you to enter the vacation time, where it is stored in the Team Repository for further use. The following screenshot shows the vacation entered by the user Trebor (`tfenstermaker`) and will be affected in the Team Load calculations for a specific project:

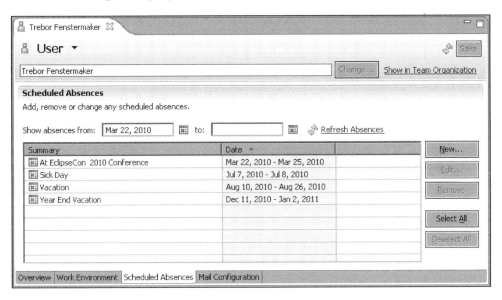

Mail Configuration

The Rational Team Concert client lets you subscribe to e-mail notifications for the events you are interested in. As seen in the following screenshot, you can subscribe to a variety of changes that happen on the work items:

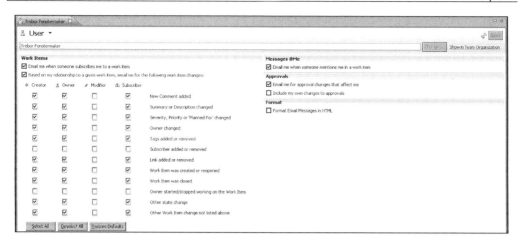

From the User Editor, you can also do several actions related to team collaboration and work items. When users are connected and online via an instant messenger service, you will be able to connect to them immediately by sending files, calling, or through text-chat. Here is also where you can find all the repository workspaces owned by a specific user and load this workspace if required. Also, when a specific user is assigned an important task, you can subscribe to all the events they generate, as shown next.

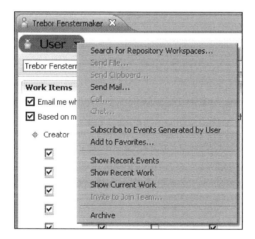

 In addition to being accessible from the User View, these functions can also be accessed by right-clicking on a user from other views, such as Team Organization.

These notification mechanisms are an important feature of the Rational Team Concert client that enables you to be alerted to those items that interest you. Without it, it could be a daunting task for you to get updates on all the things happening in a project, especially when a work item related to your module is modified.

Instant Messaging

Rational Team Concert seamlessly integrates with Instant Messaging, giving a smooth experience in team communication. Team members can do a peer-to-peer chat or group chat with other project members. Eclipse introduced the Instant Messaging platform via **Eclipse Communication Framework (ECF)**, and Rational Team Concert took this further by integrating support for IBM's Lotus Sametime Connect, Google Talk, and Jabber XMPP Server.

In this section, we will see several features of Instant Messaging by configuring Google Talk from the Eclipse client. Along with Instant Messaging, you can also do File Transfer, Voice Call, and more. The starting point for Instant Messaging is the Team Organization view in the Eclipse client. Team Organization lists all the users associated to the connected Team Area. You open this view to see all the online users and start messaging right away.

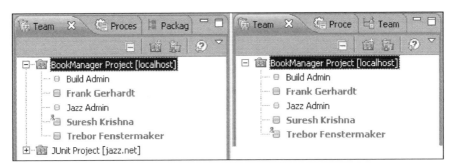

When users come online, the Eclipse client synchronizes with their status and displays the users appropriately. The previous screenshot shows two different Eclipse clients placed side-by-side for comparison. From here, you can start sending messages, and the chat client understands the different types of Work Items. The client will be able to recognize and open the Work Item description in the editor.

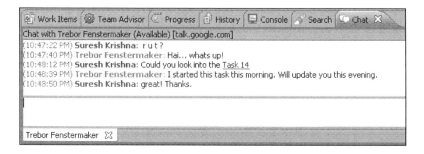

The previous chat window screenshot shows communication between two users. The important feature is that *Task 14* automatically becomes a URL, allowing the other user to click on it and open the Work Item from the discussion. This becomes the real power of integration. In the coming sections, we will see how easy it is to take a screenshot of an error in a UI and send it to the other user from the messaging infrastructure.

Events and feeds

Feeds provide a combined view of all the events that happen in a Project, Work Items, Source Control, Builds, and Plans. Feeds provide direct access of all events to team members. Rational Team Concert client automatically generates the feeds for the work items and builds as soon as you connect the Project Area in the client.

From the Team Artifacts view, expand the **Feeds** folder to look at all the available feeds. Note that these feeds are shown for all the Project Areas combined rather than per individual project. In the following example, we've opened the feed named **My Teams in BookManager Project** to see all the events generated by the entire team:

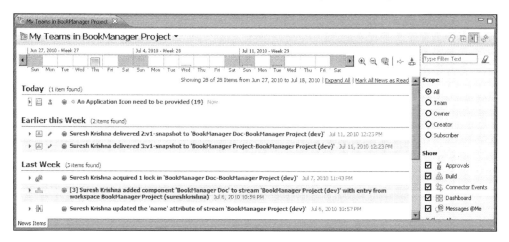

As a team member, you can choose the events that you are interested in, so you can narrow the scope. The feeds show all the events generated by Builds, Team Server, Dashboard, and messages that mentions you. As an administrator, you have a complete overview of the various events happening across all the team members. As opposed to traditional project management, you need not spend time in collecting the information from different team members on what they did. Each event has a description attached with all the details.

Subscribing to feeds is another great way you can receive information. Right-click and subscribe to a build definition or query item in addition to the ones that are added by default. In general, wherever there is a possibility to subscribe to events, the Rational Team client integrates this functionality in the context menu.

As the number of projects increase, you may want to highlight the things that you are most interested in. Therefore, you can add your most important items to your **Favorites** folder.

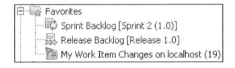

Work Items

Rational Team Concert uses the **Work Item** as a fundamental mechanism to track, plan, and assign development tasks. On an abstract level, a Work Item is a task. However, this Work Item provides a way to track progress, plan releases, and monitor the project's health. Typically, Work Items are bugs, enhancements, and tasks with varied priorities and are generally attached to a specific release. Rational Team Concert inherently supports the connection between the Work Item and source code. Thus, as a developer, you can go to Work Items from source code and vice-versa.

In the following sections, we will see how to create Work Items and customize them. In this process, we will test our BookManager application as the product owner and report our TODOs as Work Items and later assign them to team members. While creating the Work Items we will explore the various UI elements like **My Work View**, **Dashboards**, **Queries**, **Team Central**, and more.

Work Items UI

There exists multiple ways to access the Work Items from the Rational Team Concert client. Remember that the Eclipse client has two major dedicated perspectives—**Jazz Administrator** and **Work Items**. Both perspectives show the Team Artifacts view. While the Jazz Administration perspective has the Team Organization and Process Templates views, the Work Items perspective consists of Work Items view, My Work view, Team Central view, and Tag Cloud view.

Work Items view

You can create custom queries on the Work Items. When a user runs the query, the results are displayed in the Work Items view. The result can be sorted in a variety of ways and you can open any Work Item of interest by double-clicking on it as seen in the next screenshot. As an example, you can list the Work Items based on the **Depends On**, **Blocks**, **Children**, **Parents**, and other relationships.

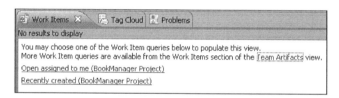

Team Artifacts view

The Team Artifacts view has all the essential details about the BookManager Project such as Repository Connections, Project Area, Favorites, Feeds, My Repository Workspaces, My Team Areas, and Work Item History. More importantly, this stages the information on the various project builds, project plans, source control modules, and Work Items. This important information is organized in the form of several folders as shown in the following screenshot:

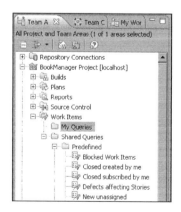

Some of the important functions that can be done from the Team Artifacts view include but are not limited to the following:

- Create and define build definitions and build engines (discussed in a later chapter)
- Create or edit the Iteration and Release plans for the project
- Create and share project reports
- Create or edit new Streams, Snapshots, and Repository Workspaces
- Run several pre-defined Work Item queries or create new ones
- View the news from subscribed feeds

My Work view

As a team member, you can open the **My Work** view to assign and plan allocated work items. You can manage the items in progress or the items that you would like to resolve in the future. My Work view gives an overview all the tasks allocated on your username as shown in the next screenshot:

Team Central view

The Team Central view, as the name suggests, gives a centralized view of all the team members' loads, as well as their event logs and open Work Items. It is important to realize the difference between the Team Central view and My Work view. While My Work view provides an in-depth view of the tasks of specific team member, the Team Central view provides an overview of the team members as shown.

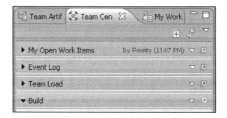

Tag Cloud view

Each time a Work Item is entered, you can add tags to it. These tags help you organize and find items. The Tag Cloud view will give us an overview of the most frequently used tags and variations in the tags.

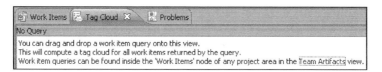

Creating Work Items

Work Item is the primary mechanism for stakeholders and the team to create and follow tasks through to completion. Depending on the project needs, a scrum master or other stakeholders can create the Work Items and track them. Remember that Rational Team Concert has the web interface that any stakeholder not using the Eclipse (or Visual Studio) client can use to create, edit, and track Work Items.

Creating Work Item can start from the Eclipse client's by **File | New | Work Item** or go to **Team Artifacts view | BookManager Project | Work Items | New | Work Item**. In either case, the action will invoke the **Create Work Item** dialog as shown in the following screenshot. You can also create Work Items in the context of a plan. This allows you to open a Sprint or Release Backlog and start creating the planned Work Items.

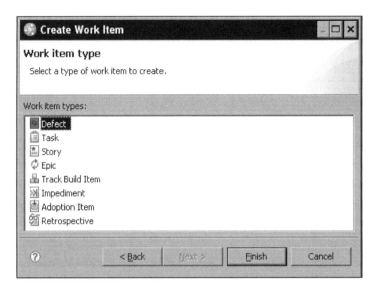

As you can see, there are several types a Work Item transforms to. Depending on the stakeholder's role, you may be using one of many Work Items quite often. For example, if you are a requirements engineer, you will be using the Task, Story, and Epic types frequently. If you are a developer, you will be using the **Defect**, **Task**, and **Track Build Item** types. Let us see what each of these items is used for:

- **Epic**: This is used when a story is too big to complete in a single sprint or when there are too many unknowns to estimate the amount of work. An **Epic** can be broken down into several stories. For example, a description of a complete banking system, explaining how the legacy system integrates with a new online system of a particular bank.

- **Story**: A **Story** is a software system requirement formulated as one or more sentences in the everyday business language of the user. For example, a **Story** that explains types of bank accounts and how they differ from each other.

- **Task**: This is a Work Item that must be completed to implement the **Story**. For example, a **Task** can be as simple as updating the copyright information in a HTML source.

- **Defect**: This specific type of Work Item is used to identify a bug. Generally, this is used when a specific feature is not working as expected. For example, when navigating from the Login page to the Account Overview page in the application, the browser throws a JavaScript exception.

- **Track Build Item**: This type is used to create an item from a build result to track the fixes needed for a failed build. For example, the build is broken due to an API change in a component and should be propagated to all the usages.

- **Impediment**: This issue type is used for tasks that block the progress of a project. For example, without the database upgrade, QA will not be able to proceed with testing. This delays the sprint timeline.

- **Adoption Item**: This is used when changes done by one team need to be adopted by another team. For example, the core framework team has changed the way e-mail and SMS is delivered to customers on demand. This change needs to be adopted by the other banking and insurance products that depend on this framework.

- **Retrospective**: Soon after the iteration is completed, it is necessary to understand all the things that went well and not. This task type is used to retrospect the iteration and can provide valuable information for the team. What went well and potential improvements should be documented for future references. For example, during one iteration, coordination between UI and UX team was good; however, we could have avoided some small issues if we had better communicated with QA team.

Traditional bug tracking and issue management tools support a limited number of issue types. However, depending on the organization and industry, we may have special task types. Rational Team Concert gives power to development teams and project stakeholders, by giving the ability to both use predefined task types and create new task ones if needed.

As a team manager, you could track the number of tasks of type **Track Build Item** and determine how much time is spent on the build failures and if there is a possibility to reduce it. At the end of a sprint or iteration, the project manager would come to know the number of project **Impediment** tasks and take preventive steps next time. With the **Adoptions Items**, you can come to know the time taken by other teams to adopt a change in the system. This could be a critical parameter to plan system-wide changes that affect more than one team. Projects typically do a review with the **Project Review Committee (PRC)**, document findings, and observations which will aid future projects. However, often the documentation used is not searchable or is unusable over time. Rational Team Server integrates all items allowing you to retrieve them any time from the system.

Let us create a few tasks in the BookManager Project Team Area. The tasks will focus on the documentation for the release, and in the process we will see how to create a task and various UI elements.

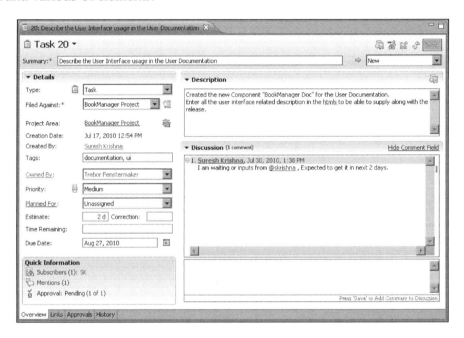

Once a task is created from one of several available context menus, the task **Description** can be entered in the Task editor. The Task editor has several tabs that separate the information into **Overview**, **Links**, **Approvals**, and **History**. In the **Overview** editor, you can see the following important information concerning a task:

- **Summary** of the task.

- **State** of the task. A task can be in any of the **New**, **Start Working**, **Complete**, or **Invalidate** states. The project administrator can customize these depending on the teams' requirements.

- **Project Area** that this task is filed against. If needed, you will be able to move the tasks from one Project Area to another one or reassign it to a different Team Area.

- **Owned By** field represents the team member that this item is being assigned to.

- **Planned For field** is used to assign this Work Item to a specific iteration or scrum release plan. This helps you to query the list of all Work Items planned for a specific iteration.

- **Created By** field is auto-populated after creation of the work item. So, you cannot see this field while creating the Work Item.

- **Tags** is an optional field where you can enter various keywords used by the tag cloud.

- As a task creator, if you know the estimate, you can enter the estimated effort for the task along with **Due date**.

- **Description** section contains the long explanation for the task along with any hints and notes for the owner.

- **Discussion** section has the complete history of the discussions across team members on this task. This feature allows the Rational Team Concert users to have a complete trace of the discussions at one place.

On the top-right corner of the **Overview** tab of the Task Editor, you can see various actions. This is one way you can avoid duplicate Work Items, as well as create new Work Items with relationships between them.

- **Find Potential Duplicates**: This action finds similar or duplicate Work Items depending on the summary of the Work Item. This is very useful in large teams and prevents you from entering duplicate bugs.

- **Subscribe Me**: As a user (if you are neither creator nor owner of the task), you could subscribe to all the updates on the Work Item. This enables you to get all the update alerts directly delivered to client.

- **Extract work item from selected text**: This is an interesting feature in Rational Team Concert client. Once a Work Item is created, you can link this Work Item with another using one of several types:
  - **Related**: This tag denotes that the two Work Items are related; for example, two items are documentation-related tasks.
  - **Block**: The newly created Work Item blocks the current one.
  - **Depends On**: The current task depends on the newly created one.
  - **Parent**: Create the Work Item with a parent relationship to the current work item.
  - **Children**: Create the Work Item with a child relationship to the current Work Item.

The **Links** tab of the Work Item editor has additional information such as attachments, subscribers, and links. In the following screenshot, you can see that a requirements document and a screenshot is attached to the Work Item. Rational Team Client has a built-in screen capture tool to very conveniently take the screenshots and attach them to the Work Item. You can see all the team members who are subscribed to this single work item.

The **Links** section is indeed very interesting, where you can establish a variety of relationships between the Work Items. In the following example, you see several relationships described in the **Links** section: *Task 20* Blocks *Task 22* and *Task 20* has two Related tasks, *Task 21* and *Task 22*.

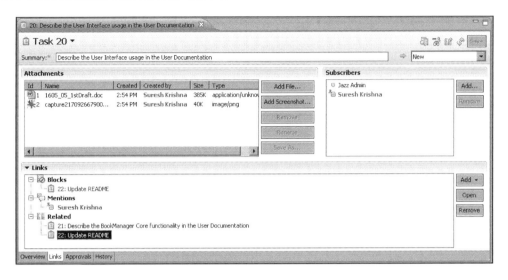

The **Approvals** tab editor enables you to add approval authority depending on the task. This is helpful in some special cases, such as when functionality needs to be reviewed by a domain specialist. A project manager or scrum master could add the domain specialist as the reviewer and this item has to undergo the defined review process. Team Server allows you to define three approval types—Approval, Review, and Verification.

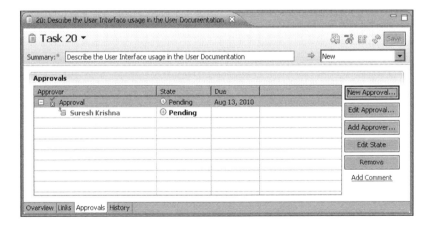

Each Work Item has the ability to track what's happening in the time line. Right from the time a Work Item is created, all the actions such as create, update, and delete events are recorded and can be viewed from the **History** tab. The timeline UI provides a unique feature to see the events between time lines. This means, as a project manager, you can see all the changes that happened in a month or a week.

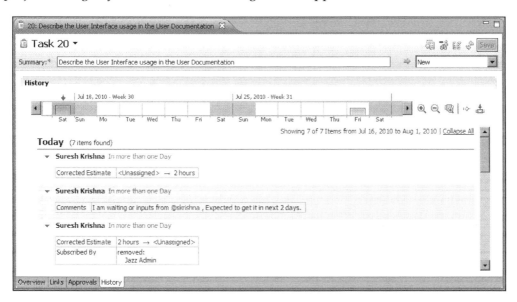

The Work Item editor is a powerful interface that lets you create and update the Work Items. Remember that at this time, we have not assigned the Work Items to any of the iterations or releases. In the next chapter, we will look in detail at the plans and iterations, and how to assign tasks to appropriate iterations. As you saw, Work Items in Rational Team Concert is much more than a bug or issue tracking system. In the next section, we will see how an individual team member sees the Work Items assigned to him from the My Work view of Eclipse client.

My Work view

We have seen how to create Work Items and now we will see how an individual team member organizes and manages them from the **My Work** view in Eclipse. My Work view is the central place for you, as a team member, to start work. My Work view has three sections that have information.

For all the My Work view description, we assume that the team member Trebor is logged in.

Inbox

This is where every new Work Item that is assigned to you appears for the first time. It's a good idea to track your Inbox regularly to see if there are any new items assigned to you. It is always recommended you organize and sort the Work Items as soon as possible.

The first time a user enters the client, there can be many Work Items under their name. They can accept all the Work Items and then start organizing and managing them. Each time a change is done on the My Work view, you can save it immediately, or you can wait for the auto-save feature.

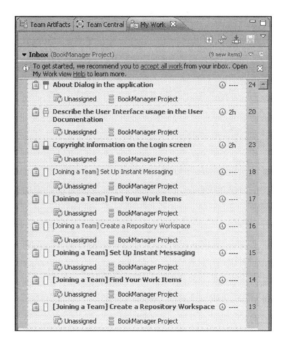

Future Work Items

Once the Work Items are accepted from the Inbox, they are moved to the **Future Work** section. All the Work Items are either unplanned or planned for some future time. You can do variety of actions on a Work Item in the Future Work section. All the actions that can be done on the work item can be categorized:

- View details and recent news about the work item
- Change the metadata about the Work Item such as Tags, Plan for, and Change filed against
- Relate the current Work Item to another one

- Start/Stop working along with finding duplicate bugs and others

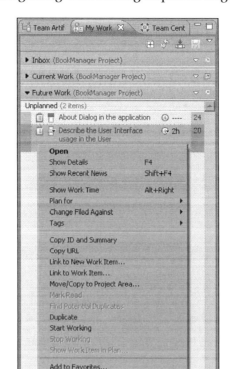

Current Work

In this section, you can see all Work Items scheduled for the coming weeks or the latest iterations. Once you start working on a Work Item, you can change the status to *In Progress*. Changing the Work Item state is highly encouraged as the state changes are reflected on all project dashboards and in the project health.

The section tool bar will let you enable the **My Work Load** analysis and **Scheduled Risk Assessment**. The horizontal bar with green and red colors represents the work load. Work load is calculated as the total number of hours of work required for all the tasks divided by the total number of available hours till the scheduled release. In our case, as shown in the next screenshot, for two days of work, we have two hours of estimated work. This is a visual representation of total work load so that the team member will be able to schedule the work accordingly. Another great feature is to be able to do a simulation on the available Work Items and visually know the Work Items that have high risk of completion.

You can see in the following screenshot that the two Work Items are in red, which means they have the risk of not meeting the schedule:

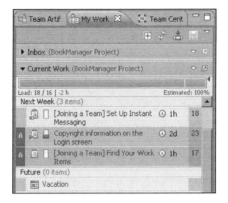

My Work view is highly customizable. You can use the toolbar to change how the view looks like. Remember that the My Work view has three sections by default. However, you can configure it to view additional sections like Preview of the Work Items, Team Load, Event Log, and others. An important aspect of the My Work view is you will be able to see the latest events or log on to the Work Item without completely opening it.

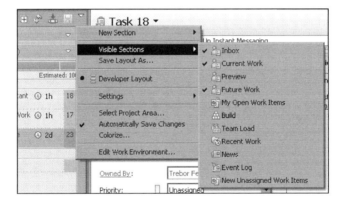

In summary, the My Work view provides an important interface to the work. We have the ability to organize, sort, and manage the items along with running the simulations on the risk assessment.

Team Central

Rational Team Concert empowers a team member not only with knowing his task progress, but also gives a high-level overview of team progress. Team Central view from the Work Items perspective can be a starting point with Event Logs, Team Load Build, and My Open Work Items.

The Team Central view has several default sections starting with My Open Work Items. This section gives an overview of the Work Items as a bar graph based on the types of the Work Items. The Event Log section has the complete trace of what's happening in the project. This will display all the events such as creation, update, and deletes on the Work Items. Team Load is a very useful visual representation of the workload of the team members. This can help team members share the work appropriately. Also, a team manager or scrum master can see this work load and distribute the tasks among other team members as needed.

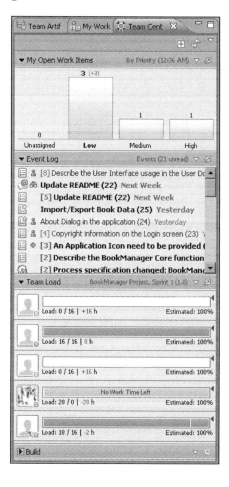

The Team Central view is enabled to be customized with other sections such as News, Recent Work Items, and New Unassigned Work Items. In the News section, you can customize the feeds that you would like to follow. Recent Work Items shows the list of all the previously worked items. Finally, all the Work Items that have not been assigned to any of the team members are shown in the New Unassigned Work Items folder.

Queries

In complex projects, we know it might be difficult to search for bugs, blockers, enhancements, tasks, stories, and issues; you can probably remember all the tasks recently worked on. However, as time passes by, it becomes more difficult to remember the details of those issues.

Rational Team Concert provides queries so that it is easy to search, discover, and populate issues depending on various conditions and filtering criteria. Queries are powerful features for management, stakeholders, and team members, and lets them find information when needed. Queries play an important role in minimizing the time needed to search work items. As an example, in any real-time project, we will be faced with generating bug reports based on various conditions:

- List of all the customer-entered bugs
- List of all the blocker bugs
- List of all the bugs raised in a month after a release
- List of all the bugs worked by each team member
- List of all the document bugs
- List of all bugs open for more than one year
- List of all open and high-severity bugs
- List of all closed bugs in the last month
- List of all bugs worked on by a specific user and reopened

This filtering mechanism can be applied to all Work Item types. Queries in general are an efficient mechanism to search Work Items based on simple to complex filtering criteria.

Predefined queries

Rational Team Concert provides several predefined queries along with any Team Area you create. Generally, these queries would be all that you need as they cover a wide range of needs. The following is a screenshot of predefined queries:

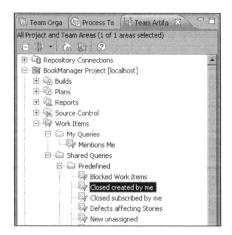

There are close to 25 predefined queries with the client. The number of predefined templates depends on the process templates that you selected for the project. You can select any query and add it to favorites, edit the contents, export work items, and run the query. The query results are displayed in the Work Items view. The Work Items view lets you create a new query, re-run a query, run a favorite query, and refresh the results from the view's toolbar.

From the Work Items view, you can access all the actions on the Work Item, such as opening, editing, duplicating, marking it as start/stop work, and many more from the same view.

Creating queries

While there are many predefined Work Item queries supplied by the Rational Team Queries, it is not uncommon that you may need to modify an existing one or create a totally new query. You could create a new query in the following ways:

- Go to **File** | **New** | **Other** to open a wizard, navigate to **Work Items** | **Work Item Query**, and click **Finish**.

- Go to Project Area in the Team Artifacts view. Navigate to **Work Items** | **New** | **Query**.

The Work Item Query editor is open and you can create the new one starting from scratch, from a simple query to a full-text query. The Query editor gives you all the power to add rules from *AND* as well as *OR* blocks, and by adding conditions. The conditions are based on the complete set of the attributes from the Work Items. You can query depending on any combination of usernames, dates, Work Item attributes, and AND/OR combinations. This will cover virtually all the combinations of queries one could think of with Work Items.

For now, we will build the query from scratch. The idea is to create a query that will give us list of Work Items based on the conditions, as shown in the following screenshot:

- Created by user `Suresh Krishna`
- Owned by user `Trebor Fenstermaker`
- Items created exactly two days ago
- Type of the Work Item is Defect and Task only

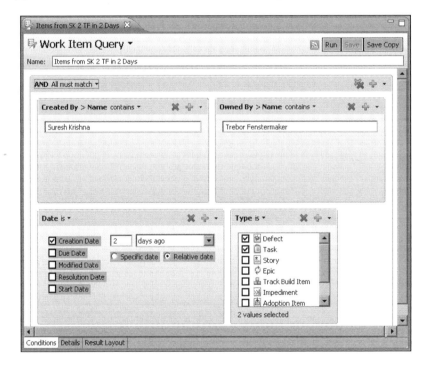

The query is created from three conditions, Created By, Owned By, and Type, and one date. Once the query is created, give it an appropriate name and save. This query appears in the My Queries folder in Work Items and is available to be run. The result of the query is displayed in the Work Items view.

Note that at the moment, the query is available only to you and is created as your private query. You can go to the **Details** tab of the Query editor and share the query with individual team members or with the entire Team Area. In our example, when the user Suresh Krishna shares the query with the user Trebor Fenstermaker, the later user can see this as the Individually Shared item in his client, as shown in the next screenshot:

As a team leader or team manager, you can take full advantage of creating queries and sharing them with team members as shown in the following screenshot. You can create the queries virtually for any combination of conditions. Once the query is created, you can right-click on it and select **Edit**. This opens up the editor, where you can change the query conditions or other details. Observe that the user Suresh has shared the work item and it appears in the client of the user Trebor.

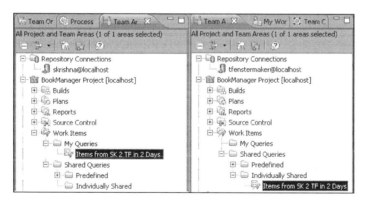

Import/Export

When working with disparate systems, it is often difficult to transfer the bugs, issues, and enhancements from one system to another. In some cases, we maintain legacy issue tracking systems, as the integration or transfer process is quite difficult.

Rational Team Concert allows you to import and export the Work Items in HTML and CSV formats. If an issue tracking system is able to export the items as CSV, we can import the issues into the Rational Team Server and map the issues and different attributes, if necessary. Eclipse client provides a variety of options to import the work items from popular issue management systems. You can import the issues from Bugzilla, ClearQuest, and any plain CSV file made of Work Items.

The import wizards of ClearQuest and Bugzilla provide a convenient way to import the Work Items. For Bugzilla import, there is an option to map the attributes to Rational Team Concert Work Items. An XML mapping file is generated when the data is being imported from Bugzilla and later on, you can map the Rational Team side of attributes. When importing the ClearQuest Work Items, make sure that ClearQuest is installed on the local machine and CLEARQUEST_HOME, RATIONAL_HOME, or CA_HOME is set. Without these required paths, the import wizard will not work. Once you connect to ClearQuest, select the query that returns the records that you want to import. Make sure that the import is done as XML files and save it in ZIP format. Finally, run the custom data mapping and test for the accuracy before a final run.

You can also import the Work Items from a CSV file. Select the CSV file and select whether the columns are to be separated by a tab, comma, or other delimiter. You could use the default mapping file or customize it as needed to complete the import process.

Import to Production System

Irrespective of import from Bugzilla, ClearQuest, or CSV files, it is recommended to do imports on a test system until the mapping seems to be good. Once you are ready to import on the production system, make sure that you back up the repository.

Often we send the Work Item lists generated by queries to stakeholders, the QA team, or higher management. Rational Team Concert provides an elegant way to export the existing Work Items from queries. We can export it either in HTML or CSV format. You can open the export wizard from **File | Export** as shown in the next screenshot. Alternatively, you can select a query from the Project Area and then right-click to export the result of the query.

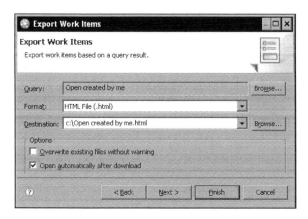

Once you select the query, output format, and destination (with full file extension) you can add and remove additional columns to display in the output file, as shown next:

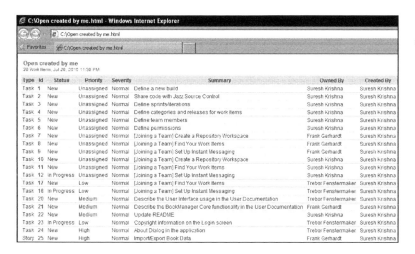

The exported file can further be used to generate reports. In a real-time scenario, you may create a Work Item query and then export it to HTML or CSV for further processing.

Customization

As the project gets more complex, the need to document detailed information on the Work Items also increases. This is especially true when fixing a customer-reported bug or targeting issues for a major release. Traditionally, we have dealt with these situations by entering the extra information in the body of the issue or as a special comment. The limitation with this kind of approach is that it's not at all effective for tracking and reporting. Searching through thousands of bugs and tasks may be exhausting and inaccurate.

Make sure that you are logged in as the Rational Team administrator and you have administrator and developer rights. Rational Team Concert gives the power to the project administrator to completely customize the Work Items. Depending on the organization, team, and customer needs, the process can be tailored to fit the team. There are numerous customizations that can be done on the Work Items.

- The complete **Editor Presentations** can be customized with a team member's preferences.
- Several **Enumerations** in the Work Items can be customized like story complexity, priority, severity, and impact.
- For various types of the Work Items, you can add custom attributes that immediately reflect in the Work Item Editor.
- **Approval Trackings** and its workflow actions can be customized.
- A personal query could become so popular that we can it to the **Predefined queries**. This makes it available to everyone.
- **Workflow** can be configured to have new states and transition actions.

To start the customization, open the **BookManager Project** Team Area and navigate to the **Process Configuration** tab of the editor. Open the **Project Configuration | Configuration Data | Work Items** folder. Here you will see several options to configure. As an example, let's configure all Work Item type priority to have additional enumerations. This means that apart from the Unassigned, Low, Medium, and High priority, we want to represent how soon the bug/task needs to be processed:

- Earliest Possible
- Next Release
- Immediate Patch

In the Team Area editor, navigate to the **Work Items | Enumerations** section. Choose the enumeration to edit (in our case **priority**) and then add the enumerations in the following section. If needed, the default value can be changed too.

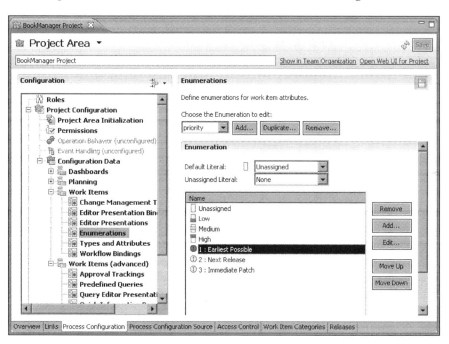

Once the enumerations are entered, save the changes. Once the enumerations are successfully added, they should be visible when you try to create a new task.

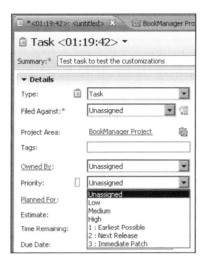

Finally, we will add custom fields to the Defect type of Work Item. We would like to know if a defect is entered by a customer and the name of that customer. This might be interesting for us as we can prioritize tasks depending on the customer (perhaps some customers are more important than others).

To achieve this, navigate to **Work Items | Types and Attributes** and choose the Work Item type. In our case, choose the Defect type. Add two custom attributes, **Customer Defect** as a Boolean type and **Customer Name** as Small String, and save the Team Area after changes.

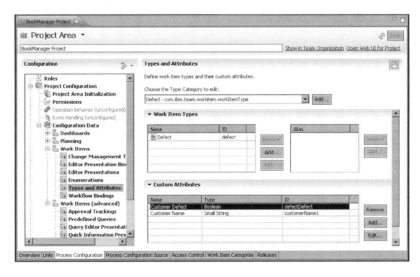

Once all the changes are saved, create a new defect. In the new Defect editor, a new tab named **Custom** appears that has the newly added attributes.

Customizing the Work Items is a powerful feature when we have to deal with a lot of custom processes and workflows. There are several customizations that you can explore.

Interestingly, Rational Team Concert provides the same powerful features on the Web UI too. You can log in to the Web UI and create the Work Item or create the query in the same way as you did in the Eclipse client. This feature is extremely useful in a scenario where a requirements engineer or product manager at a customer site can enter the user stories, epics, defects, and others without having the client set up.

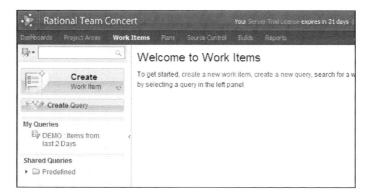

As you can see from the online system, the complete feature set of the Work Items is provided and users can see their private queries along with the shared ones.

Dashboards

Dashboards are light weight Web UI components intended to provide overview about the project status. It provides an easy drill-down mechanism to get more complete information. A group of portlets constitutes a dashboard. Each portlet is a UI element that displays a report of piece of information from the Rational Team Server data in real time.

Traditionally, stakeholders or team members may have to search and organize the data from disparate systems such as source control, issue tracking tools, requirements management tools, and others.

Dashboards makes it possible that everyone who has access to the system sees the same information at all times. Each time you access the dashboard, the reports are computed real-time. This has multiple advantages for the team like:

- The project manager can track the project health and trends at a single place
- Teams can use the dashboard data for the team meetings
- Team leads can see the individual project load and team progress and balance the workload
- Developers can track their workload
- Depending on the stakeholder, the dashboard can be customized and relevant information can be added

Explore dashboard

Log in to the Rational Team Server and select the BookManager project team area. Dashboards can be accessed from the main menu and has all the default portlets needed for a quick project overview. The default dashboard has some main components:

- **Release Burndown**: This report visualizes the remaining story points at the beginning of each iteration in a release.
- **Team Velocity**: This report visualizes the achieved story points grouped by iteration.
- **Estimated Vs Actual**: This report plots the ratio of estimated versus actual work of a team over time.
- **Current Plans**: Lists the Sprints, Releases, and Backlogs for a time line.
- **Project Events**: List of all the latest events that have happened on the project. You can drill down to see more details on an event.
- **Open Impediments**: Lists all the impediments related to the project.

- **Sprint Burndown**: This report plots the remaining backlog of work in terms of the time estimated to complete it.

- **Open Vs Closed Work Items**: This report plots all work items over time.

- **Blocked Work Items**: List of all the blocked Work Items.

- **Project Builds**: List of all the project builds.

- **Build Health**: Health calculated on the number of successes and failures of the build.

The general dashboard is fully customizable—you can add new portlets or modify the existing ones. You can create a new portlet from the existing ones by duplicating the existing one. Dashboards provide an efficient way to view the real-time reports that all project members can use.

Customize dashboards

When the project grows complex, you may feel the need for additional portlets or new tabs. The additional tabs can be easily added from the web UI and you can add the required portlets.

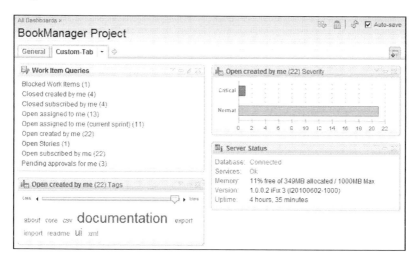

The previous screenshot shows the newly created **Custom-Tab** with the Work Item-related portlets. You can see the Work Item Queries, Tag Cloud, and Severity-based reports. You can see that the server status portlet is also added, which gives a quick overview of the server activity. You can always refresh all the portlets when you feel the data may be stale.

When you create a personal dashboard, it is not shared with other team members by default. You can select to share the dashboard with specific projects. All the team members of that project will be able to search for this dashboard and use it.

In this section you have seen how to access the dashboards, analyze various project health attributes, and customize the dashboards. Customization is a powerful feature for the dashboards where any team member can configure what they are interested in and the way they want it.

Summary

In this chapter, we've seen the various concepts of the Team Collaboration, Work Items, and Dashboards. Initially, we saw how the collaboration supports seamless transparency in the working of the project teams. We saw how to configure instant messaging, events, and feeds from the Rational Team Server.

Later, we were introduced to Work Items. The Work Item is the integral part of Rational Team Concert. Especially during the development time, the Eclipse client My Work and Team Central views are very useful. You have also seen how to create queries and run them.

Finally, we saw how to leverage the Dashboards. Dashboards provide real-time data reporting UI widgets that helps the entire team to understand the project status better. You can add a new Dashboard tab and then add new portlets. You can also share the Dashboard depending on the need.

In the next chapter we will get introduced to Planning and Release Management. You will see basic concepts such as Iterations, Releases, and Sprints in the context of Rational Team Concert. Once we get familiarized with the release and planning, we will assign the Work Items to a specific Sprint and see how a release is made. We will also make some feature enhancements to the BookManager Project.

6

Development Process and Release Planning

A program is never less than 90% complete, and never more than 95% complete.

–Terry Baker

A modern software development project is difficult to imagine without some form of development process. A software development process, simple or complex, comprises a set of rules, recommendations, standards, tools, and of course, people. Software release planning is very much an integral part of the development process and deals with how tasks are grouped, how releases are planned, and ways to track the release progress. Remember that tracking tasks is not the same as tracking releases.

In this chapter, we will explore various aspects of the software development process and release planning and management:

- For the software development process, we will be introduced to the software process templates, configuring the templates, and team roles
- From the Release Planning, we will get introduced to an overview of iterations, sprints, backlogs, and tracking releases

We have seen various features of Rational Team Concert, such as Repository Connections, Team Area, Workspace repository, Work Items, Team Collaboration, and others. We have also set up the team area for the BookManager application and tested its functionality. As a project administrator, we have added a few stories, tasks, and defects for the team. As a natural consequence, we would like to create a new release plan, schedule the stories and tasks, assign stories and tasks to this release, and track it to finish.

Development process

Software development processes can be conceived as a sequence of steps and practices to accomplish the software product development in a predictable manner. While this gives a broad definition of the development process, it may become more specific depending on the organization, domain, and expertise. Typically, any development process needs a set of practices, methodologies, tools, and supporting functions.

- Tasks and practices:
    - Requirements management
    - Architecting or/and designing the solution
    - Implementation
    - Integration
    - Testing
    - Release management
    - Maintenance/Patching

- Methodologies:
    - Waterfall
    - V-Model
    - RUP
    - Agile
    - Spiral and others

- Tools:
    - Compiler / Debugger
    - Build
    - Release
    - Issue

- Support
    - Project management
    - Configuration management
    - Quality assurance
    - Documentation

The development process will vary with the complexity of the project, its size, and the number of teams assigned to it. Rational Team Concert improves the productivity of the teams and quality of the work by letting the teams teach the best practices to the tool. Rational Team Concert and the Jazz platform support this in the following ways:

- Out-of-the-box process templates that provide a blueprint for the project area's initial process and iteration structure. After the project area is created, these process templates can be modified to fit the project and team needs.

- Rather than having to consult documentation and remember what processes you should follow, Rational Team Concert uses the process knowledge it is configured with to automatically detect violations of your team's process the instant they happen.

- Process is hierarchical. The general project-wide process is defined at the project level. The process can then be modified to meet the needs of team areas within the project.

- The process is explicit and all the work that team members do within the system happens within a context of a defined process.

- The Jazz platform is process neutral. Each project team can define an appropriate level of control and guidance. This means that each and every project team can choose the process.

There is no single process that applies to all team members and all phases of a project. You can use process behavior to customize the process in specific team areas and iterations. The project process specification addresses project-wide, team, and role-specific behavior and permissions such as the following:

- Predefined project reports and queries

- Work item types, workflows, and enumerations

- Roles available for a team

- Team and role-specific permissions for client and server-side operations

- Team and role-specific preconditions that define the conditions under which client-side and server-side operations are allowed to proceed

- Team and role-specific follow-up actions for client-side and server-side operations

Process templates provide a new project area with an initial process configuration and iteration structure. In the next sections, we will see an overview of the available process templates and how to use them. Also, Scrum being the most popular agile development methodology, we will look into various aspects of using and customizing the Scrum process template.

Process templates

Rational Team Concert provides several out-of-the-box process templates that can be used as a starting point. You select a process template when you create a project area to help you get started with the initial process. After creation, the project area's process and iteration structure can be modified independent of the template.

You can create a process template with no initial content, except for the process configuration structure and placeholder iterations. Or you can create a process template from an existing project area. The latter option enables your team to create projects based on a successful process that is implemented in an existing project.

You can create templates from scratch or from existing project areas. Templates are specified in XML using a schema that can be extended by configuration-point declarations. You can edit templates using source and high-level editors.

Typically after starting the project, you may need to change the process behavior to suit your team. This can be done right with the existing team process template and you can save this as either a new template or overwrite the existing one.

Out-of-the-box templates

Rational Team Concert provides a few templates out of the box and these can be installed any time from the web UI. Optionally, you can import and install the custom templates from the Eclipse client from **File | Import | Team Process | Process Template**. This action will either take a directory that contains templates or an archive of templates. Remember that each project area can choose its own project template and that templates exist on the server level. The set of out-of-the-box process templates available from Rational Team Concert are shown in the following screenshot:

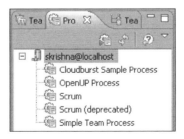

Depending on the team size, project, and other requirements, you can apply any one of the templates to your project area. Based on this template, the work item's workflow will change. We will now see an overview of the available templates.

Cloudburst

The Cloudburst process template is designed to support the Cloudburst reference project from the Jazz technology platform. This template includes two development lines — development and maintenance, each with different delivery milestones and process requirements. The development team includes two sub-teams — one for client development and the other for server development. One project lead is defined at the project area. Other project members are defined within the team areas.

OpenUp

The OpenUp process preserves the essential characteristics of the Rational Unified Process, which includes iterative development, use cases and scenarios driving development, risk management, and an architecture-centric approach.

OpenUp is one of the processes defined by the Eclipse Process Framework project. It provides an example of how to integrate third-party processes into Jazz. OpenUp structures the project lifecycle into four phase iterations — Inception, Elaboration, Construction, and Transition. There are additional iterations within these phases.

Scrum

The Scrum process template supports a popular approach to managing projects in an agile way. This template includes a single development line (Main Development) with a release 1.0. The release is subdivided into a number of fixed-length sprints.

Simple Team

The Simple Team process template enables teams to get started quickly. Team members have permissions to perform any modification in the project.

Translatable templates

Translatable process templates are supported starting with Rational Team Concert 1.0.1. A translatable process template has user-visible strings packaged so that they can be translated into languages other than English. It can be used to create a project area with translated work item workflows, reports, dashboards, process preconditions, role names, iteration names, and so on.

Various important aspects such as process templates, project areas, team areas, roles, preconditions, and follow-up actions exist in the process templates. You need to be a member of the JazzAdmins group in your repository to configure the process templates. A typical Scrum process template is shown as follows, which can be opened from the Process Templates view of Jazz Administration perspective:

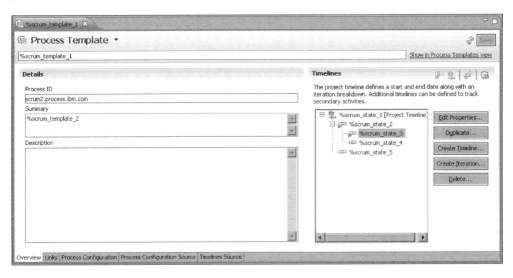

Multiple files can be specified, each with the strings for a certain locale. The name of each file reveals the locale of the strings it contains. For example, consider a process template that supports two locales—English (United States) and Deutsch (Germany). The template has two files attached to it, one named `template_en_US.messages` and the other named `template_de.messages`. A typical translation file looks like a property file with a `name=value` format:

```
scrum_spec_0=Produkteigner
scrum_spec_1=Scrum-Master
scrum_spec_2=Teammitglied
scrum_spec_3=Projektinitiator
scrum_spec_6=Ein Mitglied des funktionsübergreifenden Teams.
scrum_spec_7=Der Projektinitiator.
scrum_spec_9=Projekt konfigurieren
scrum_spec_10=Team 1
scrum_spec_40=Projekt für Berichte einrichten
scrum_spec_41=Blockierende Arbeitselemente
scrum_spec_43=Buildzustand
scrum_spec_46=Buildergebnisse
scrum_spec_48=Burndown
```

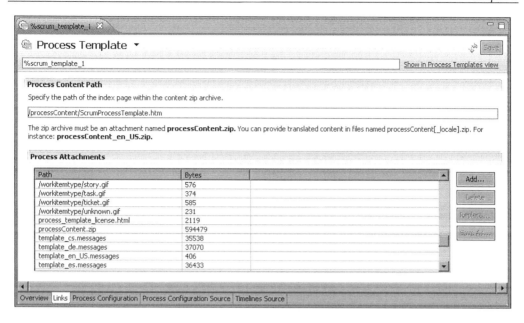

The previous screenshot shows the **Process Template** with the process attachments with translated content. When a project area is created, one of the template's supported locales must be selected. Work items, reports, dashboards, and process messages for the project area and related team areas will be in the language of the chosen locale. For instance, if you created a project area with the German version of the template described above, fields in work items would have German names, reports and dashboards would have German text, and messages in the Team Advisor view would be in German.

Complete internationalization of the workflow in Rational Team Concert is provided by these translations. You can easily look at the process templates and translate the relevant message in the message files.

Process configuration

In the previous section we have seen an overview of various process templates and how they are used. Project Area, Team Area, and Process templates have high-level editors to configure and customize the process flow. With the help of these high-level editors, you can configure numerous process attributes. For example, you can add roles, change the various permissions for the roles, modify operation behaviors, change work item types, and many more as shown in the following screenshot:

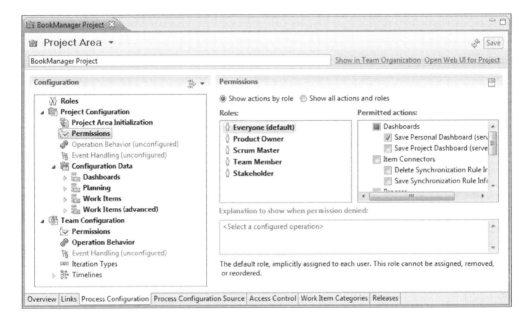

As you can see from about screenshot, Rational Team Concert provides a convenient way to configure the process without exposing the XML source behind it. When you prefer to directly edit the XML, you can do so from the Process Configuration Source tab. However, it is recommended to use the Process Configuration editor to avoid XML editing errors.

If you want to share the process that you configured with other projects, you can do so from the Project Area. Once you capture and save the changes for your Project Area, you are ready to share the process right from the Project Area context menu. From the context menu of the Project Area, click **Create Process Template**. Enter the necessary details and create a new process template representing all the changes that we made to current project area, shown as follows:

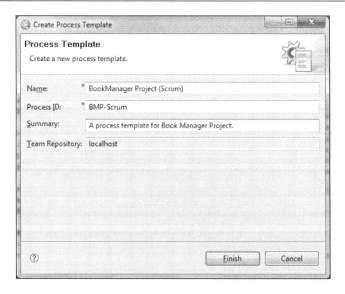

Once the process template is created, it's visible in the Process Templates view. This template now has all the process configurations we saved before. If needed, this process template itself can be configured again before sharing with other projects.

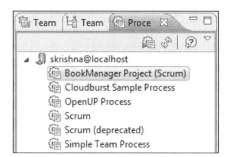

From the Process Templates view, select the template, and from the context menu, select **Export**. Enter the destination folder to make this template readily available for other teams. This template can be imported by other projects and can be applied to their project areas. This makes it easy for the projects to share their best practices in the form of the process template.

Agile development

Scrum is a concrete discipline of Agile software engineering. While Agile methodologies place emphasis on the principles and benefits of the iterative and incremental software development, Scrum constitutes a concrete set of management practices for highly flexible and productive teams.

Scrum is a popular form of Agile methodology practiced these days. In this book, the BookManager application uses the Scrum development template. As you would have noticed in the previous chapters, we have leveraged the Scrum process template and release management.

The central idea behind this section is to be aware of the process-oriented workflow in Rational Team Concert. We will describe this by using the Scrum process and see its integration into Rational Team Concert.

We will now see various aspects of how Scrum is supported and practiced through Rational Team Concert.

Project Area

Rational Team Concert starts the infusion of the process right at the time of the **Project Area** creation. This means that you can decide to choose a process from the available templates and attach it to the Project Area. From then on, the project and team has the ability to conform to the chosen process. If the project has more than one team, different teams may participate at different times and may follow a different process. In this situation, you can create **Team Areas** for different teams and add team members, roles, and customize process, if needed.

You could deploy the default available templates or create a templates from an existing one that suites your team and organizational needs. Creating a new template or initializing the project with available template is only the starting point. With the progress of the project, you can change the template to fit your team. In traditional software development, we see various tools that are bundled without seamless integration, and often the user needs to navigate from one tool to another to get a task done. Typically the process conformity is achieved with the help of various team meetings, spreadsheets, checklists, and others that are outside the tools or software development infrastructure. However, with Rational Team Concert, the process, team, and development tools are all integrated into one. As a team member, you don't have to worry about the process conformity or process knowledge as long as the administrator configures the process templates as shown in the following screenshot:

The ability of the tools to understand the project and process is one of the core concepts of Rational Team Concert, called **Process aware tools**.

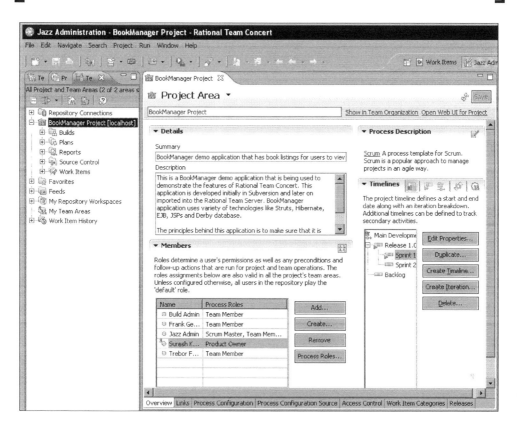

Open the Project Area description of BookManager Project from the Team Organization view. The Project Area editor has several editor tabs that describe members, release plans, process configuration, work item categories, and others.

The Project Area's **Overview** tab contains the crucial information about the process. It has the name and short description about the process attached to this Project Area. In our case, you see Scrum as the selected process template. This tab also has the list of project members. Depending on the process selection, the process roles assigned to a user may change. Rational Team Concert has widely accepted user roles from the Scrum process such as:

- **Scrum Master**: A person responsible for the project.

- **Product Owner**: Person responsible for managing the product. He is also the person who will manage the product backlog.

- **Stakeholder**: Any party interested in the outcome of the product, such as internal management, a partner, or a customer.

- **Team Member**: A member of the cross-functional team who works for this project.

During the Project Area creation, the second step is to choose the process template. As an administrator, you need to make sure that the available templates are deployed. By default, the **English (United States)** locale is selected for the selected Scrum template. Depending on your country and language, you will adjust the locale. Be sure the project is initialized by ensuring that the default setting that says **Automatically initialize the Project Area on Finish as specified in the process template** is selected, as shown in the next screenshot:

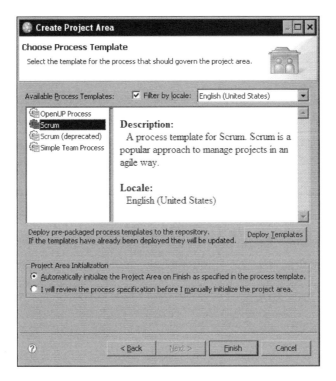

Project Area also defines the project time lines. When we create a Project Area with Scrum process template, by default Rational Team Concert creates a main release, **Release 1,** with two sprints namely **Sprint 1** and **Sprint 2**. It also creates a product backlog. As an administrator, you will attach the process template to the project. The rest of the work is done by Rational Team Concert, giving you a ready-to-use system.

Role definition

The Scrum process template comes with default user roles, namely Stakeholder, Product Owner, Scrum Master, and Team Member. You can also add additional roles that are in your organization, as shown in the following screenshot:

To define a new role, go to the **Process Configuration** tab of the Project Area. In the **Defined Roles** section, you can add a new role by clicking on the **Add New Role** icon. You can define **Cardinality** to allow this role to be assigned to multiple members or to a single member, as shown in the following screenshot:

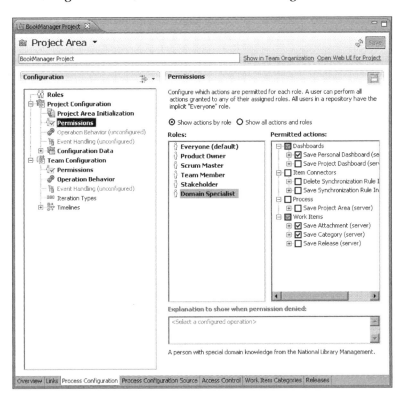

Every role defined in a process template needs to have permitted actions. This is configured by navigating to **Project Configuration | Permissions** in the **Process Configuration** tab. Select the **Domain Specialist** role and grant the necessary actions. In our case, we have given access to the Domain Specialist so that he is able to create and save dashboards and review the work items.

Configure the permissions and behavior of operations, that are associated with a team area from **Team Configuration | Permissions**. The options in this section can be further customized in Team Areas. These options can also be configured differently for a particular timeline, iteration, or type of iteration.

Optionally, you can enter a custom message explaining why permission is denied for a combination of a role and action.

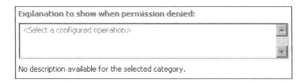

You have seen that the Scrum template not only gives default roles and permissions in the context of Rational Team Concert, but also gives you the power to add and further customize the roles and permissions

Team collaboration

One of the guiding principles of the Agile methodology is emphasis on *individuals and interactions over processes and tools*. Rational Team Concert gives every possible emphasis on people and teams by providing an integrated approach on collaboration. Team and individual interaction is supported via a variety of tools within.

At a bare minimum, teams can interact with the work item-aware Instant Messaging via Google Talk. In a more sophisticated integrated approach, you can use Lotus Sametime, which is a client-server application and middleware platform that provides real-time and unified communication and collaboration for enterprises. These capabilities include presence information, enterprise instant messaging, web conferencing, community collaboration, and telephony capabilities and integration.

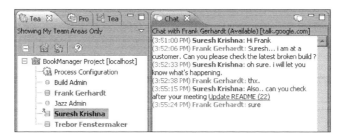

Team members have the ability to share their availability with the entire team as seen in the previous screenshot. This makes it possible for all the members to be aware of what's happening in the team. You can quickly look at the scheduled absence view of team member to know why a team member is not online or responding to e-mails. This information is also considered for the calculation of the team load and burn down charts. In traditional tools, this information needs to be updated in several spreadsheets or disparate systems, and any project report needs to pull the data from different systems, which is time consuming and error prone.

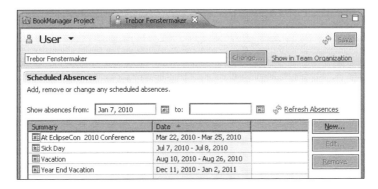

As seen in the previous screenshot, individuals can define their availability for the project. In a globally distributed team, it is necessary to know a team member's time zone and project availability. This can be captured by the team member in the **Work Environment** tab of the User editor.

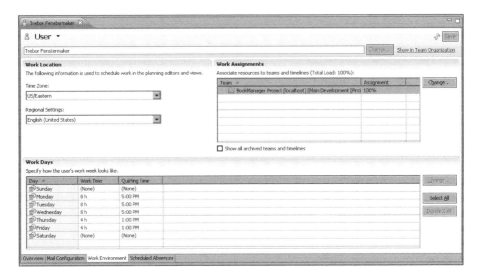

You, as a team member, can enter the time zone, work day schedule, and work assignments. Work assignments have the interesting aspect that you can see who is dedicated to multiple projects, if any. These integrated collaboration features, combined with the powerful features from work items, increase the team's productivity.

Work items

Work items are a way to keep track of issues and tasks in a project during the development lifecycle. They are the indicators of the project progress. Depending on the process template attached to the project, the types of the work items will change. In the case of the Scrum process, the work items are a combination of the generic work items and types specific to Scrum:

- Defect
- Task
- Story
- Epic
- Track Build Item
- Impediment
- Adoption Item
- Retrospective

Attaching the Scrum template to the Project Area creates all the necessary work item types. You can observe that we did not create any new work items types for the Scrum process and as soon as the Project Area is created, we have everything ready concerning the Scrum process.

Product Managers or Product Owners can create Epics or Stories as work items and start tracking them. A work item has several features integrated into Rational Team Concert and provide a way that you can leverage to increase team productivity, such as:

- Assign the work items for a specific Sprint or Backlog.
- Attach needed information such as documents, spreadsheets, presentations, and other external information.
- Link other work items and maintain various relationships such as parent, child, related, duplicate, and depend-on relationships.
- Add one or more team members or stakeholders as subscribers to an Epic or Story.

- Add one or more approvers to the work item. In practice, you could add a stakeholder or a domain specialist as reviewer for this Story or Epic.

- Finally, each work item has the complete changes on it recorded and can be seen in the **History** tab.

Project administrators and team members benefit from the work item changes that happen on the various project reports in real time. Work items are neatly integrated into the team, process, and source control system of Rational Team Concert. Automatic generation of the work item infrastructure is a powerful feature that reduces a significant manual effort.

Repository workspace

A repository workspace is a private development area where you can keep your work. Your work remains private to the workspace until you decide to deliver it to a team flow target such as a shared stream.

In traditional software development, it is difficult to deal with constantly incoming changes, such as when you, as a team member, are working on a work item and another higher priority task comes up. If your manager asks you to work on this higher priority task immediately, then you are left in a messy state with your previous work. You will manually copy these files to a temporary location and start working on the new task. We are not always in a position to revert the working files as considerable work may have already been done. So, in a situation where there are many high-priority tasks coming in and the dynamic workplace leaves you to juggle with the working files, the real challenge in this scenario is the manual effort of merging the conflicting files later on.

Rational Team Concert enables you to respond to dynamic environments and unscheduled work priorities. With the help of the repository workspaces and change sets, you can do various actions to work with the new work items such as:

- **Deliver**: The change set is marked as complete if not already completed, and then flows to the workspace's current flow target.

- **Suspend**: The change set is removed from the local workspace but preserved in the repository so that it can be restored when you want to resume work on it.

- **Discard**: The change set is discarded and the items revert to the state they were in before the first change was made. This operation permanently undoes all the changes in the change set.

As an example, consider a scenario where you are working on a task and make considerable changes to source files. When an urgent task comes in, Rational Team Concert empowers you to make variety of decisions. You can deliver the current changes if they are complete, suspend the changes to complete this urgent task, or discard the changes made till now to work on the new urgent task. From the context menu of the change set in the Pending changes view, you can take the most appropriate action. Without this capability, you may need to manually back up the incomplete changes to work on them at a later time. The following screenshot shows the context menu on a change set:

Responding to change is one of the primary principles of the Scrum, and Rational Team Concert enables a controlled and careful change mechanism. You can check-in your changes into your own repository workspace and later decide if you want to deliver into a flow target. This way all your work is preserved and you can adapt to the ever-changing priorities.

Reporting

Scrum Master, Product Owner, Team Member, and other stakeholders need to have a real-time view of the project progress, including any impediments. Rational Team Concert provides a real-time view of the overall project progress via dashboards accessed from the web interface, as seen in the following screenshot. Remember that the source control, work items, and process templates are all seamlessly integrated, which gives a real-time view of the project progress.

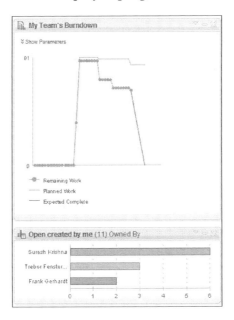

In the previous screenshot you can see the Sprint burn down chart and the open work items. Teams can use the burn down charts for the daily Scrum meetings. This report plots the remaining backlog of work in terms of the time estimated to complete it. Ideally, the chart will show a trend toward zero hours of remaining work as the sprint comes to a close. Only work items that are open, are in progress, and have an estimate specified are included in the calculation.

As an administrator you can get various reports based on the work items and assignments. This helps understand the number of outstanding work items for each team member. For any stakeholder of the project, reports give a real-time view of the project progress and you can generate reports on what you feel is important for you.

Release planning

Scrum advocates the continuous release of the working software and getting immediate feedback from the customer. At the time of Project Area creation, Rational Team Concert will also create the Main Release as **Release 1.0** and two sprints, Sprint 1 and Sprint 2, by default.

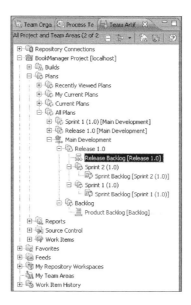

As seen in the previous screenshot, depending on your project requirements, you can create one or more Sprints that would constitute a main release. In our case, we have Sprint 1 and Sprint 2 that would get released as Release 1.0. From each of the Backlogs you see in the Team Artifacts view, you can see the items that are yet to be worked on. The idea is that the Product Backlog has the list of all the tasks that are yet to be scheduled, and the Release backlog has list of all items that actually planned for the release. The Scrum Master would schedule tasks from Product Backlog to a specific Sprint, which would also show up in the Release backlog.

Build management

Your team can use the Rational Team Concert Build component of the Jazz technology platform to define and manage the builds. Your team can have **build awareness** through build monitoring, build alerts, build result viewing, and linkage of builds with other artifacts such as change sets and work items.

When you create a build definition, you have the option to create a dedicated repository workspace for the build. Dedicated build workspaces enable you to identify changes and work items that go into a build, and to create snapshots of the build source content.

In the next chapter, we will see an in-depth view of how to define, configure, and start builds. With the help of the Team Build component, Rational Team Concert provides support for continuous integration and nightly builds. As an administrator you can schedule the builds at a specific time, and team members can request a build on-demand. You can leverage any existing ant scripts in the project.

You saw in the above sections that once the Scrum process template is associated with the Project Area, you get a fully functional process infused into the client. Various aspects of the project and team, such as Work Item types, release management, Role definitions, and others, are defined by the process template selection. You have also seen that Rational Team Concert completely supports the various aspects of the Scrum process.

Release management

The process of release management is the way to plan, schedule, build, and make the software available to the end users in a defined timeline. Release management involves several interrelated and overlapping tasks that sum up to provide a meaningful release. They are as follows:

- Define a top-level release plan along with timelines. This becomes the release that goes to the end customers.
- Divide the timeline into the smaller and manageable Iterations. In the Agile development scenario, these are called Sprints.
- Define and prioritize the Stories for a release and Tasks for Iterations.
- Make sure that all the must have stories of the release are scheduled across the defined iterations.
- Assign Stories to releases and Tasks to individual team members.
- Track the progress of the tasks in each iteration.
- Manage the constantly incoming change requests and add them to product backlog.
- Risk assessment of tasks and iterations.
- Generate reports to the project stakeholders.

Rational Team Concert provides a way to accomplish all the above-mentioned tasks right from the client or from the web application. We will now explore different aspects of the release planning and iteration tracking from the client.

 The goal of this section is to track **Sprint 1** of the BookManager application and then plan for the future release. This will give us an overview of how to create and schedule releases. At the end of this section, you will have an overview of the release planning, and how to track the iterations and releases with the dashboard reports.

A Project Release plan is the highest-level plan in Rational Team Concert that provides an overview of the project goals. A Project Release plan displays top-level work items, such as Stories and Epics associated to a project area or team area, current iteration, and its child iterations. You can create a Project Release plan for any iteration. However, it is advisable to create a Project Release plan for the top iteration. The other plan types, such as Team Release plan and Iteration plan, can be created for child iterations. As mentioned earlier, in Agile methodology, iterations are called Sprints.

In general, a Project Release plan groups work items based on backlog, iterations, teams, and work breakdown. You can create a plan overview, create and modify work item assignments for team members, and track the progress of the work. Projects are organized into a series of fixed-length development periods called iterations (Sprints in Agile methodology). Each timeline has its own set of iterations. Timeline, iterations, start and end dates, and the current iteration designation are defined in the project area editor.

Changes in a work item are reflected in the plan and vice versa. As an example, when a work item's estimated duration is changed or closed, that status is reflected in the plan. This keeps the plan synchronized with current project activity and minimizes the need for redundant documentation and manual collection of data.

Iteration planning

Rational Team Concert projects are organized into a series of fixed-length development periods called iterations. Each timeline has its own set of iterations as shown in the next screenshot. You can create an iteration plan and assign work items to each iteration.

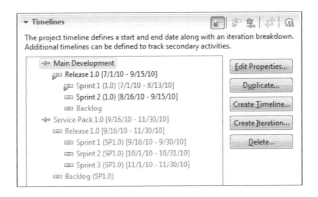

You can see the project timeline from the Project Area's Overview editor. BookManager Application's project timeline is created as **Main Development**, which has a main iteration named **Release 1.0**. The main **Release 1.0** iteration is split across two sprints, namely **Sprint 1** and **Sprint 2**. The project timeline also has the product **Backlog** that consists of prioritized work items. BookManager Project follows the Scrum process and hence we call the iterations Sprints. You can see that the Sprints are time bound and the final release sums up both the sprints that we defined.

A future timeline **Service Pack 1.0** delivery is planned as soon as the current timeline is finished. This project timeline consists of the three sprints and one project backlog. Planning the iterations in advance gives you a chance to allocate the work items accordingly. Work items can be initially placed in the project backlog and before the start of the sprint; you can assign the work items to the right team member.

Every iteration plan can be configured either to broaden or narrow down the permission levels from the **Project Area Editor | Process Configuration**; select **Team Configuration | Timelines**.

Project tracking

Project tracking is fundamentally different in Rational Team Concert when compared to traditional systems. At any point in time, all the stakeholders will get a real-time view of the project progress. As a project manager, you can simply leverage the pre-defined templates, use them directly, or modify them as you need to. Rational Team Concert provides different reports that are suitable for a team leader, team member, and other stakeholders. In *Chapter 5, Team Collaboration and Work Items*, we saw a short introduction to the reports and dashboards. We will now see an in-depth view of the sprint and iteration tracking.

In traditional systems, we are typically collecting the data from different places, often spreadsheets. As a project manager, you would look for the spreadsheet where all the release tasks are mentioned. Collecting data from different spreadsheets and various systems to see the project progress is time consuming and error prone.

With Rational Team Concert each release iteration knows the set of tasks, and each task is aware of the status. All this information is very well connected with the code editor and source control. This close integration makes it possible to see release data in real-time and generate on-the-fly reports.

Let's start looking at the Sprint and Release Backlog user interface from the Team Artifacts view as shown in the following screenshot. The current Sprint backlog can be accessed from many places in the project area.

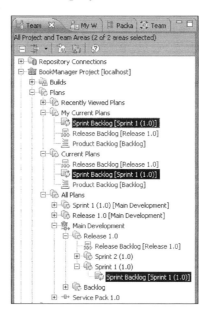

Open the Team Artifacts view and then open the **BookManager Project | Plans**. **My Current Plans** shows the list of all plans that are relevant to you as a user. Typically, this will have all the plans from the team iterations in which you are participating. In the cases when there are no team iterations, the plans are the same as the current iteration plans. Notice that the plans related to the current user are shown in blue, while the others are in black. If there are multiple team iterations then **Current Plans** will contain all the team iterations even when you are not part of one.

All Plans, as the name suggests, contains all the Project Timelines in that project. In our **BookManager Project**, **Main Development** and **Service Pack 1.0** are shown.

Opening the Sprint Backlog from the Team Artifacts view will open the **Sprint Backlog** editor as shown in the next screenshot:

The **Sprint Backlog** editor contains three tabs—**Overview**, **Planned Items**, and **Charts**. The **Overview** tab uses a WikiCreole wiki editing syntax text editor. Formatting includes bold text, bullets and numbered lists, tables, and links to work items and external websites. You can also add color to the foreground and background of the page. When viewing pages in edit mode, you can add or download attachments.

In our case, the **Overview** tab has the introduction to the BookManager application, a list of features for the current Sprint, and the list of team members as shown in the next screenshot. If required, you can add more wiki pages to this tab.

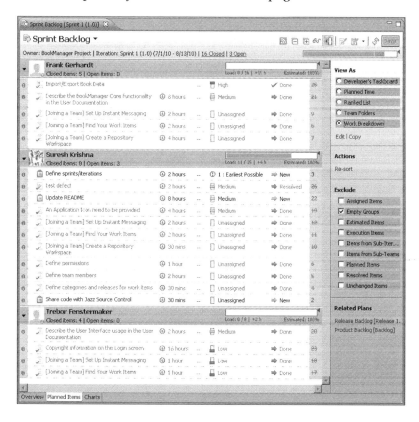

The **Planned Items** tab of the Sprint editor gives a very good view of the list of all the work items for the current Sprint. This tab shows you the work items for each user, status, priorities, and the initial estimate of the tasks. The Sprint Backlog is a sophisticated editor with a facility to show a criteria filter, preview the work items, and the ability to add the RSS feed of this Sprint to your local feeds.

The **Planned Items** editor can be filtered in various ways to make sense of the work items or for reporting. A very interesting feature of this editor is that you can view the tasks as Developer's Taskboard that gives a report useful for daily scrums as shown in the following screenshot. Typically, as a team manager, you can use this to view the team's progress and discuss the impediments. You may wish to not show the completed tasks by filtering the tasks to see only the information relevant to you.

The third tab, labeled **Charts** in the Sprint Backlog editor, shows the burn down chart for the current Sprint. You can choose the most relevant ones from the templates and gauge the Sprint progress. These real-time charts not only provide a great source of information about progress, but they also provide trends in the work items burn down as shown in the following screenshot. These observations may become crucial lessons at the time of the Sprint Retrospective phase.

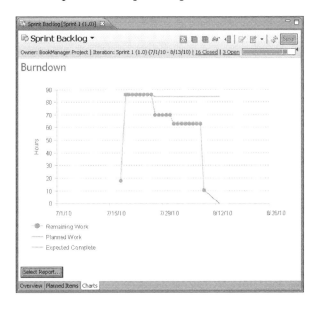

You have seen that the Sprint Backlog editor provides a wealth of information, including the wiki style description, work items, status, priorities, team members, and charts. You can fully leverage the information for daily scrums and management reporting.

As a project manager, you can see open and closed work items grouped by priority. This gives an overview of the types of tasks that are relevant for a sprint, and some hints to make the next plan better.

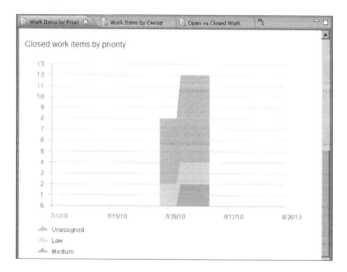

As an example, the **Closed work items by priority** chart has many **Unassigned** priority items. This observation can be carried forward to make for better planning for the next Sprint, and to make sure that all the work items are prioritized.

Often you would like to have an overview of the number of tasks resolved by each team member, as well as what kind of priority tasks they handle. As seen previously, the Developer's Taskboard view is an all-in-one view that associates the team member, work items, and its status. However, the **Work Items by Owner** report template gives you an overview of the number of tasks that are divided among team members and the open versus closed work items assigned to a specific team member:

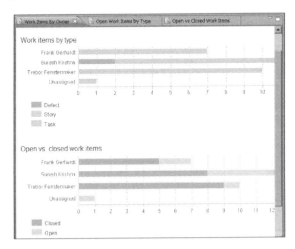

Analyzing the above **Work Items by Owner** chart, we can observe who is working on the most number of defects, who is responsible for stories, and how many work items have an owner as **Unassigned**. Another metric we use often is the number of issues or tasks that are closed by a team member. This metric helps the team manager to see if any team member has excess work, so they can redistribute it to the team. A combination of these two charts will give you an idea of each team member's load, and what kind and how many tasks are being worked on.

Another report that helps monitor the sprint progress and team performance is **Open vs Closed Work Items**. **Open**, **In Progress**, and **Closed** items are represented in the chart by a different color. This report plots all work items over time. As shown in the next screenshot, if an iteration is specified, only those work items planned for that iteration are shown:

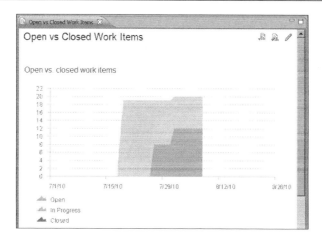

During the analysis of the chart, you need to watch to see if the open work items are growing faster than those that are closed. This indicates that a backlog is growing. You can also see if work items are not being closed at all if the number remains constant. Additionally, you may want to monitor the number of work items in progress. It is a good practice in Agile development to limit the number of items in progress.

You have seen several template charts that will give you a great analysis of the real-time data that Rational Team Concert has. There are several other charts that indicate the project, team, and work item health that can be obtained from **Team Artifacts view | BookManager Project | Reports | Shared Project or Report Templates**.

If you are a team member, you have access to team progress from the Team Central view in the Team Load section and also the Recent Work section. The Recent Work section in particular gives a great view of the tasks that have started or completed as shown in the following screenshot:

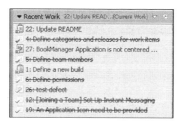

A team member, as well as a team manager, can use various resources in Rational Team Concert to get an overview of the work items, team member work load, open and closed items, and others, and be confident on the Release plan and Release schedule.

- Team Manager or Stakeholder:
    - ° Team Artifacts view gives an in-depth view of the various Release Plans and Iteration Plans
    - ° Iteration Plan Editor has various capabilities such as Wiki overview, charts, and various views of the Work items
    - ° Developer Taskboard view gives an overview of the tasks that are in Start, In progress, and Completed states on every team member
    - ° Leverage the powerful report templates by configuring and viewing reports of your interest

- Team Member:
    - ° My Work view to see the current and future work for a specific team member
    - ° Team Central view gives a crisp view of the entire team's load and how they are performing on the scheduled tasks
    - ° In addition to the team manager, you as a team member can use the same report templates from the Team Artifacts view

 Release tracking is indirectly done by tracking work items connected to that specific Sprint.

Reality check

Several features of the BookManager application have been developed by the team for Sprint 1. We will now use the Ant build file for the application to generate the runtime artifacts and deploy it to a standard Servlet container. In our case, we will use Tomcat as the application server. In Chapter 3, we deployed the BookManager application from the subversion control system into Rational Team Concert Team source control. Since then, several features were introduced for Sprint 1:

- Non-admin users will not be able to delete books
- Admin user will be able to export the available books in XML or CSV format
- Application has an **About** dialog that shows the build ID
- Application has a special icon

Sprint 2 will focus on the documentation, code quality, and build system. We will define and run the build system in Sprint 2 (which will be covered in the next chapter).

Let us build, deploy, and run the application. We will need to initially use the admin utility of the BookManager application to create users. For now we will quickly check for the above mentioned Stories and then release Sprint 1.

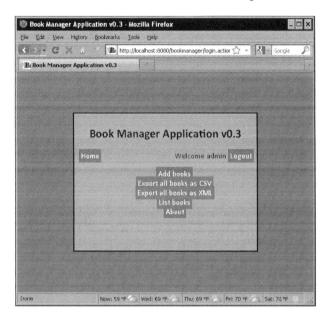

As seen in the previous screenshot, BookManager can now export the books. It also has its own application icon. We will now quickly do the following operations and then release Sprint 1:

- Add books
- List books
- Modify books
- Delete books
- Export books to CSV
- Export books to XML
- About application
- Breadcrumbs in every page
- Login and logout with admin and non-admin accounts

We will test all the features, including the Export to XML features. This feature serializes the books to a standard Java object XML as shown in the following screenshot:

```xml
<?xml version="1.0" encoding="UTF-8" ?>
- <java version="1.6.0_06" class="java.beans.XMLDecoder">
  - <object class="java.util.ArrayList">
    - <void method="add">
      - <object class="server.beans.Book">
        - <void property="author">
            <string>Mark Kurlansky</string>
          </void>
        - <void property="binding">
            <string>Hardcover</string>
          </void>
        - <void property="book_id">
            <long>1</long>
          </void>
        - <void property="catalog">
            <string>TN900.K865</string>
          </void>
        - <void property="copyright">
            <int>2002</int>
          </void>
        - <void property="title">
            <string>Salt: A World History</string>
          </void>
        </object>
      </void>
```

As shown in the next screenshot, once you serialize a book to a CSV file, you will be able to open it with Microsoft Excel or any text editor.

A	B	C	D	E	F
book_id	catalog	title	author	copyright	binding
1	TN900.K86	Salt: A World History	Mark Kurlansky	2002	Hardcover
2	0	The Book of General Ignorance	Deckle Edge	2007	Hardcover
3	0	Head First Java 2nd Edition	Kathy Sierra	2009	Paperback
4	0	Effective Java (2nd Edition)	Joshua Bloch	2008	Paperback
5	0	Sams Teach Yourself Java in 24 Ho	Rogers Cadenhead	2009	Paperback
6	0	Core Java(TM) Volume I--Fundamen	Cay S. Horstmann	2007	Paperback
7	0	Beginning Programming with Java F	Barry A. Burd	2005	Paperback
8	0	Java In A Nutshell 5th Edition	David Flanagan	2005	Paperback
9	0	Core Java Vol. 2: Advanced Feature	Cay S. Horstmann	2008	Paperback
10	0	Introduction to Java Programming C	Y. Daniel Liang	2010	Paperback
11	0	Thinking in Java (4th Edition)	Bruce Eckel	2006	Paperback
12	0	SCJP Sun Certified Programmer for	Katherine Sierra	2008	Hardcover
13	0	Java Concurrency in Practice	Brian Goetz	2006	Paperback

Once all the features are tested, we can start to prepare for the release. Let us do a few checks before we release:

- Open the Sprint 1 backlog from Team Artifacts and check that there are no remaining work items in the **Planned Items** tab

- Open the **Charts** tab editor and check that the burn down chart shows **Remaining work** as **0**

- Open the My Work view and verify that you have no current work

- Open the Team Central view and note that none of the team members have work items in Sprint 1

Now we will take the snapshot of the components *BookManager Doc* and *BookManager Project* for future reference as shown in the next screenshot. Initially the snapshot will be associated to the project workspace, and then we can promote it to the stream.

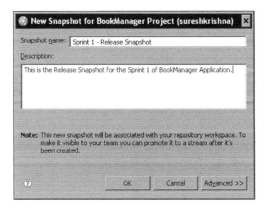

When the snapshots are created, the version numbers are automatically incremented by one and you can see it in the component history. Select the component and then click on the **Show | Baselines** to see the previous baselines as shown in the next screenshot:

Before we start the next Sprint, we need to make sure that the previous one is marked as completed and set the current Sprint. Open the BookManager Project Area and navigate to the **Timelines** section in the **Overview** tab. Select Sprint 2, and then right-click and select Set as Current Iteration.

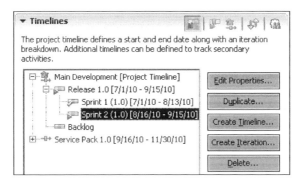

Optionally, we can create a release in the **Release** tab editor. Use this page to define the releases that your project team creates and maintains. Users can associate work items with specific releases by selecting a release for the **Found In** attribute as seen below. Once the release entry is successfully created, we can now create work items against this release entry. The release entry gives the team a history of the release timelines. With this, we are ready to start development on the next iteration.

Once the release entry is successfully created, we can now create work items against this release entry. The release entry gives the team a history of the release timelines. With this, we are ready to start development on the next iteration.

Summary

Initially we looked at an introduction to the software development process in general. Then we discussed the advantages of Rational Team Concert by seamlessly integrating the coding, issue management, source control, release management, and build management. We saw the power of the Process templates and an overview of the templates that are available.

In this chapter, we have used the Scrum process for the BookManager application. We did a deep dive into the Scrum development and integrated support from Rational Team Concert. We have seen how team members and Scrum Masters can leverage various features and reports.

Finally, we have seen an in-depth approach to Release management. We have looked at the project and iteration plans and then configured the release schedules. We have also defined a future release plan for the BookManager application. We have deployed the BookManager application and tested its new features. Later on, we looked into several check points, took a snapshot of the code, and then released Sprint 1.

In the next chapter, we will focus on the BookManager Documentation, Code Quality, and finally the Build management. With these features we will release Sprint 2, which will be the final sprint for Release 1.0. We will see in detail about the build engine, defining builds, and using the existing ant configuration.

7
Build Management

Make it work, make it right, make it fast.

-Kent Beck

Software build is the process of gathering the source code and other artifacts to churn them into executable software. Modern builds also provide traceability, association between artifacts and work items, reproducibility, IDE integration, and build comparison. With the increasing complexity of the software, builds too are becoming complex to manage. In this chapter, we will:

- See an overview of the build engine, build a toolkit, learn how to define the build, and track progress from Eclipse and the Web UI

- Work for Sprint 2 completion of the BookManager Project and deliver Release 1.0 to the main development line

- Define builds, set up the build engine, and track the BookManager Project's builds from a developer and build user's perspectives

Continuous integration

Continuous integration is a software development best practice that distributed teams use more and more as a way to mitigate integration problems and facilitate more rapid development of cohesive software. We have seen various aspects of Team Source Control, collaboration, work items, planning, and release management in Rational Team Concert. We will now see ways to manage continuous integration with the help of the Rational Team Concert build toolkit. The following is a quote by Martin Fowler about Continuous Integration:

> *Continuous Integration is a software development practice where members of a team integrate their work frequently; usually each person integrates at least daily, leading to multiple integrations per day. Each integration is verified by an automated build (including test) to detect integration errors as quickly as possible. Many teams find that this approach leads to significantly reduced integration problems and allows a team to develop cohesive software more rapidly.*

Continuous integration has become a rather default step in any software development lifecycle. To achieve continuous integration, you need teams to check on daily basis, both code and the appropriate tools to support the process. In Rational Team Concert, the build toolkit supports continuous integration.

Benefits

Without continuous integration in practice, you will see disconnect between code that the team has developed and code that is integrated. Often, team members have to rework certain aspects of their module as interfaces do not match. Team members may also need to merge code and resolve conflicts in shared libraries. In extreme cases, team members may have to completely redo the module due to a wide gap between the design and implementation. To reduce the amount of rework and unexpected surprises, continuous integration helps the team to keep track of integration each time a team member checks the source code.

Continuous integration comprises of a set of common practices including, but not limited to, the following:

- **Source code repository**: The project should have all the artifacts required to build the software in a single source code repository.
- **Automate the build**: By leveraging tools such as Ant, Maven, Make, and others, build should be automated to build the artifacts and push the executables into a test or QA environment.
- **Run the unit tests**: Once the source code compiles, make sure to run the unit tests, to increase team confidence in code behavior.

- **Frequent commits**: Checking the code frequently with small features gives an opportunity to quickly respond to changes. Also, responding to many weeks or months of changes is more difficult than responding to a day's worth.

- **Test in production environment**: Once the software is built, it should be tested in a QA environment (equivalent to the production environment) so that any assumptions made in the development environment are removed.

- **Package the software**: Package the software in such a way that development, QA, or customer teams can be easily deployed if needed.

- **Publish the build results**: Software builds should be published to the right audience and should be easily accessible via HTTP, FTP, or any widely used protocol.

The effort required to integrate a system increases exponentially with time. By integrating the system more frequently, integration issues are identified earlier, when they are easier to fix, and the overall integration effort is reduced. The result is a higher-quality product and more predictable delivery schedules.

Continuous integration provides the following benefits:

- **Improved feedback**: Continuous integration shows constant and demonstrable progress.

- **Improved bug detection**: Continuous integration enables you to detect and remove errors early, often minutes after they've been injected into the product.

- **Improved collaboration**: Continuous integration enables team members to work together safely. They know they can make a change to their code, integrate it into the system, and determine very quickly whether or not their change conflicts with others.

- **Improved system integration**: By integrating continuously throughout your product, you know that you can actually build the system, thereby mitigating integration surprises at the end of the lifecycle.

- Reduced number of parallel changes that need to be merged and tested.

- **Reduced number of errors found during system testing**: All conflicts are resolved before making new change sets available, and they are resolved by the person who is in the best position to do so (namely the original team member).

- **Reduced technical risk**: You always have an up-to-date system to test against.

- **Reduced management risk**: By continuously integrating your system, you know exactly how much functionality you have built to date, thereby improving your ability to predict when you will be able to deliver the promised functionality.

Build module

For the Rational Team Concert Enterprise edition, the build system toolkit needs to be downloaded separately from Jazz.net. The downloaded and extracted build toolkit consists of the build engine and toolkit modules. We can use the build component to define and manage builds. This module provides us with build awareness through build progress monitoring, build alerts, build result viewing, and linkage of builds with other artifacts such as change sets and work items. While the build toolkit is best suited for Ant builds, you can use any scripting technology that can invoke Ant such as Perl, batch files, or Make.

The extracted source has the `Buildengine` and `Buildtoolkit` directories. The `Buildengine` directory has the Jazz build engine, which runs as a client to the Jazz server, polling, and processing build requests. The `Buildtoolkit` directory is the Ant build toolkit, a set of Ant tasks available for use from your Ant scripts for publishing artifacts (for example, downloads, logs, compilation, and JUnit results) back to the build result on the server, reporting build progress, and other tasks. Out of the box, the Rational Team Concert build includes support for Ant, Maven, and command-line builds.

Rational Team Concert builds can have traceability between change sets and work items. You typically run a build against files that come from a designated build repository workspace that has incoming flows from the team's main development stream. Before running the build, all the latest changes are accepted from the team's stream and a reproducible snapshot of the files is created. The change sets and work items included in the build are recorded for consumers of the build to view.

After a build is considered good, you can create a Release from the build. You can then set the **Found in** field of a work item to the particular release associated with the build. The following figure illustrates the traceability between change sets and work items when you run a build against files from a team stream:

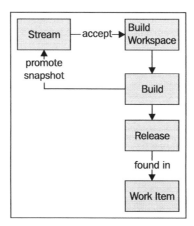

Build setup

Team build is a first-class component in Rational Team Concert, meaning there is a crisp integration of the build engine and build tools into the Web and Eclipse client. The IDE, source code, source control, team process, and team builds are all interrelated and you can trace builds to artifacts and vice versa.

In general, you, as the team's release engineer, install the build engine and Ant toolkit on a dedicated build machine. The build engine and toolkit are clients of the Rational Concert Team Server. The release engineer creates a corresponding build engine in the Jazz repository, and specifies the build definitions it will support, by writing a build script for each definition.

A build definition can use a schedule to run a build. For example, you can set up a build to run at a continuous time interval and, optionally, choose to build or not build based on source code changes in the Jazz repository. You can also set up a build to run at a specific time each day. Build tasks vary among projects. In addition to compiling source code and packaging the corresponding content into an appropriate executable form, a build can include other steps, such as running automated tests or running code quality tools over the code base.

A typical build process looks as follows:

- The release engineer starts the Jazz Build Engine on the build machine. The build engine polls the Jazz Team Server for build requests.

- The build engine retrieves a request to run a build. The build request identifies the build definition and can include property settings that override the default settings. The build definition tells the build engine which script to run.

- Each build definition has an associated build script, which is typically a versioned artifact under Rational Team Concert source control.

- The build engine runs the build script, which runs Ant tasks that communicate with the Jazz Team Server to fetch source files from a stream or workspace, report progress, and create the build output, including artifacts, logs, and links.

- The build outputs are stored in the repository, so that developers can view the logs and download the build artifacts.

Recommendations

Individual team members can run team builds and then publish the results. However, to get the most out of the build module and continuous integration, it is recommended you set up the Rational Team Concert builds in a certain way. These are only generic recommendations; depending on your team's requirements, you may choose to take a different approach.

- **Build user**: The Build toolkit and the Build Engine requires a user. It is recommended to create a special user dedicated to builds. Assign a Build System client access license to the build user.

- **Password encryption**: Do not specify build user passwords in Ant build files or the Jazz Build Engine command line. Use the Jazz Build Engine `createPasswordFile` option to create an encrypted password file that you can use with Ant tasks and the build engine.

- **Workspace owner**: Create a Rational Team Concert source control workspace for the build and set the build user as the workspace owner.

Build Engine and Toolkit

The Build Engine processes the build requests, starts and completes builds, and finishes by publishing build logs. If your organization uses a different build system, you can still use the same build mechanism and leverage the Ant tasks from the toolkit. Tasks in the buildtoolkit can perform each of these functions. Typically, you can invoke the buildtoolkit tasks from your selected build engine or within your build scripts.

You can use buildtoolkit tasks to perform various tasks, including getting the next build request, starting a build, completing a build, and publishing logs. You can find an example build script that does not use the Jazz Build Engine at `installdir/buildsystem/buildtoolkit/examples/standalone`, where `installdir` is the Build System Toolkit installation directory.

When you create a build definition, you have the option to create a dedicated repository workspace for the build. Dedicated build workspaces enable you to identify changes and work items that go into a build, and to create snapshots of the build source content.

When your build definition specifies a build repository workspace, the Jazz Build Engine, which is connected to the Jazz repository, uses this repository workspace to identify the content to build. The build engine accepts any incoming changes from the team's stream and loads the repository workspace contents into the local file system for processing.

There is a Jazz Source Control pre-build step that can be added to a build to make it easy to fetch files from a Jazz repository workspace or stream. The Source Control step will add a page to the build definition and allows you to configure how to fetch the files.

The snapshot and baselines created by the build are private to the build workspace. If you want to make them official, you can promote and rename them to a stream to make them easier to find for team members.

If you already have a build script and don't want to migrate to a Jazz Source Control build, you can use the Ant fetch task to fetch code from the Rational Team Concert repository from within your script.

We have seen an overview of the Build toolkit in Rational Tool Concert, and various modules such as Build Engine and Toolkit. Depending on your organization's preference, you can reuse the existing Build Engine and use the toolkit to invoke the various team repository tasks. Remember that in the previous chapters, we successfully built the BookManager Project with Ant. Now we will see how to use a combination of the Build Engine and Toolkit to configure and build the BookManager Project using the existing Ant script.

Working with Eclipse

In Rational Team Concert, the build environment will use a deck of tools consisting of at least one build engine and one or more build scripts. In our case, the Jazz Build Engine launches the process that will run the Ant build script and collect its output. You must provide the build scripts that perform the detailed tasks to compile and test the code to build artifacts as shown in the following figure:

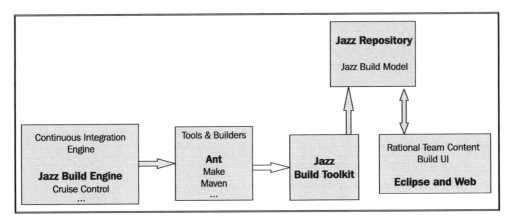

The Rational Team Concert build brings together the work items, change sets, builds, and releases. This allows for the builds to be repeatable and traceable over time. Creating a new Jazz build requires you to create a build engine and build definition in the Jazz repository. The build engine identifies the build system that will perform builds (in our case an Ant build). The build definition identifies a particular build and its properties.

Before we proceed with defining the builds and build engines, make sure that a build user is defined and a valid Rational Team Concert Build System license is assigned. As a best practice, let us encrypt and create a password file for the build user:

1. From the command prompt go to `<root>\buildsystem\buildengine\eclipse`.

2. Run the `jbe -createPasswordFile <passwordFileName>` command as follows:

   ```
   >jbe -createPasswordFile buildPass.txt

   *** Warning: password will be printed to the screen.
   password: ******

   Password stored in file: "D:\RTC\Jazz\buildsystem\buildengine\
   eclipse\buildPass.txt"
   ```

```
*** Warning: The password is encrypted to prevent casual
observation, but a determined attacker may discover the password.
The password file should be protected with operating system file
permissions.
```

We have created an encrypted password to use with the Ant task at build time.

Build definition

Launch an Eclipse client with build admin as the user and connect to the BookManager Project project repository. As we are launching the build admin client for the first time, this user does not have any repository workspaces. Create a repository workspace and declare the build admin (with username `build-admin`) as the owner. This will be the workspace (BookManager Project build) that is used for all the project builds. It is always recommended to use a special build admin user and build workspace so that builds are clean and any issues can be easily isolated.

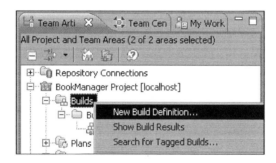

As shown in the previous screenshot, from the Team Artifacts view, go to **BookManager Project** repository, right-click on the **Builds** section, and select **New Build Definition**. Follow the wizard that will create a new Build Definition as follows:

1. In the **Build Definition** wizard, select **Create a New Build** and click **Next**.

2. Enter a valid build name in the **ID** field and select an appropriate build template. In our case, we use **Ant – Jazz Build Engine** to make use of our existing Ant build script. Click **Next**.

3. The pre-build wizard page lists all the available source control systems. Select the **Jazz Source Control** system, so all the sources are loaded from this source control. Click **Next**.

4. The post-build wizard page lists a few options you can select that will be executed after build. For example, ECJ Publishing creates logs generated by Eclipse Compiler for Java. Select **ECJ Publishing** and click **Next**.

5. The **Additional Configuration** wizard page contains **General, Schedule**, and **Properties** options. By default, these are selected and can be configured in the **Build Definition** editor. Click **Finish**.

The wizard will open the **Build Definition** editor. Here we will enter some critical information as shown in the following screenshot:

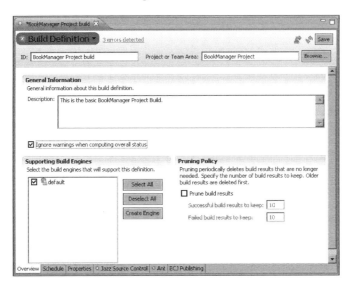

The **Build Definition** editor has all it needs for the build. The **Overview** tab contains the basic information such as build definition ID, Project Area, Build Engine, and whether we need pruning of the build results. If you wish to have pruning, select the option and specify a number of successful and failed builds.

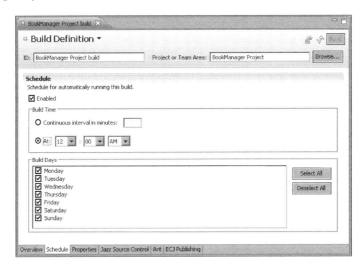

The **Schedule** tab has automatic build scheduling information. By default, it is not set. You can enable the automatic schedule and then select various parameters. To have it at regular intervals, you can use the **Continuous interval in minutes** option or you can use once-a-day time slots. Select one that suits your requirement.

The **Properties** tab allows you to define custom properties that you would like to use in your build script or in other configuration tabs as shown in the following screenshot:

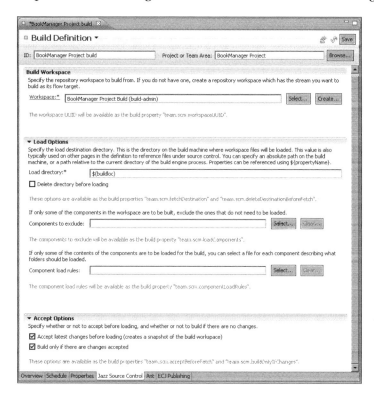

The **Jazz Source Control** tab has many available options. You need to specify the Repository Workspace to build from. During build time, the sources will be copied onto physical disks. The **Load directory** property specifies the absolute path or a path relative to the build engine process. Here is where you can also exclude one or more components from the build, if you need to. Finally, select how the change sets need to be treated by the build.

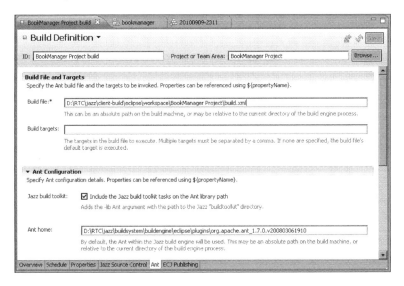

As shown in previous screenshot, in the **Ant** configuration tab, enter the **Build file** that needs to be executed. Optionally, you can enter a specific **Build target** and other Ant-specific settings that include the Ant and Java homes, JVM arguments, and any additional property files. Only the Ant file is mandatory. Once all this required information is entered, you can save the build specification without any errors. This build definition is now visible under the **Builds** section of the BookManager project in Team Artifacts.

Next, open the *default* build engine from the BookManager Project's build section as shown in the following screenshot:

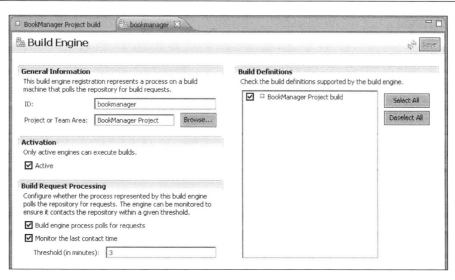

Give a meaningful name to the build engine and select the project area that this build engine caters to. This editor will also have the list of all the build definitions that this build engine supports. These build definitions can be organized by how they build for various operating systems. Remember to check the build engine process polls requests. If we need to schedule the builds in the build definition, then the build engine should have polling capability. Finally, you can specify the properties that are available to the builder, such as Ant. Property values can reference other properties using $\{property\}$ syntax. Build definition properties override build engine properties of the same name.

Now we are ready to start the build engine and test the build performance.

Start the build engine

The build system we installed during our initial setup has all the tools necessary for us to start the build process and poll for a build on a regular basis. Go to the Rational Team Concert root directory and navigate to the build engine directory (that is, `D:\rtc\Jazz\buildsystem\buildengine`). The following is an example usage of the build engine from command line:

```
// example usage of the build engine command line
jbe -repository https://localhost:9444/Jazz
    -userId     build-admin
    -pass       admin
    -engineId   bookmanager
    -sleeptime  1
```

When testing builds, it's a good idea to run with the options `-verbose` and `-sleepTime 1`. The `sleepTime` argument will ensure that the build engine sleeps for the specified time before start of the next build request. In production use, the default `sleepTime` (30 seconds) is more appropriate, particularly if running many build engines. The `verbose` option provides detailed logging of the build activity.

```
// example usage of the build engine command line with usage of verbose
and passwordFile options


jbe -repository    https://localhost:9444/Jazz

    -userId        build-admin

    -passwordFile buildPass.txt

    -engineId      bookmanager

    -verbose
```

In production environments, it makes sense to use password encryption and not show the password in the build engine arguments. You can use the `passwordFile` that we created earlier, and supply it as an argument to the build engine. This `passwordFile` path could be an absolute path or relative to the `jbe` executable as shown in the following screenshot:

From the command line, go to the `jbe` executable directory in the build engine, and start the build engine with the appropriate arguments. Notice that we have used the `passwordFile` that has an encrypted password instead of plain text for security. The build engine is now started and ready to take build requests from clients.

Test the build

Testing the build involves submitting the build request either with the Web UI or the Eclipse client. From the Eclipse client, go to the Team Artifacts view and navigate to the **Builds** section. You will see the **BookManager Project build** definition. Right-click the build definition, select the **Request Build** option, and submit the build:

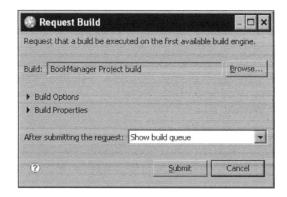

Select all the default settings and click **Submit**. This will trigger a build on the bookmanager build engine as shown in the following screenshot:

As the verbose mode is on, the build engine gives detailed information for us to understand the process. You can observe that as a pre-build step, the build engine checks if there is a need to synchronize the sources due to changes in source control. Then the Ant build system is invoked where the appropriate Ant target from the script is executed. Finally, the post-build steps, if any, are executed. Each build is identified with the complete date and time stamp. For example, 20100912-2107 is the build identifier.

Once the build engine's console shows a successful build, there are several options to see the build result details. Go to Eclipse's build definition in Team Artifacts and right-click to select **Show Build Results**. This will open the Build results view with all the successful, failed, and current builds corresponding to that build definition.

The Build results view shows a list of all the builds that happened on that build definition. The build typically has the label as the identifier, progress information (if it is Completed or In Progress), the total duration of the build, and the build's start time. You can filter the list based on the build definitions and submit a build request from the same view.

Build administration

As a project administrator or build administrator, it is important to know the build's performance and reasons for failed builds. From the Build Results view, one can double-click to open the Build Result editor as shown in the following screenshot:

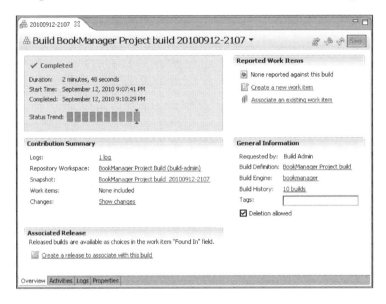

The Build Result editor has most of the information any administrator would need, such as:

- Repository workspace that this build is based on.

- Workspace repository snapshot taken during that specific build.

- Any work items and change sets associated with the build.

- To facilitate the QA process, any QA engineer or team leader can quickly create a work item against this build. This establishes a bi-directional relation on work items and builds.

- Generic information that identifies the Build Definition, Build Engine, and requested username.

- Any pre-build and post-build activity details, if defined.

- Detailed logs of the build script's execution.
- Build properties used for this instance.

As an administrator, you can leverage the power of Rational Team Concert by quickly creating the release from the build editor. You could choose if the release is global or only for your project's teams. In essence, you could build and pass on the build ID to the QA team. Once you get a go sign from QA, you can quickly create the release of the build and make it available for customer release.

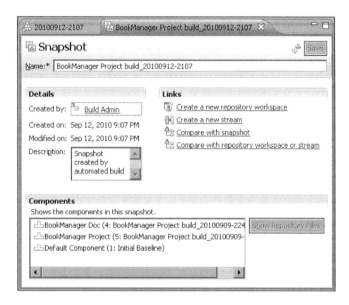

From the Build result editor page, you can navigate to the code snapshot created by the build as seen in previous screenshot. The code snapshot consists of the latest component code, and has basic information about the owner and creation date. On this snapshot, you can do a variety of operations. You can create a new workspace repository, or create a new stream for another user so he can start working on a fresh release right away.

Finally, as an administrator, you can also see a list of all the created snapshots by all the builds. From Team Artifacts, go to **My Repository Workspaces | BookManager Project Build (build-admin)**. Right-click and select **Show | Snapshots**. This would open the search view with all the snapshots as shown in the next screenshot:

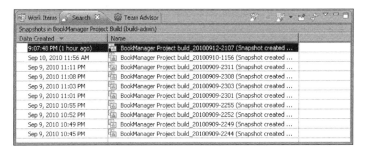

All the snapshots created by build manager are shown. Remember that these snapshots are local to the Workspace repository and are not visible to other users. With the snapshot search results, you can compare two snapshots and see any code changes.

Rational Team Concert made the build administration very easy by providing a complete integration of the Build Engine, Build Definition, Source Code, Work Items, and users. As a build administrator, the traditional problem of the build traceability is very well taken care of.

Working with the Web UI

Most of the capabilities available in the Eclipse client are also available on the Web UI. At times, it is easier to work on the web client with its lightweight interface. As seen in the following screenshot, log in to the Web UI and navigate to the BookManager Project project area and click on the **Builds** screen:

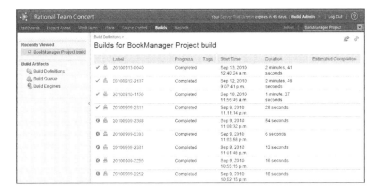

From the Web UI, you can explore several features of build definitions, build engines, and the build queue, such as the following:

- Submit a request for build
- Copy and share the build result URL with colleagues
- View build definitions and build engines for a project area
- View a list of all the completed builds
- View build results in detail

Another great place to explore the build results and statistics around them is the Project Dashboard. It allows several viewlets to be added and configured. As seen in the BookManager application example, the build statistics and health reports get better as the project has more builds and it accumulates more data.

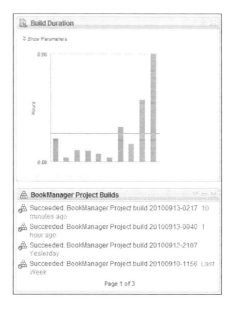

Typically, having the build health and build duration reports would help the entire team follow-up on any issues. In the **Build Duration** report, the horizontal line shows the average build time for all the builds considered in the report. The team needs to be watchful of the scenarios when there are long build durations and many failed builds. This may point to a compilation or unit testing problem in the code.

In general, the Web UI provides a great overview of all the build-related statistics and also lets you manage the build results. In the next section, we will see how to use the build result to release a project to the customer.

Releasing the project

The activities involved in a project depend on the software's complexity, the team's distribution, and the organization's processes. Smaller projects may simply involve building the software, updating the installation and user documentation, and then shipping it to the customer. Complex projects may involve iteratively building a multitude of components until approved by QA branching the code, creating the installation and user documentation, creating demo data for the users, tuning for performance based on deployment, and concluding with a discussion of lessons learned and best practices.

As we have already seen, Rational Team Concert allows us to create releases right from the build results. In our case, we are working on Sprint–2 and we can probably release the project once all the work items are closed on Sprint–1, Sprint–2, and Release Backlog. Notice that Sprint–1 and Sprint–2 are attached to the release plan Release–1. To do a quick reality check of the release situation, go to **Release Backlog** in the current plans from the Team Artifacts view.

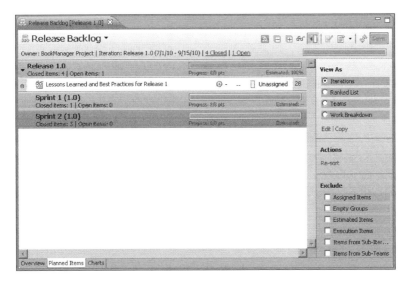

Test the application

Remember the Release Backlog editor is found by selecting the **Iterations** option from **View As** in the **Planned Items** tab. This gives a clear view of the major release and the sprints associated with it. You can see that *Sprint–1* and *Sprint–2* have no work items to be completed as shown by a green bar. However, the Release backlog has a single work item to be closed. Let's quickly test the application distribution. If we see the expected functionality, we will release *Sprint–2*. Quickly deploy and test the application.

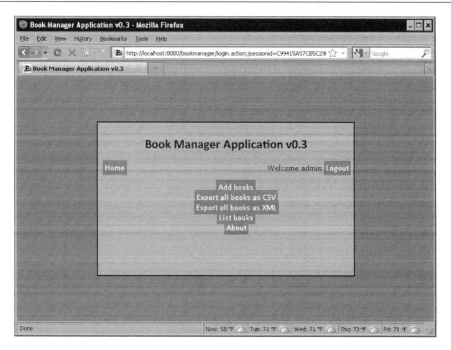

Deploy the application in Tomcat, and run the admin utility to create the users and load the demo data. Test for the expected functionality before passing QA and getting ready to release the latest successful build:

- Admin user is able to add, modify, and delete books
- Admin user is able to export books in CSV and XML format
- Admin user is able to list all available books
- Non-admin user is able to list the books and see the **About** dialog
- Admin and non-admin users are able to navigate via bread crumbs and log out of the session
- Once the user is logged verify that the session is expired and the user needs to log in again

Once the test cases are passed, the current iteration Sprint–2 is ready to be released.

Release the application

The previous release for Sprint–1 was a manual effort, where the build was done manually and the release defined in the project area. For Sprint–2, the build process is stabilized to the point where we can use the automatic build to create the results for the release.

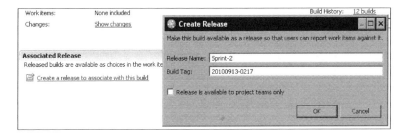

As seen in previous screenshot, go to the Build Results view and open the latest build that we tested against. From the Build Results editor, select the **Create a release to associate this build** option. This will open a dialog; enter **Release Name** and **Build tag** appropriately. Click **OK** to create the Release definition.

At times you will want to share the release only with the project teams and not with the users or customers. Rational Team Concert provides an option while creating Releases from Build Results to do so.

As a project administrator, you can leverage this feature to push releases only to project teams.

Creating the release definition on the build results leads to the creation of a release entry in the **Releases** tab section of the project area as shown in the following screenshot:

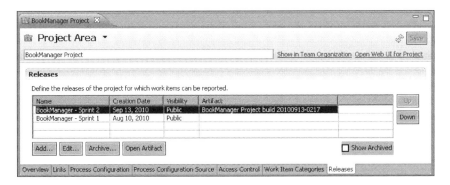

These release names are used to create bugs against a specific release. One can mark the field **Found In** when entering the bug against a specific release. As both sprints are released, we are now ready to make the main release of the product.

Traceability and retrospective

In the Release Backlog, there is a work item of type Retrospective, and this needs to be closed before the release can be made. It typically discusses the lessons learned and best practices with the team and documents the findings in the form of a retrospective. Remember that in the Scrum process, it is very important to understand what could be improved and what we did best in a sprint. Rational Team Concert makes this retrospective available for future reference.

The most interesting aspect of Releases and Build Results is that Rational Team Concert solves the classic traceability problem. As a project manager or administrator, you have the complete flexibility to trace the Releases, Build Results, Change Sets, and Work Items from top to bottom or from the bottom up. Traditionally, the traceability is not straightforward:

- Some teams use a spreadsheet to trace the Work Items and Releases
- In many cases the builds are not reproducible
- Very often teams reproduce builds by branching, which is not desirable and becomes an overhead in bigger teams
- Some source code control systems allow tagging or labeling but they can still be moved

Rational Team Concert allows project teams to have fine-grained traceability integrated into the clients. The following figure is an attempt to show the complete overview of the hierarchy and a connection between Releases, Build Results, Work Items, and Change Sets. Also, each build takes a snapshot that records the current baselines of each component in a repository workspace. It is a repository object that you use if you need to return your workspace to an earlier configuration.

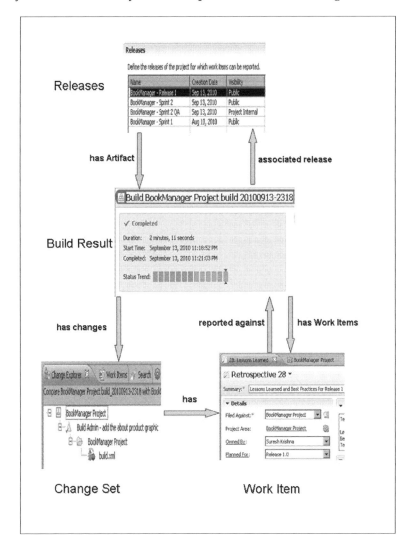

Rational Team Concert provides an easy and integrated way to approach the traceability problem as seen in the previous figure. When a problem is reported on a release, one can quickly go to the build, get the project snapshot, and find the root cause.

Web dashboard

We have seen how Sprints and Releases are made from the Eclipse client. A sense of the completeness can also be gotten from the web dashboards. As a team member, you can log in to the web client and explore several available portlets as shown in the following screenshot:

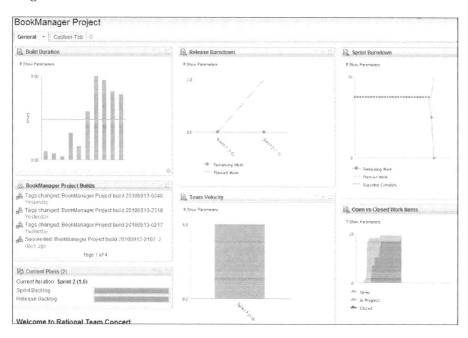

The project dashboard gives an overview of several components of a project's progress:

- The Build Duration portlet gives an overview of the build times over a specified period. If there is an unusual sudden spike in the build duration, you may need to check if the build is frozen or if the tests are slow.

- The Project Builds feed allows you to see how the builds are executing. You can navigate to the build results and explore the details.

- The Current Plans portlet lets you visualize the remaining work.

- The Release Burndown portlet visualizes the remaining story points at the beginning of each iteration in a release. Each dot represents the start of one iteration, and the height of the line represents the total of all story points in the open story work items.

- Sprint Burndown plots the remaining backlog of work in terms of the time estimated to complete it. Agile development methodologies such as Scrum use a burn down to plot the daily progress towards the end of a sprint.

- Finally, the Open vs Closed work item portlet plots all work items over time. The work item state is color coded. If an iteration is specified, only those work items planned for that iteration are shown.

You can add and configure your own portlets. Like the Eclipse client, the Web UI also gives an overview of the release and work item status.

Recommended practices

Build is one task that happens very often and care must be taken to makes sure the build system performs as expected. The following simple household rules will keep the build system and the build process healthy:

- **Use personal builds**: Before the code is checked in and delivered to the stream, it is recommended to run personal builds and test the code. This prevents the code becoming fragile.

- **Create build user**: For the QA builds or for the main releases, create a separate build user. This ensures that the code is synchronized from all the team members and built in a clean environment.

- **Create workspace repository**: A new workspace repository with the owner as the build user will help to maintain exclusivity. This is not a developer repository and will never have code changes or stale data.

- **Build on a separate machine**: Very often we see that the customer and developer environments are different, which can lead to many problems. Building and testing on a separate machine that simulates the customer environment helps reduce these problems.

- **Password encryption**: It is perhaps alright to specify the password in plain text format in development and QA environments. However, in production environments, plain text passwords should be avoided. For this reason, you can encrypt the password and store it in a protected file relative to the `jbe` execution directory.

Summary

Build is one task that is very common during software development. Integration of the build tools and interconnection between the build tools, source control, development environment, and tasks is essential in modern software development.

At the beginning of this chapter we saw the various components of build tools. A build engine is used to run the continuous builds and is supplied with Rational Team Concert. The build tools module consists of the Ant tasks necessary to interact with the Jazz source control and build the software.

We then worked with the Eclipse client to create the build definition and set up the build engine. Once the build engine is started, a build is submitted from the Eclipse client and the build results are explored. Build Results are then used to create a Release. We saw that complete traceability was given between Releases, Build Results, Change Sets, and Work Items.

Finally, we saw how to explore the build results from the web client and reiterated a few recommended practices. In the next chapter, we will see how to leverage the Jazz technology platform and build on top of it.

8

Extending RTC

Simplicity, carried to the extreme, becomes elegance.

-Jon Franklin

Rational Team Concert is a collaborative environment that integrates work items, source control, process, planning, and builds. It enables developers, architects, product owners, management, and other stakeholders to build highly customizable and configurable software. All this is made possible by building Rational Team Concert on top of the Jazz technology platform.

Jazz is an infrastructure platform built on the principles of openness and extensibility. The central idea of the Jazz infrastructure is to provide a set of common software development lifecycle services that any tool could implement or extend. The service implementation is based on the **Open Services for Lifecycle Collaboration** (OSLC), which is an industry initiative to enable interoperability of tools and resources across vendors. Organizations typically use tools from multiple vendors to capture and manage the data across various steps in the development lifecycle. The consumption of data is typically done by the tools that created it. The lack of common APIs across the lifecycle steps makes it difficult to manage the software delivery process. The Jazz platform solves this puzzle by providing domain-specific services with a language-neutral, RESTful interface so that arbitrary clients can access them.

In this chapter, we will see the Jazz extension architecture and explore various ways to extend Rational Team Concert. We will do the following:

- Get an overview of the Extension architecture
- Install the Rational Team Concert SDK and set up the target platform
- Create, test, and deploy client and server extensions

Extension architecture

The core idea of the Jazz Services Architecture is not to create tools that replace existing ones, but to provide hooks for existing tools in an organization. Regular customizations, such as work item types and processes, are covered in Team Concert. Developers who need to extend the current Team Concert functionality will probably be using the Java or RESTful APIs, as shown in the next figure:

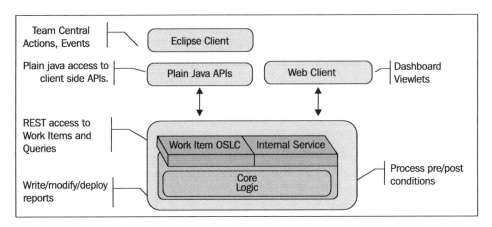

We broadly classify the Jazz extensions into client-and server-side APIs.

On the client side, you can use the Java APIs for Eclipse client, or use RESTful services for a web client. On the web client, you can contribute new viewlets to the dashboard. On the Eclipse side, you can add various actions and events into the Team Central view. You can develop server-side extensions with process preconditions. Rational Team Concert has many example reports that you may use to gain insight into your software development process. However, you are not limited to these reports.

SDK setup

When developing extensions for Rational Team Concert, you'll need to install a client and server locally, the ZIP files of the source, and the plain Java client libraries. Required files can be downloaded from the Jazz.net website. All target platform plugins are packaged in a single ZIP file that has all the client, server, tests, and source code.

Go to Jazz.net and find the appropriate Rational Team Concert downloads. Switch to the **All Downloads** page and download the Client for Eclipse IDE, Plain Java Client Libraries, and Rational Team Concert SDK. The SDK includes binaries and source for client, server, and JUnit tests as seen in the next screenshot. Unzip the SDK ZIP file into your Eclipse client location, for example: `C:/RTC/jazz/client/eclipse`. Unzip the plain Java client into the Jazz client, for example: `C:/RTC/jazz/client/plainjava`.

> For client and server extension development, we will make use of the Express-C installation. Once we develop, debug, and deploy on this test environment, we can take the respective extensions and deploy them onto a production server.

A common way to develop against the server in development mode is to run a *real* server installation such as the Express-C server with Tomcat, and connect to it remotely to debug. The advantage of using Tomcat is that it is a real deployment environment and is easy to debug a running live server using Java tools in Eclipse.

Target platform

Start the Eclipse client from Express-C all-in-one edition. Eclipse has a default target environment with Rational Team Concert, Eclipse RCP, and other plugins. However, we should develop these extensions using the Rational Team Concert SDK that we just downloaded. This ensures that Eclipse has all the required compile and runtime libraries at the time of development.

The **target platform** refers to the plugins, which your workspace will be built and run against. It describes the platform that you are developing for. Target platform refers to your currently active bundles and a *target definition* is a way of determining the plugins to add to the state. You can have multiple target definitions but only one definition can be selected as the target platform.

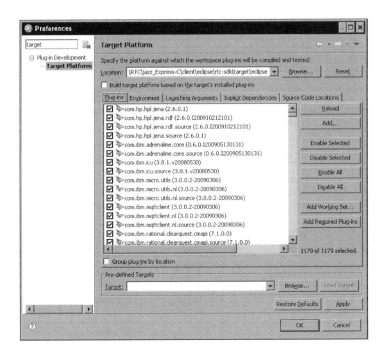

As seen in the previous screenshot, go to **Window | Preferences | Plug-in Development | Target Platform** to open the Target Platform configuration in Eclipse. From the **Location** field, browse and select the location where the `rtc-sdk` is unzipped. Eclipse will automatically parse all the available plugins into the target plugins section. Click **OK** to make sure that the target platform plugins have been changed. This will ensure that all RTC SDK plugins are available for development.

Simple tests

Once Eclipse is configured with the target environment, it's time to run the Java client examples as a first step. The `plainjava` library we downloaded has a few Java snippets that can be quickly tested by creating a Java project. In Eclipse, create a Java project from the existing source of the `plainjava` directory as seen in the next screenshot:

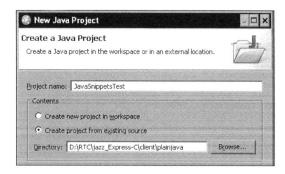

In the next step, add all the libraries within the project folder, which are required for the snippets to run successfully. Add the libraries and create the Java project as seen in the next screenshot:

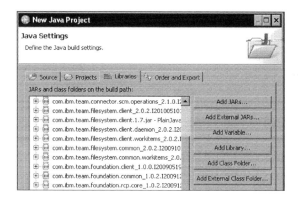

The Jazz platform is implemented as several plugins that run in an Eclipse OSGi runtime. However, a layer of client code has been designed to run as a standalone Java application. Non-Eclipse clients can make use of this mechanism to run as scripts or other tools. To run the snippets you'll also need a running Jazz server with administrative permissions. See Jazz.net for instructions on installing the simple all-in-one Jazz server. The PlainJava client library includes a set of snippets that show you how to perform the basics such as creating a work item, creating streams and delivering changes, and creating team and project areas. The following table shows the Java snippets from PlainJava download:

Java Class	Description
Snippet1	Connects to a Jazz repository and prints if the connection is successful.
Snippet2	Creates a stream, a repository workspace, and delivers changes to the stream from the repository workspace.
Snippet3	Creates a project area and team area.
Snippet4	Prints all the contents of a repository workspace or stream.
Snippet5	Creates a work item.

These snippets create exemplary workspaces, work items, team areas, and so forth. This is a quick way to test if the target environment is set up correctly and that the PlainJava APIs work. Select `Snippet2` from the package explorer, right-click, and select **Run as Java Application**. This program will take a few moments to complete the execution and show its progress in the console, as seen in next screenshot:

`Snippet2` does many things and uses a variety of Jazz APIs to deliver changes into the stream, as shown in the following code snippet:

```
// Creates a stream, a repository workspace, and deliver changes to
the stream from the repository workspace

public class Snippet2 {
  public static void main(String[] args) {
    // Start the team platform
    TeamPlatform.startup();
    try {
      IProgressMonitor monitor = new SysoutProgressMonitor();
      // Connect to the ream repository and if successfully login,
        then get the teamRepository.
      ITeamRepository repo = Snippet1.login(monitor);
      addFilesToStream(repo, monitor);
    } catch (TeamRepositoryException e) {
      System.out.println("Unable to login: "+e.getMessage());
    } finally {
      TeamPlatform.shutdown();
    }
  }
}
```

```
public static IWorkspaceConnection addFilesToStream(ITeamRepository
  repo, IProgressMonitor monitor) throws TeamRepositoryException,
  ItemNotFoundException, ComponentNotInWorkspaceException {

  // create a team area
  ITeamAreaHandle teamArea = Snippet3.createProject(repo,
    "Snippet 2");
  IWorkspaceManager wm = SCMPlatform.getWorkspaceManager(repo);

  // create the workspace
  IWorkspaceConnection workspace =
    wm.createWorkspace(repo.loggedInContributor(),
    "Example Workspace", "Description", monitor);
  //create the compoent
  IComponentHandle component = wm.createComponent("Component",
    repo.loggedInContributor(), monitor);
  // add component to workspace
  workspace.addComponent(component, false, monitor);

  // create the stream seeded from the workspace
  IWorkspaceConnection stream = wm.createStream(teamArea,
    "Example Stream", "Description", monitor);
  stream.addComponent(component, workspace, false, monitor);

  // The root folder is created when the component is created.
  // add a folder called 'project' to the workspace
  IChangeSetHandle cs1 = workspace.createChangeSet(component,
    monitor);
  IFolder rootFolder = (IFolder)
    workspace.configuration(component).rootFolderHandle(monitor);

  // create source folder ("/project")
  IFolder projectFolder= (IFolder)IFolder.ITEM_TYPE.createItem();
  projectFolder.setParent(rootFolder);
  projectFolder.setName("project");
  // commit the workspace with the project folder
  workspace.commit(cs1, Collections.singletonList(
    workspace.configurationOpFactory().save(projectFolder))
    , monitor);

  // add a file called 'file.txt' under the 'project' folder.
  IFileItem file = (IFileItem) IFileItem.ITEM_TYPE.createItem();
  file.setName("file.txt");
  file.setParent(projectFolder);
  IFileContentManager contentManager =
    FileSystemCore.getContentManager(repo);
```

```
        IFileContent storedContent = contentManager.storeContent(
                IFileContent.ENCODING_US_ASCII,
                FileLineDelimiter.LINE_DELIMITER_PLATFORM,
                new
                VersionedContentManagerByteArrayInputStreamPovider(
                "The contents of my file.txt".getBytes()),
                null, monitor);
        file.setContentType(IFileItem.CONTENT_TYPE_TEXT);
        file.setContent(storedContent);
        file.setFileTimestamp(new Date());
        // commit the workspace with file contents
        workspace.commit(cs1, Collections.singletonList(
          workspace.configurationOpFactory().save(file)), monitor);

        // deliver the changes to the stream
        IChangeHistorySyncReport sync =
                workspace.compareTo(stream,
                WorkspaceComparisonFlags.CHANGE_SET_COMPARISON_ONLY,
                Collections.EMPTY_LIST, monitor);
        workspace.deliver(stream, sync, Collections.EMPTY_LIST,
          sync.outgoingChangeSets(component), monitor);
        monitor.subTask("Created changes and delivered to " +
          stream.getName());
        return workspace;
    }
}
```

The following functionality is provided by Snippet2, using Snippet1 to log in and Snippet3 to create a project area:

- Get the Team Repository Service and log in with admin credentials
- Create the project area and team area
- Create the example workspace called Example Workspace
- Create a new stream called Example Stream
- Add a component called Component to the stream
- Create a change set with the workspace and component
- Create a folder named project and commit the workspace with the project.
- Create a file named file.txt and commit the workspace with that file
- Commit and deliver the workspace

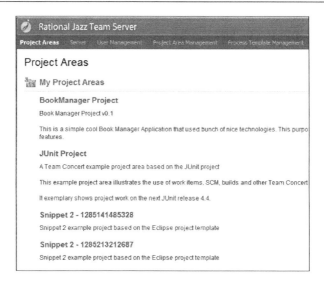

As a quick test, we can log into the Rational Team Concert web client and see that an example project is already created, as shown in the previous screenshot. Go to the Project Area Management of this project and navigate to the Source Control. As you can see in the next screenshot, the example stream, component, and file are created. This completes the simple test to see if the SDK setup and the PlainJava APIs work.

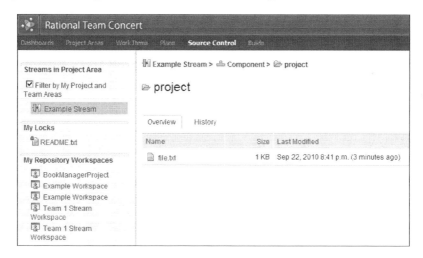

RESTful API

This section assumes that you are familiar with RESTful architecture and how to use it. RESTful APIs allows you to get, create, modify, and query work items and other resources using standard HTTP methods, allowing integration with minimal requirements for the clients. The API adheres to the OSLC CM specification. It shouldn't take much more than an HTTP client and an XML or JSON parser to use the APIs. These APIs provide you convenient dialogs where needed and you can do a variety of things, such as the following:

- Load work items in different formats such as JSON, XML, ATOM, and HTML, and in different levels of granularity
- Create work items by obtaining an HTML creation dialog module
- Create work items by posting their JSON or XML representation to a factory URL
- Query work items (full text and structured queries)
- Query work items by obtaining an HTML picker module

The OSLC specification describes a discovery chain where clients need to know just a single entry point to find all other necessary URLs. You, as a client, can use the discovery chain offered by Jazz Server and do not have to remember any hardcoded URLs. In essence, any client who follows the OSLC standards will be able to operate on the services without knowing exact details.

The root document is exposed at `https://<server>:<port>/jazz/rootservices`. Fetch this document and extract the Change Management Catalog URL (pointed to by `rdf:resource`) of the element, as seen in the following snippet:

```
<oslc_cm:cmServiceProviders
  rdf:resource="
  https://localhost:9443/jazz/oslc/workitems/catalog"/>
```

The document behind this URL contains a list of `ServiceProvider` elements that point to the documents that contain the actual service descriptions. In the case of RTC, there is one `ServiceProvider` element for each project area. Typically, an application would use the title of this element to allow the user to choose between the project areas. In the next snippet, you can see the URLs that will give you details of the BookManager Project and its various services:

```
<oslc_disc:ServiceProvider>

  <dc:title>BookManager Project</dc:title>
```

```
<oslc_disc:details
  rdf:resource="https://localhost:9443/jazz/process/project-
  areas/_bXsA0GXDEd-yVOv1HQe_JA"/>

<oslc_disc:services
  rdf:resource="https://localhost:9443/jazz/oslc/contexts/
  _bXsA0GXDEd-yVOv1HQe_JA/workitems/services.xml"/>

<jp:consumerRegistry
  rdf:resource="https://localhost:9443/jazz/process/project-
  areas/_bXsA0GXDEd-yVOv1HQe_JA/links"/>

</oslc_disc:ServiceProvider>
```

Fetch the services document pointed by `oslc_disc:services`. This document contains links to the dialog modules, to the factory URL to create new work items, and to the work item collection URL that allows the querying work items. This document has many important URLs from an application point of view. Your custom applications can leverage the **New Defect** creation dialog or the **Defect Selection** dialog embedded in the custom applications as seen in next code snippet. These dialogs provide a convenient way to present the data and enter search information when necessary.

```
<oslc_cm:creationDialog oslc_cm:default="true" calm:id="defect"
  oslc_cm:hintWidth="740px" oslc_cm:hintHeight="510px">

  <dc:title>New Defect</dc:title>

  <oslc_cm:url>https://localhost:9443/jazz/_ajax-
    modules/com.ibm.team.workitem.WICreationDialog?projectAreaName=
    BookManager%20Project&dc%3Atype=defect</oslc_cm:url>

</oslc_cm:creationDialog>

<oslc_cm:selectionDialog calm:id="defect" oslc_cm:hintWidth="550px"
  oslc_cm:hintHeight="360px">

  <dc:title>Defect Selection</dc:title>

  <oslc_cm:url>https://localhost:9443/jazz/_ajax-
    modules/com.ibm.team.workitem.WIPicker?projectAreaName=
    BookManager%20Project&dc%3Atype=defect</oslc_cm:url>

</oslc_cm:selectionDialog>
```

RESTful APIs provide a minimal interface to do the job. As an example, the **Defect Selection** dialog can be used to pick a specific defect based on search criteria, as shown in the next screenshot:

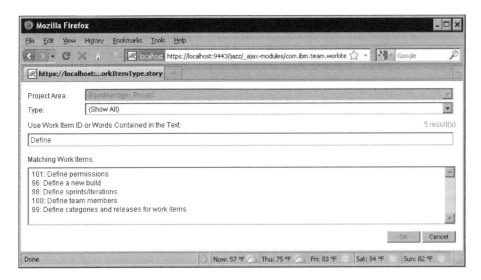

In a similar way, custom applications can use the **New Defect** dialog as shown in next screenshot:

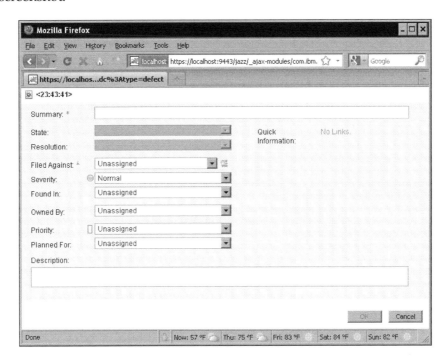

Applications can also make use of the different file formats the server can return in its response. For example, XML and JSON using either of `https://localhost:9443/jazz/oslc/workitems/96.xml` or `https://localhost:9443/jazz/oslc/workitems/96.json` style URLs.

In summary, RESTful APIs combined with the OSLC standards become a powerful tool in the hands of developers. Applications that are built on the Jazz platform can take advantage of the root document URL to infer the service endpoints. It is common to imagine a scenario of embedding the service URLs like New Defect or Defect Selection in custom or existing applications for a seamless integration.

Client extensions

Client extensions can be written either on the Eclipse client or web client. On the Eclipse client, you can extend several aspects of Team Central, Actions, Events, and others to make it more relevant to the organization and team. You can extend the web client to have specific custom-built viewlets on the Dashboard. In both cases, you would need to set up the Eclipse client and make use of the Rational Team Concert's SDK libraries.

Extension development

We will now develop, debug, and deploy a simple Extension to Rational Team Concert's Eclipse client. Specifically, we will contribute a whole new section to the Rational Team Concert's Team Central view.

Start the Eclipse client that's configured with the SDK target environment plugins. Create a plugin project with a meaningful name and open the `plugin.xml` editor. Add `org.eclipse.ui`, `org.eclipse.core.runtime` and `com.ibm.team.jface` to the plugin dependencies in the **Dependencies** tab. Go to the **Extensions** tab in the editor and add `com.ibm.team.jface.expandableSection` as an extension point. Fill the following properties with appropriate details and then save the extension point:

- **id**: Enter a unique extension ID to be recognized by the Eclipse runtime.
- **name**: Human-readable Extension name. This is the same name that the new section will have.
- **class**: Contributing class either implementing the `ISection` interface or extending the `Section` abstract class.
- **icon**: Icon that is shown next to the Name in the UI.
- **isOpenable**: When set to `true`, will show a small button that will open the section content in a view or editor.

- **isTemplate**: When set to `true`, will allow creation of a new instance of the section from the New-Menu in Team Central.

- **isCloneable**: When set to `true`, will allow duplicating the section to have more than one instance.

- **isDeletable**: When set to `true`, will allow deleting the section from Team Central.

- **hideChevron** and **requiredInstance**: Both attributes are deprecated.

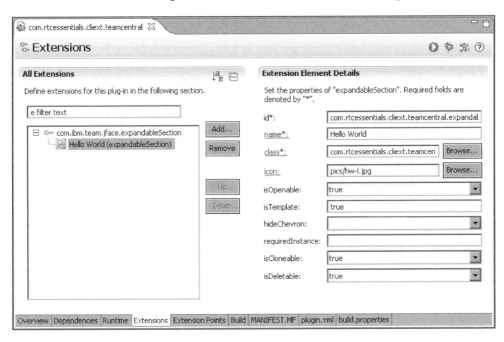

If you associate an icon to the new section, make sure that this icon is added to the build configuration. This will ensure that the icon is also copied at the time of building the deployable plugins. Now, create a contributing class to the new `expandableSection` called `HelloWorldSection`. As much of the default functionality is embedded in the `Section` class, our new `HelloWorldSection` class will extend the `Section` class. We will implement the `ISection.createContent` and `ISection.setFocus` methods of the `Section` class. Functionally, this new section is simple and demonstrates the extension capabilities of Eclipse. The following code snippet shows the `HelloWorldSection` implementation:

```
// com.ibm.team.jface.expandableSection extension uses the
// Section delegate to contribute to the Team Central.

// Section is the Abstract default implementation of the
```

```
// Isection. The section is capable of expanding or collapsing
// a single client that is its direct child.

public class HelloWorldSection extends Section {

  private Link hwLink;

  public void createContent(final Composite parent) {
    GridLayout grid= new GridLayout(1, false);
    grid.marginHeight= 1;
    parent.setLayout(grid);

    // Show ClickMe Link
    hwLink= new Link(parent, SWT.NONE);
    hwLink.setText("RTC Client Extention. <a>Click Me!</a>");
    hwLink.setLayoutData(new GridData(SWT.BEGINNING, SWT.BEGINNING,
      false, false));
    hwLink.setBackground(parent.getBackground());
    hwLink.addSelectionListener(new SelectionAdapter() {
    public void widgetSelected(SelectionEvent e) {
      MessageDialog.openInformation(parent.getShell(),
        "RTC Client Extension Demo", "This is a quick demo of the
        extending the \nRational Team Concert's Eclipse client.");
      }
    });

    // Label Separator
    Label separator = new Label(parent, SWT.HORIZONTAL |
      SWT.SEPARATOR);
    separator.setLayoutData(new GridData(GridData.FILL_HORIZONTAL));

    // Show Info Image Label
    Label infoImgLabel= new Label(parent, SWT.NONE);
    infoImgLabel.setBackground(parent.getBackground());
    infoImgLabel.setLayoutData(new GridData(SWT.CENTER, SWT.CENTER,
      false, false));
    infoImgLabel.setImage(parent.getDisplay().getSystemImage(
      SWT.ICON_INFORMATION));

    // Label Separator
    separator = new Label(parent, SWT.HORIZONTAL | SWT.SEPARATOR);
    separator.setLayoutData(new GridData(GridData.FILL_HORIZONTAL));

    // Show Message
```

```
StyledText warningMsg= new StyledText(parent, SWT.MULTI |
   SWT.READ_ONLY);
warningMsg.setBackground(parent.getBackground());
warningMsg.setLayoutData(new GridData(SWT.FILL, SWT.FILL, true,
   false, 1, 2));
warningMsg.setText("Extending RTC Client is really easy.\n
   "Make use of the various extensions and\n drop the plugins
   into the Eclipse client.");
}


@Override
public void setFocus() {
   hwLink.setFocus();
}


}
```

The HelloWorldSection has a simple interface with a **Click Me** link, an **Information Icon**, and a **Short Description** with a Link widget. Now that the extension is created and the contributing class is ready, we can start testing the plugin by running it as an Eclipse application on the target platform.

Eclipse **Plug-in Development Environment** (PDE) provides an application launcher that allows you to run and debug your plugin by launching a separate Eclipse application. As with all other launchers in Eclipse (like Java Application), the Eclipse application launcher can be invoked via a shortcut and its launch configurations are centrally managed in the **Launch Configuration** dialog.

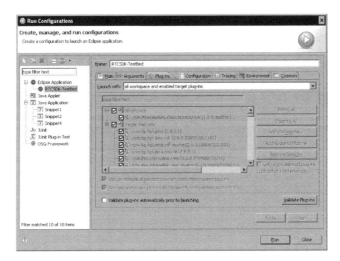

As seen in the previous screenshot, the launch configuration window makes sure that our newly created plugin is included and runs it. This will open another Eclipse Application with our `HelloWorldSection` in Team Central. If not already opened, go to **Window | Show View | Other**. From the **Show View** dialog, select **Collaboration | Team Central**. Once Team Central is opened, you can configure and add sections to the view by clicking the *Menu* icon at the top and selecting **New Section**, as seen in the next screenshot:

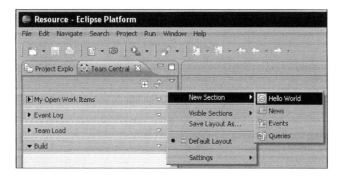

Select the **Hello World** section from the **New Section** menu, which will add the section to the Team Central View. Remember that at the time of the extension definition, we enabled the attribute **isOpenable**, which enables and shows a small arrow button towards the right-side of Hello World entry, as seen in the next screenshot. This functionality is helpful when we want to elaborate or expand the information in the section.

Extension deployment

The Hello World section stacks to the bottom of the Team Central view and is in the expanded state once it is opened. From the `HelloWorldSection` class, the Link Label, Information Icon, and Long Description are shown in the section. Clicking on the **Click Me** link should open an information dialog. Once we are satisfied with the plugin, we can export the plugin as **Deployable plug-ins and fragments** to a temporary location, as seen in the next screenshot. Once the plugin JAR file is created, copy the JAR file into the client's Eclipse `dropins` directory. This will make sure that Eclipse will pick up the plugin at the next start up.

Extension deployment

In production environments, it is recommended to create an Eclipse Update site that has the new plugins and features. This helps Eclipse keep track of updates, and users can avoid having to work with individual JAR files.

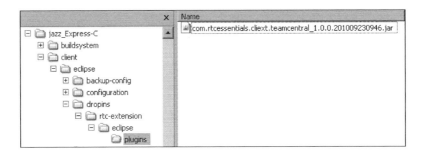

After the plugins are in the `dropins` directory, start the Eclipse client and open the Team Central view. Open the Hello World section and test for the expected functionality, as shown in the next screenshot:

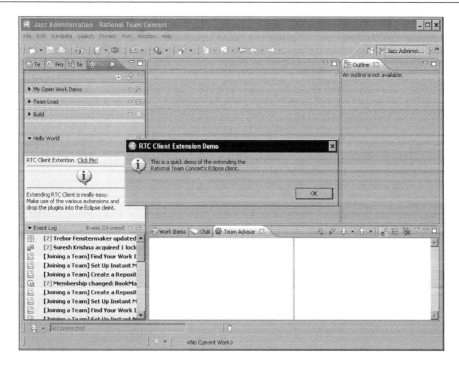

Developing extensions for the Eclipse client is indeed an easy task with the Rational Team Concert's SDK. In summary, here is what we did to develop, debug, and deploy the plugin that extends Rational Team Concert's functionality:

1. Set up the Eclipse client's *target platform* with SDK plugins.

2. Open the Eclipse client and create a new plugin.

3. Use the extension point `com.ibm.team.jface.expandableSection` to contribute to the Team Central Section.

4. Create a new class `HelloWorldSection` that extends the `Section` abstract class.

5. Test the functionality using the *Eclipse PDE launch*.

6. Deploy the new plugin as *deployable plugins and features*.

7. Copy the new plugin JAR file into the `dropins` directory of the Eclipse client.

8. Start the Eclipse client and open Team Central to test the new section.

Server extensions

Rational Team Concert provides several APIs to build server-side extensions. Client extensions are written for a specific individual client such as Eclipse, Visual Studio, or a web UI. Server-side extensions are triggered independent of the client that is used to perform an action. Depending on the situation, you may find that client extensions may not be appropriate and you instead need a powerful server-side mechanism. You can implement several extensions like dynamic action providers, event handlers, operation advisors, operation participants, process validators, and several others.

Server extension is a vast topic with many possibilities. In this book, we will focus on creating an example operation advisor that will give us an idea on how to build server extensions. For example, you, as a product owner, can see that some of the Blocker Work Items are created without any description or due dates, causing you to spend considerable time gathering this information. Given such a scenario, we will build an operation advisor extension that would enforce our preconditions on a Work Item. Thus, every time a project member creates a Work Item of type Defect with Blocker severity, the extension will make sure that Due Date and Description are entered. It is such a combination of these two conditions (mandatory Due Date and Description) that requires us to build a operation advisor on the server side.

Server-side extensions need a real server installation for us to develop, debug, and test against. Once the extension is tested on the test server, it is just a matter of copying the update site and configuring the project on the production server. We will use the Rational Team Concert Express-C installation for development. The Express-C version download and setup is described in detail in *Appendix A, Quick Reference*. The extension needs a debugging environment to be set up even before we start development. Following is an overview of the steps for developing and deploying the extension:

1. Download, install, and configure the Express-C Server on Tomcat.
2. Configure Tomcat for debugging and OSGi console.
3. Start the Eclipse client and create a extension plugin, feature, and update site.
4. Deploy the extension to the Tomcat test server and test the functionality.
5. From Eclipse, test the functionality and debug via Tomcat server.
6. Deploy the extension to a production environment.

Extension development

Even before we start the development in Eclipse, we must configure the debug server on Tomcat. Go to the WEB-INF folder of the deployed Jazz server on Tomcat and open the web.xml file (for example, <express-c_path>\server\tomcat\webapps\ jazz\WEB-INF\web.xml). Uncomment the following XML snippet to enable the OSGi console. This will allow you to test if your plugin is installed and configured correctly on the server.

```
<init-param>
  <param-name>commandline</param-name>
  <param-value>-console</param-value>
</init-param>
```

Once the OSGi console is enabled, go to the server.startup.bat script in the Express-C server directory. Open the file and change JAVA_OPTS to the following:

```
set JAVA_OPTS=-Djava.awt.headless=true -Xdebug
-Xrunjdwp:transport=dt_socket,server=y,suspend=n,address=1044
-DSQLSERVER_JDBC="%SQLSERVER_JDBC%"
```

This will enable you to connect to the Tomcat server and debug the breakpoints in the code.

From the Eclipse client, create a plugin. This plugin does not need an activator and does not contribute to the UI. Add the com.ibm.team.process.service. operationAdvisors extension point and fill in the required attributes as shown in the following screenshot. The important aspect is that we make this advisor respond to the WorkItem Save action and the **id** (com.ibm.team.workitem.operation. workItemSave) must be reflected in the **operationId** attribute.

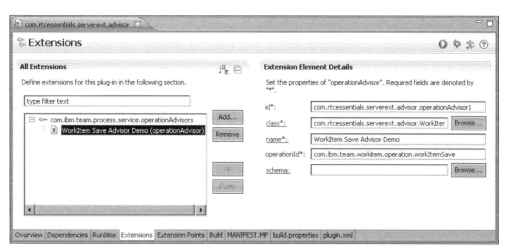

Create the class `WorkItemSaveAdvisor` that implements `IOperationAdvisor`. Essentially, this class provides the piece of functionality that gets executed when a Defect type Work Item is saved. The following code describes the functionality of the advisor:

```
public class WorkItemSaveAdvisor implements IOperationAdvisor {
  public void run(AdvisableOperation operation,
    IProcessConfigurationElement advisorConfiguration,
    IAdvisorInfoCollector collector, IProgressMonitor monitor)
    throws TeamRepositoryException {
// Returns the operation-specific data associated with the
  operation
Object data= operation.getOperationData();
if (data instanceof ISaveParameter) {
  ISaveParameter saveParameter= (ISaveParameter) data;
  // get the new auditable state
  IAuditable auditable= saveParameter.getNewState();
  // we are interested in the auditable item only if it's a
    WorkItem
  if (auditable instanceof IWorkItem) {
  // get the common auditable object from the team repository
    IAuditableCommon auditableCommon=
    saveParameter.getSaveOperationParameter().getAuditableCommon();
    // get the specific workitem, workitemtype and severity
    IWorkItemCommon workItemCommon=
        auditableCommon.getPeer(IWorkItemCommon.class);
    IWorkItem workItem= (IWorkItem) auditable;
    IWorkItemType workItemType=
        workItemCommon.findWorkItemType(workItem.getProjectArea(),
        workItem.getWorkItemType(), monitor);
    Identifier<ISeverity> severity = workItem.getSeverity();
    // if workitem is a defect, make sure that Due Date and
      Description fields are filled in.
    if (workItemType.getIdentifier().equals("defect")) {
      if
        (severity.getStringIdentifier().equals(
        "severity.literal.16"))    {
        Timestamp dueDate = workItem.getDueDate();
        if (dueDate == null) {
        IAdvisorInfo info = collector.createProblemInfo("
        Blocking Work Item", "Blocking workitem must have a Due
        Date", "error");
        collector.addInfo(info);
        }
        String plainDesc =
            workItem.getHTMLDescription().getPlainText();
        if (plainDesc == null || plainDesc.equals("")) {
        IAdvisorInfo info =
          collector.createProblemInfo("Blocking Work Item",
          "Blocking workitem must have a Description", "error");
```

```
            collector.addInfo(info);
          }
        }
      }
    }
  }
}
```

`AdvisableOperation` provides a lot of information about the current operation. Check that this operation is a `SaveParameter` and get the Auditable items state. If this Auditable item is an instance of the `WorkItem`, then get the common API (`IWorkItemCommon`). This `WorkItem` API will give the necessary information to retrieve all the fields from the user interface. Determine the type of the Work Item and then, depending on the severity type, check for the Due Date and Description. This code provides an introduction to the set of common APIs that we would use for other uses.

Update site and deployment

Create an `EclipseFeature` from the Eclipse client and add the Action Advisor plugin as an included plugin. The extension deployment on the server is made via an update site. Create the Eclipse update site and add the advisor feature to the included features. When creating the update site, uncheck the **Use default location** option and enter a directory directly on the top level of the Express-C server directory. This is the test deploy directory that our plugin deploy script will update, and the Jazz application will use the same folder for reading the extension, as shown in the following screenshot:

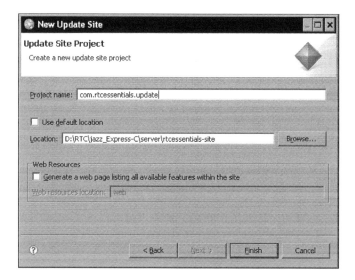

Once the update site is created, add the new feature (`com.rtcessentials.feature`) in the site editor. You can build the plugin and feature to make an update site by using the *Build* action. Alternatively, you can right-click on the `site.xml` file from the **Project Explorer** and select **PDE Tools | Build Site**.

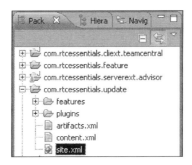

The update site contains all the necessary JAR files for the Jazz server, as seen in the previous screenshot. We now need to create a configuration file that will tell the Jazz server to pick the newly created extension. Go to `<express-c_path>\server\conf\jazz\provision_profiles` and create a configuration file `rtcessentials-profile.ini` that has the following details:

```
url=file:../rtcessentials-site
featureid=com.rtcessentials.feature
```

This file contains the path of the extension relative to the top-level server directory and `featureid` of the extension. A final configuration step is to add the Save Advisor to the project process configuration. This step lets the project know about the new advisor and adds it to the preconditions section of the `workitemSave` operation. Once you add the XML snippet as shown in the following screenshot, save the Project configuration:

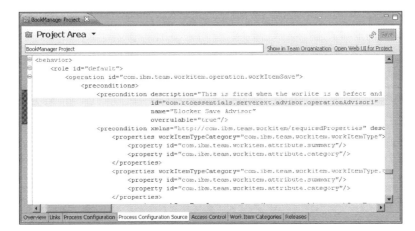

Testing the extension

Once the extension deployment is done on the Tomcat server, stop it, delete the temporary work directory from `<expressC-path>\server\tomcat\work`, and restart. This will ensure there is no cache of the old JAR files. Tomcat will start in the OSGI debug mode where you can query for the service status. Remember that all Jazz plugins are OSGI services, and are activated depending on need. To test if the new advisor extension is activated, type `ss rtcessentials` on the server console.

This tells us that the extension is recognized by the Jazz Server and the extension service is activated. To debug the code from the Eclipse client, create a new debug launch configuration. Enter the port number that we specified in the Tomcat start script, and connect to the server as shown in the next screenshot. Depending on where we want to inspect, we can create break points and step through.

Remember that the Eclipse client is set up with the complete Rational Team Concert's SDK. Hence, we have all the sources available at debug time.

Now open the web client and log in to the BookManager Project. Go to the Work Items section and create a new Defect type Work Item. Enter the **Summary, Filed Against,** and **Severity,** and create the work item by saving it as shown in the next screenshot:

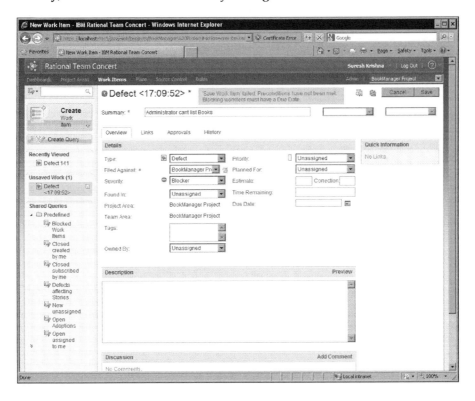

The Jazz server enforces the first rule in our `WorkItemSaveAdvisor` that the **Due Date** must be filled in. As shown in the next screenshot, once you fill in the **Due Date** and save, the server checks for the **Description** as well. Thus, the `WorkItemSaveAdvisor` takes care of the default pre-conditions and also the ones we added.

As is typical of web applications, the conditions are enforced one at a time with the error messages displayed sequentially. On Eclipse, the true power of the Work Advisor becomes evident. Open the Eclipse client and try to create the Work Item on the BookManager Project. Once you enter the **Summary** of a Blocking item and save, the server checks for pre-conditions and throws errors. The Eclipse client shows the total number of errors and an in-depth description of each of those items in Team Advisor.

Once the functionality is thoroughly tested, server extensions can be deployed on the production environment using the following simple steps. Server administrators can plan these activities by communicating downtime to the team.

- Copy the update site of the server extension into the Jazz server directory (for example, `D:\RTC\jazz\server4WSA`). This is the same directory that is used to deploy Jazz on the WebSphere application server.

- Go to the provision profiles directory (for example, `D:\RTC\jazz\server\ conf\jazz\provision_profiles`) and create a configuration file that has the server extension feature name and location of the update site.

Project teams can use the Jazz platform and Rational Team Concert out of the box as it is. Or they can extend and customize the team process, work items, team member role management, and much more.

Summary

In this chapter, you have seen how to develop extensions on the Rational Team Concert's client and server. Even though we have not discussed the whole gamut of extensions, you should have an idea of the possibilities.

We have used the Express-C edition of Rational Team Concert as the development and testing platform. We have set up the Eclipse client's target platform in Express-C with the SDK libraries, which enables us to develop against the client and server code. We have briefly explored the various options and usages of the RESTful APIs.

On the Eclipse client, we developed a Team Central extension that has a `HelloWorld` section. This section can be added from the view's menu and a minimal UI is constructed to demonstrate the extension functionality.

For the server extension, we have set up our Tomcat in debug mode and created a plugin with the required extension. Once the extension point is added, we coded the functionality for the `WorkItemSaveAdvisor` and deployed it onto the server via an update site. We tested the functionality on the web UI and Eclipse UI where the Save Advisors guided through the errors.

The Express-C testing environment is used to develop, debug, and deploy the client and server extensions. The extension JAR files can then be deployed on the production environment with confidence.

As an advanced user, you can make use of the powerful Jazz extension architecture to fulfill your team's needs. Depending on the usage characteristics, you can decide to extend the Eclipse or web client, as well as provide server-side extensions.

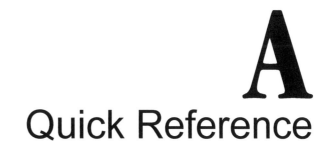

Quick Reference

This appendix explains many frequently used terms for a quick reference.

Book Manager Application

A real-world Book Manager Application walks you through all the core features of the Rational Team Concert during different phases of development and release. This application uses a variety of technologies such as Apache Struts, Hibernate Persistence, EJB, and Derby database. The application will be imported and further developed and enhanced using the various Rational Team Concert Server and Client capabilities.

Change sets

A Change set is a collection of changed resources in a single component, which can be either checked-in and delivered, or suspended till a later time. Change sets flow between a repository workspace and its flow targets. Workspaces usually have at least one flow target and many have more than one.

Component

A Component is a collection of artifacts (analogous to a module in conventional software development). You can make any component in the repository a part of a stream. Typically, the components in a stream are related functionally so that they are grouped together. After you have created a stream, you can use the Stream editor to manage components.

Dashboards

Dashboards are light-weight Web UI components intended to provide an overview about the project status. It provides an easy drill-down mechanism to get more complete information. A group of portlets or viewlets constitute a dashboard. Each portlet or viewlet is a UI element that displays a report of a piece of information from the Ration Team Server data in real-time. Dashboards make it possible for every team member to see the same information all the time. Each time you access the dashboard, the reports are computed in real time.

Eclipse

Eclipse is a software development environment comprising an **Integrated Development Environment (IDE)** and an extensible plugin system. Initially it was perceived as a Java IDE, a **Rich Client Platform (RCP)**, and a Tool Integration Platform. However, with time, Eclipse transformed into an eco-system of platform, application frameworks, tools, and runtimes. Eclipse is a universal tool platform—an open, extensible IDE for anything and everything, but nothing in particular.

Flow target

Flow target is the target area where the delivered changes flow into. The flow target for repository workspaces can be a stream or another workspace. Flow target can be modified from the Repository Workspace editor.

Iteration plan

Rational Team Concert projects are organized into a series of fixed-length development periods called iterations. Each timeline has its own set of iterations. An iteration plan displays the goals to be achieved in an iteration. You can create an iteration plan and assign work items that are to be completed in an iteration.

Jazz-based products

Jazz stands as an open, extensible platform where several tools are developed on it. Tools such as Rational Team Concert, Rational Quality Manager, and Rational Requirements Composer are some examples of the tools built on the Jazz platform.

Jazz platform

Jazz is a technology platform for collaborative software delivery. Uniquely attuned to global and distributed teams, Jazz is designed to transform how people work together to build software, making software delivery more collaborative, productive, and transparent. You can think of Jazz as an extensible framework that dynamically integrates and synchronizes people, processes, and assets associated with software development projects. Jazz is not a product. Product offerings that are built on the Jazz platform can leverage a rich set of capabilities for team-based software development and delivery.

Jazz Sandbox

Rational Team Concert lets you play and explore the complete product from Sandbox. You can access the Sandbox at `https://jazz.net/sandbox` and log in with the Jazz.net credentials. Sandbox is accessed via any standard web browser and you can create your own project and work on it right away. Once you have the Jazz. net user credentials, it just takes a few minutes to set up a project. Sandbox provides two example read-only projects, JUnit and Call Center, which you can explore and play with.

Jazz Team Server

This provides the foundation services or APIs that provide the access to the Team, Dashboards, Security, Event Notification, Search, and Collaboration aspects. The JTS is built on the **Open Lifecycle Service Collaboration** (OSLC) platform so that any tool that conforms to the OSLC can be easily plugged in.

My Work view

Use this view to triage new work items assigned to you, manage work items in progress, and manage work items that you plan to resolve in a future iteration. The **My Work** view from the Eclipse client is used to organize and manage the team member's work items. The My Work view is the central place for you as a team member to start work. My Work view has three sections that have information such as Inbox, Future Work Items, and Current Work.

Open Lifecycle Service Collaboration

Open Services for Lifecycle Collaboration (OSLC) is a community effort to help product and software delivery teams by making it easier to use lifecycle tools in combination. The OSLC community is creating open, public descriptions of resources and interfaces for sharing the things that teams rely on, such as change requests, test cases, defects, requirements, and user stories.

Project area

The project area is the system's representation of a project. The project area defines the project deliverables, team structure, process, and schedule. A project area is stored as a top-level or root item in a repository. A project area references project artifacts and stores the relationships between these artifacts. Access to a project area and its artifacts is controlled by permissions.

Project Area Management

Project Area Management lets you create and manage the project areas. You can't delete a project area after you create it but you can archive it. Project Area Management lets you define the project area, team members, process, permission, access control, and roles.

Process templates

A process template provides a new project area with an initial process configuration and iteration structure. You can create a process template with no initial content, except the process configuration structure and placeholder iterations. You can also create a process template from an existing project area. The latter option enables your team to create projects based on a successful process that is implemented in an existing project.

Process

Process is the collection of roles, practices, rules, and guidelines used to organize and control the flow of work. The project process is defined in a project area and can be further customized in a team area. In Rational Team Concert, you use process to define user roles and their permissions for performing operations within the tool, such as changing the state of a work item.

Project Release plan

A Project Release plan is the highest-level plan in Rational Team Concert that provides a brief overview of the project goals. A Project Release plan displays top-level work items, such as Stories and Epics associated to a project area or team area, child team areas, current iteration, and its child iterations.

Queries

Rational Team Concert provides queries that allow you to discover and populate the work items depending on different criteria. Queries are a powerful feature for the management, stakeholders, and team members so that they can extract the information as and when needed. Queries play an important role to minimize the time to analyze and generate reports.

Rational Team Concert

IBM Rational Team Concert is a complete, collaborative development environment providing agile and traditional planning, project health, integrated reporting, customizable process support, work item management, change management, source code management, and build management.

Rational Team Concert is built on the Jazz platform.

Reporting

Scrum Master, Product Owner, Team Member, and other stakeholders need to have a real-time view of the project progress including any impediments. Rational Team Concert provides a real-time view of the project progress via dashboards, queries, and reports.

Repository Workspace

A **Repository Workspace** is a mirror of the repository artifacts available on the local machine from server repository. You can create a repository workspace and add/create new components that contain project artefacts. You can **deliver** the project artifacts to make sure that the client's local workspace and repository workspace are in sync.

Scrum development

Agile methodologies emphasis on the principles and benefits of the iterative and incremental software. Scrum is a concrete discipline of an Agile process management method and a process skeleton that contains a set of practices and predefined roles.

Stream

A Stream is a repository object that includes one or more components. Streams are typically used to integrate the work done in workspaces. As a team member, you deliver changes to the stream and accept other team members' changes from the stream into your Repository Workspace.

Tag Cloud view

Use this view to create a tag cloud. For a given query, a tag cloud displays the number of work items by tag attribute. Each time a work item is entered, you can add the tags to the work item. These tags help you organize and find the frequently used tags in a project. The Tag Cloud view will give us an overview of the frequently used tags and variations in the tags.

Team Advisor

Every operation in Rational Team Concert enforces a set of pre-conditions and post-conditions. When an operation needs to be executed and pre-conditions are not met, the error and reasons are communicated to the user with the help of the Team Advisor view. This view shows the list of all the operations that violated the pre-conditions and the explanations. Team Advisor increases confidence in team members as it describes the reasons why an operation did not work.

Team area

The structure of the project teams is defined by a hierarchy of team areas. The team area manages team membership, roles assignments, and team artifacts. It defines the team members on the team and specifies their roles and defines the timeline in which the team is participating. Team areas are optional. A simple project with a small number of users might not need to separate team areas. Instead, all work is done in the context of the project area.

Team Artifact view

Your project area within the Team Artifact view contains a Work Items folder. The Work Items folder contains the queries available to you.

Team Build

The Jazz Team Build component of the Jazz technology platform provides support for the automation, monitoring, and awareness of a team's regular builds. The Jazz Team Build provides a model for representing the team's build definitions, build engines, and build results. The model supports teams with different build technologies.

Team Central view

The Team Central view is organized into multiple News, Events, and Queries sections, which are updated continually with the latest developments such as build operations, change set deliveries, and work item modifications that affect your project.

Timeline

A timeline represents an area of activity within a project that typically has its own schedule, deliverables, teams, and processes. For example, a project with both new product release development and current product maintenance might define these two efforts in separate timelines because they have different delivery schedules, teams, and processes. Project intervals or phases are defined within a timeline and expressed as a hierarchy of iterations.

Work items

Rational Team Concert has the **work item** as a fundamental mechanism to track, plan, and assign development tasks. A work item provides a way to track the progress, plan the releases, and monitor system health. Work items are, for example, bugs, enhancements, and tasks with varied priorities and generally attached to a specific release. Rational Team Concert inherently supports the connection between the work item and source code. Thus, as a developer, you can go to work items from source code and vice versa.

Work items perspective

The Work items perspective includes Work Items, Team Artifacts, Team Central, My Work, and Tag Cloud. All these views provide tools to help you create, triage, and work on work items.

Work Items view

When you run a query, the Work Items view displays the results in a table. You can sort the results according to column heading by clicking a column heading. Click the column heading again to change the sort order (ascending or descending).

B

Installing the Express-C Edition with the Tomcat Server

Simplicity is prerequisite for reliability.

--Edsger W.Dijkstra

In *Chapter 2, Installing RTC and WebSphere*, you downloaded and installed the Enterprise version of Rational Team Concert, and configured it to use IBM WebSphere. This appendix assumes you have read and are familiar with that procedure, but instead are interested in installing Rational Team Concert Express-C for use with Apache Tomcat. Here, you will see the differences between the setups.

Once we install the server and client, you will do an initial setup and check the basic functionality. Throughout the book, the Rational Team Concert server runs on the built-in Tomcat server, and the Rational Team Concert client is based on Eclipse. Rational Team Concert comes with an example *JUnit Project*, which can be set up to get used to the different aspects of the system.

Finally, a sample project *BookManager* is set up in the Rational Team Concert's server. We are assuming that *BookManager* is already developed and stored in a Subversion source control system, where we will import it into the Rational Team Concert server. This exercise will show you the power of Rational Team Concert in importing existing source code.

You will set up the project in the Rational Team Concert server, access it through the client, and configure it for deployment in Tomcat. We will finish the chapter by looking at *BookManager's* modules and functionality.

Rational Team Concert Express-C features

Recall from the discussion in Chapter 2 that there are, in fact, four different editions of Rational Team Concert available. The Express-C version is suitable for teams of ten or less, and comes with a free license.

Apache Tomcat is a robust, open source servlet container suitable, and for convenience, comes bundled with Rational Team Concert for a quick out-of-the-box setup.

Together, these provide a free environment for a small team that is very quick to get running.

Installing Rational Team Concert Express-C

In this chapter, we will run *Express-C* on the following configuration:

- Derby database
- Tomcat as application server
- Eclipse as IDE
- Subversion—import existing demo application into Jazz Repository

Our examples and screenshots are from a Windows 32-bit installation. The ideal hardware configuration suggested by IBM RTC experts is as follows:

- Intel Pentium Xeon (32 bit or 64 bit)
- 1024 x 786 screen resolution
- 2 GB RAM
- 1 GB disk space

As with the Enterprise edition, you can get the Rational Team Concert *Express–C* distribution from either the IBM or Jazz websites. Once you've downloaded the Express-C ZIP file, installation, and configuration are only few clicks away. If you download the full client for Eclipse IDE and server distribution, after installation you will have *Express-C* the server, client, build system, report tools, and SCM tools. Alternatively, you can download each piece separately. Our steps here assume you've downloaded the complete bundle.

A quick installation has several easy steps to follow. The idea is to install, set up, and configure project on the server.

Installing Express-C

Extract the contents of the Express-C ZIP to a directory of your choice. It is that simple.

 The installation directory for the Rational Team Concert is now referred to as `<root>`.

As with the Enterprise version, the extracted contents will contain the build system, client, repository tools, SCM tools, and server.

Express-C basic setup

Go to the `<root>\server` folder and run the `server.startup.bat` command to start the server. This will start the Tomcat server, and deploy the Jazz Team Server application, `jazz.war`, in `<root>\server\tomcat\webapps`. As the server starts, you will see information messages as shown in the following screenshot. Notice that the server starts on a http port **9080** and on https port **9443**. You can connect to it on either of these:

Once the server is started, you are ready to set up and configure the Rational Team Concert. You can now create projects, workspaces, and users from the web interface.

Connection error

By default, the server starts on http port 9080. When you start the Rational Team Concert, you may get an exception that may read **java.net.BindException**: **Address already in use**.

This error points you to check the already used and running ports on the machine. Change the server port by editing the `server.xml` file in the `<root>\server\tomcat\conf` folder.

Using a web browser, navigate to `http://localhost:9080/jazz` or `https://localhost:9443/jazz`. Like in Enterprise installation, you will see a screen similar to the following one, where you sign-on to administer the installation. For the initial login, use the default of ADMIN/ADMIN. As always, be sure to change it from this default immediately.

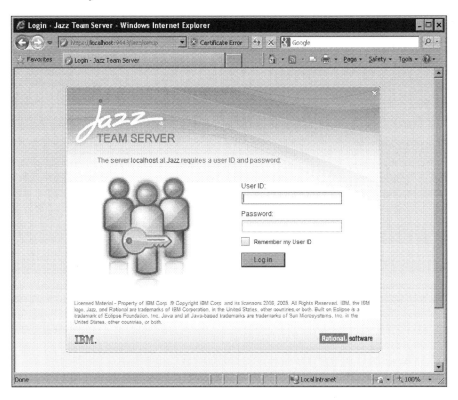

Once logged in, you are presented with the setup screens, as shown next. Walk through these to configure e-mail, database, and public repository URI settings or choose the **Fast Path Setup**:

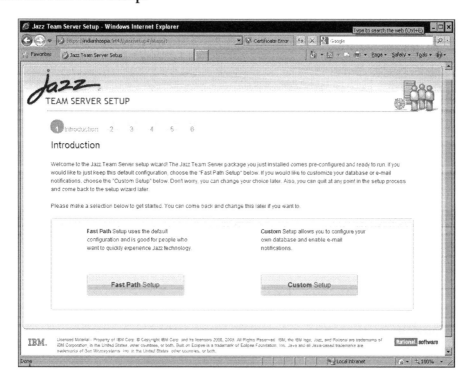

With Express–C, you have a choice of administering users through a non-LDAP registry, or through Tomcat. During the Setup User Registry screen (seen next), choose which you intend to use. This step is also where you should change the default administrative login and password.

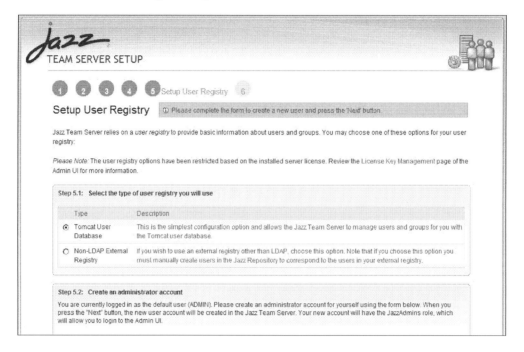

Admin setup

The remainder of the administrative setup, including establishing project areas, assigning user roles, and the like, are identical to the steps we followed in the Enterprise setup. Refer to Chapter 2 for the details.

Client setup

As with the Enterprise setup, the Rational Team Concert client is provided with its own JDK, and is available at `<rtcRoot>\jazz\client\eclipse\eclipse.exe`. Follow the steps in Chapter 2 to do the following client tasks:

- Accept a team invitation
- Connect to a project area
- Create a project area
- Create project plans

- Create work items
- Define process templates
- Import the source code from SVN, ClearCase
- Create team builds

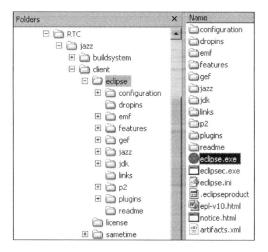

Rational Team Concert client asks for the location of the workspace. This is the workspace location for any new projects that are created and/or imported to, as shown in the next screenshot:

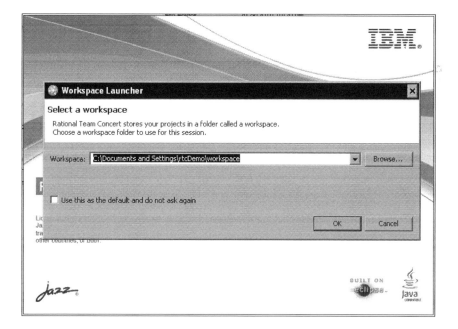

Once the workspace is selected, the Rational Team Concert's client is started and the welcome screen appears.

JUnit Project example

The JUnit example is bundled with Express-C and provides a realistic software development project; in this case, it was actually used by the JUnit Project team to plan, track, and collaborate on JUnit Version 4.4. Notice that in Chapter 2, we connected to the Jazz SandBox to access the JUnit Project. Out of the box, the Express-C team server comes with the JUnit Project that you can connect and play with. Follow the steps in Chapter 2 to set up this project as an example.

Summary

In this appendix, you have installed and configured the Express-C edition of Rational Team Concert's client and server running on Apache Tomcat, with emphasis on the differences between this and the previous steps you followed for the Enterprise edition running on IBM WebSphere. Express-C is the ideal version to use for a small team or a group seeking to quickly explore the features of the Rational Team Concert suite.

C

The BookManager
Application Architecture

BookManager Application is used throughout this book to describe the functionality of the Rational Team Concert. In this appendix, you will see the architecture and functionality of the BookManager Application.

Architecture

For our sample BookManager project, we chose a mix of well-understood, mature, and widely available open source technologies to implement a standard n-tiered, web-based application. This is a typical JEE app that has a Presentation layer made with JSPs, a Services layer made with Struts actions, and a Persistence layer that uses Hibernate as a front-end to a Derby database. This architecture is shown in the following figure:

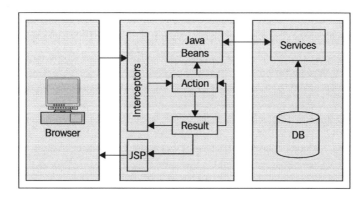

Let's examine each of these logical tiers.

Presentation tier

The client is presented as a series of web pages, generated by JSP, using the Apache Struts 2.x framework. Struts is a very mature set of servlets and JSP tag libraries that provides a classic **MVC** (**Model-View-Controller**) pattern for web-based presentation tiers written in Java. The look and feel is enhanced through the use of basic **CSS** (**Cascading Style Sheets**). You can learn more about Struts from the project's home page at `struts.apache.org`.

Services tier

The services are written as Java servlets, the majority of which are implemented as Struts Actions. This provides the *controller* piece of the MVC implementation of Apache Struts. The work of validating input, persisting the data, and retrieving them is handled by these servlets. This approach allows us to deploy our application on any Sun-compliant servlet container; in our case, Apache Tomcat.

Many of the features such as exception handling, file uploading, lifecycle callbacks, and validation are provided by Interceptors (these are conceptually the same as servlet filters) or the JDK's `Proxy` class. They provide a way to supply pre-processing and post-processing around an action.

The Struts framework is completely configurable via XML files.

Persistence tier

The data is stored in a relational database (RDBMS) that is abstracted by the open source Hibernate 3.x framework. Hibernate provides a simple object-relational (OR) mapping construct that makes it easy to persist Java beans in a relational database, without having to write **Structured Query Language** (**SQL**) or hand-coded mapping logic. The mapping is stored in easily modifiable and distributable XML files, which are read by Hibernate. In turn, Hibernate wraps the complexity of all database activity, including connecting, communicating, and performing typical Create, Read, Update, and Delete (CRUD) functions.

Hibernate is an abstraction of Persistence, which still requires an implementation of some sort. For our project, we are using the Apache Derby embedded database. Derby is a lightweight, completely pure Java database that can be bundled with an application and distributed as part of the final software package, without need for a separate installation and setup. Likewise, it is instantiated and used at run-time and thus, does not require a separate process that must be managed independent of BookManager Application. While this is suitable for our purposes, the configuration we're using does not scale, and must be replaced either with a server-based Derby install or another RDBMS system (such as MySQL, Oracle, and so on). Fortunately, Hibernate makes it easy to switch; a few changes to one of the configuration files and the inclusion of the proper JDBC library (that is, the library that facilitates communication with the database from Java) is all that's needed to migrate the BookManager Application to a different database product.

Control flow

The Struts framework is the backbone of the BookManager Application and we use it to specify the flow of control based on user actions. These are configured in a `struts.xml` file that describes which JSPs work with which Actions and under what conditions. The following is the Struts configuration XML source code:

```
<!DOCTYPE struts PUBLIC "-//Apache Software Foundation//DTD Struts
Configuration 2.0//EN"  "http://struts.apache.org/dtds/struts-
2.0.dtd">

<struts>
  <package name="default" extends="struts-default">
    <interceptors>
      <interceptor name="checkAuthentication"
        class="client.interceptor.LoginInterceptor" />
      <interceptor-stack name="booklookDefaultStackNoAuth">
        <interceptor-ref name="createSession"/>
        <interceptor-ref name="defaultStack"/>
      </interceptor-stack>
    </interceptors>

    <default-interceptor-ref name="booklookDefaultStack" />

    <!-- This section provides a single routing point for any errors
       thrown by the server, as well as forcing the user back to the
       login page in the event he is not authenticated. -->
    <global-results>
      <result name="error">/error.jsp</result>
        <result name="login">/login.jsp</result>
```

```
    </global-results>
    <global-exception-mappings>
      <exception-mapping exception=
      "org.apache.struts.register.exceptions.SecurityBreachException"
      result="securityerror" />
      <exception-mapping exception="java.lang.Exception"
        result="error" />
    </global-exception-mappings>

    <!-- This section maps the individual servlets to the pages that
      should be displayed as a result.  Each servlet is an action
      that corresponds to an activity the user can perform. The login
      action is different from the others in that if an error occurs,
      we display the login page again, rather than an error page -->
    <action name="login" class="client.action.LoginAction">
      <interceptor-ref name="booklookDefaultStackNoAuth"/>
      <result name="success">welcome.jsp</result>
      <result name="error">login.jsp</result>
    </action>
    <action name="addbookscreen"
      class="client.action.AddBookScreenAction">
      <result>addbook.jsp</result>
    </action>
    <action name="addbook" class="client.action.AddBookAction">
      <result name="success" type="redirectAction">listbooks</result>
    </action>
    <action name="listbooks" class="client.action.ListBooksAction">
      <result>listbooks.jsp</result>
    </action>
    <action name="editbookscreen"
      class="client.action.EditBookScreenAction">
      <result>editbook.jsp</result>
    </action>
    <action name="editbook" class="client.action.EditBookAction">
      <result name="success" type="redirectAction">listbooks</result>
    </action>
    <action name="deletebook" class="client.action.DeleteBookAction">
      <result name="success" type="redirectAction">listbooks</result>
    </action>
    <action name="logout" class="client.action.LogoutAction">
      <interceptor-ref name="booklookDefaultStackNoAuth"/>
    </action>
  </package>
</struts>
```

Interceptors

Struts 2 has an interceptor feature that allows a developer to process the workflow of any Struts request, prior to it being served to the user. We added a `LoginInterceptor` class to the existing chain of Struts interceptors (defined by the line `defaultStack`) to check if a `USER` object is present in the `HTTP` session prior to each Struts action being served. If it is the case, we assume the user has authenticated via the login page and continue the user onto their originally requested action. If not, we bypass the original user's action and force him to the `login.jsp` page to enter his credentials. These credentials are sent to a `LoginAction` in Struts, which builds a `BookManagerUser` object and queries the Derby database via Hibernate to see if the user's login and password are a match. If so, it creates a `USER` session variable with a `BookplaneUser Javabean` object in it. This variable contains not only the user's login and SHA-encrypted password but also his role. Any user with a role of *admin* will be permitted to add and update book information; all other user roles can only view the book list.

In the current BookManager Application, the `struts.xml` file is configured with interceptors, global results, and actions. It is typical to have several interceptors assigned per action. As you can imagine, having to configure every interceptor for each action would quickly become extremely unmanageable. For this reason, interceptors can be grouped into named stacks. In our case, we've created an interceptor stack named `booklookDefaultStackNoAuth` that combines the out of the box `defaultStack` and `createSession` interceptors, and attaches them to the login and logout actions. The following is the code for the `LoginInterceptor`:

```
package client.interceptor;

import java.util.Map;
import com.opensymphony.xwork2.Action;
import com.opensymphony.xwork2.ActionContext;
import com.opensymphony.xwork2.ActionInvocation;
import com.opensymphony.xwork2.interceptor.AbstractInterceptor;

@SuppressWarnings("serial")
public class LoginInterceptor extends AbstractInterceptor {

    public String intercept(ActionInvocation actionInvocation) throws
      Exception {
      Map<String, Object> session =
                    ActionContext.getContext().getSession();
      Object booklookUserObject = session.get("USER");

      if (booklookUserObject == null) {
        return Action.LOGIN;
```

```
        }
        return actionInvocation.invoke();
    }
}
```

From the above `LoginInterceptor.java` source, the class has a single method implementation, `intercept()`. Using custom interceptors in your application is an elegant way to provide cross-cutting application features. The `AbstractInterceptor` class provides a default no-op implementation of both the `destroy` as well as the `init` method.

To allow a user to logout, we added a `LogoutAction` and links to it on each page of the application. When a user selects this, his USER session variable is deleted, which in turn forces the `LoginInterceptor` to return the user to the `login.jsp`. As the entire `BackplaneUser` object is present in the session, we can access it from inside each of the JSPs. We use this to add the user's login name to a welcome message at the top of each screen in the application.

The `LoginInterceptor` is configured to run by default on all actions except the login and logout actions. This is because if we were to force a check on the login during a login, we'd wind up in an infinite loop! We provide this login-free path for the login and logout by defining an alternate interceptor stack that does not contain the `LoginInterceptor` and assigning it as the path for `LoginAction` and `LogoutAction`.

Actions

Actions are a fundamental concept in most web application frameworks and they are the basic unit of work that can be associated with an HTTP request coming from a browser. The very basic usage of an action is to perform work with a single result always being returned.

```
package client.action;

import java.util.Map;

import server.beans.BooklookUser;
import server.services.PasswordEncrypter;
import server.services.Persistence;

import com.opensymphony.xwork2.ActionContext;
import com.opensymphony.xwork2.ActionSupport;

@SuppressWarnings("serial")
public class LoginAction extends ActionSupport {
```

```
    private String username;
    private String password;

    public String getUsername(){
        return username;
    }
    public void setUsername(String username) {
        this.username = username;
    }

    public String getPassword() {
        return password;
    }

    public void setPassword(String password){
        this.password = password;
    }

    public String execute() throws Exception {
        Map<String, Object> session =
                ActionContext.getContext().getSession();

        String encryptedPassword = PasswordEncrypter.encrypt(password);
        BooklookUser user = Persistence.getInstance().getUser(username,
                encryptedPassword);
        if (user == null) {
            session.put("LOGINSUCCESS", "false");
            return ERROR;
        }
        session.put("LOGINSUCCESS", "true");
        session.put("USER", user);
        return SUCCESS;
    }
}
```

From the above code listing of the LoginAction, the execute method gets the session, retrieves the user with that username-password, and finally sets the session. Thus, you can imagine the Action doing a piece of work from the execute method and returning a string.

You can see from the above `struts.xml` listing, the action name is associated to the action class, which is responsible for the `execute` method. Optionally, the interceptor reference name is also mentioned, which takes care of the additional orthogonal functionality. The interesting thing here is, if the result is a success, then `welcome.jsp` is invoked; otherwise the user is served `login.jsp`. Remember that the result of the `execute()` method of `LoginAction` is a String.

```
<action name="login" class="client.action.LoginAction">
  <interceptor-ref name="booklookDefaultStackNoAuth"/>
  <result name="success">welcome.jsp</result>
  <result name="error">login.jsp</result>
</action>
```

`PasswordEncrypter` and Persistence are two services that are used in most of our Action classes. More importantly, the Persistence class provides several APIs for retrieving the sessions, looking up users, and maintaining the book data.

Admin

Admin is a simple utility module for administering the users and their access to the BookManager Application. It is an executable JAR with a main class that accepts command line input, and makes static calls to a `UserAdmin` class. This class handles building the necessary Hibernate objects and adding or retrieving them from the Derby database via Hibernate calls.

The Admin utility needs to be run before the application war is actually deployed on to the servlet container, to create and populate the Derby database schema and add users and administrators for application access.

Flow summary

We have seen how different aspects of the Interceptors, Actions, and Admin module work together. Now, we will see how a single request to log in from the browser translates to different actions:

1. The browser requests the `login.action`.

2. The Filter Dispatcher of the Struts 2 framework looks at the request and determines the appropriate Action—in this case `LoginAction` (defined in the `struts.xml` file).

3. Next, the Interceptors are applied. In this case, the `booklookDefaultStackNoAuth` interceptor is applied to the action (defined in the `struts.xml` file).

4. Next, the Action method is executed. In our example, the appropriate method on the action login is executed to authenticate the user from the database and a welcome page (`welcome.jsp`) is shown. If the authentication fails, the user is shown an error message and the login page (`login.jsp`).

In case of other action such as `addbook`, the Action is executed and redirected to the `listbooks` action. You can observe that Actions and redirections are mentioned declaratively in the `struts.xml` configuration file:

```
<action name="addbook" class="client.action.AddBookAction">
  <result name="success" type="redirectAction">
    listbooks
  </result>
</action>
```

Functionality

Our system is meant to exercise simple CRUD functions for a collection of books. The screen flow reflects the following functions.

Login

The application's start page has the login page that has the username and password fields, allowing users with both admin and user rolls to login and authenticate.

Welcome page

After successfully authenticating, the Welcome page acts as a launching point for the rest of the application's functions, including adding, listing, modifying, and deleting books.

Add book

Adding produces a simple input screen with fields and labels allowing the user to enter basic information about the book, including the title, author, and a catalog number.

List books

After adding the book, the user is presented with a simple list of books in the database. This screen can also be reached from the **List** page on the welcome screen.

Update book

Clicking on a title will take the user to a screen similar to the add page, allowing the user to update information. After saving the update, the user again sees the list of books, this time with the updated information.

Delete book

On each line is a **delete** checkbox which, when checked and submitted, will delete the record from the database. The user is presented with the updated list of books after deletion.

Initially, our application only has the Add and List functions. In the later chapters, Update and Delete are added.

Summary

In this appendix you saw the architecture of the BookManager Application that uses the JEE technologies such as JSPs, servlets, Struts, and Hibernate. The application architecture was described as presentation, services, and persistence tiers along with control flow. Later, you saw the various capabilities of the application.

D
What's New in RTC v3.0

Rational Team Concert 3.0 is available as a general release as of November 2010. This book is based on Rational Team Concert version 2.0.0.3. While most of the features discussed are provided in version 3, some new ones have been added, such as a new licensing model for the server, better integration with the Rational Quality Manager, support for distributed source control management, additional methods for more traditional planning models, and adoption of the OpenSocial standard for the Dashboard, allowing integration with Gmail or iGoogle. This Appendix gives a brief overview of these new features of Jazz Team Server and Rational Team Concert 3.0.

Features overview

The following is an overview of enhancements in the Rational Team Concert 3.0:

- **General features**:
    - *Enterprise process projects*: This adds the ability to share processes between a set of projects on the same server.
    - *New process pre-conditions*: A lot of new pre-conditions help teams better control how they work. This includes support for enforcing that all change sets be accepted before delivering, parent work items can't be closed until all children are closed, and work item state-based required properties.
    - *Navigation*: The Web UI is redesigned to improve navigation and ease of use. The navigation bar is replaced with the mini dashboard, and has additional features such as global search, common filtering to find artifacts, a home menu, and component menus.
    - *SmartCard and SSL certificates*: Support is added in the Eclipse, build, web, and command line clients to allow users to authenticate with SmartCard and SSL certificates.

- **Packaging and licencing**:
  - ○ Packaging and platform support is simplified in 3.0. There is only one product that supports all our platforms. Instead of the model in 2.X with separate products and servers for these platforms (RTC, RTC for System Z, RTC for Power), they have been merged.
  - ○ As an administrator, the first thing you'll notice is that there are now two applications running on your server—the **CCM (Change and Configuration Management)** and the **JTS (Jazz Team Server)**.
  - ○ As new applications are available, you will be able to install licenses into the same JTS and share users and licenses across the applications. This will be useful because new versions of RQM and RRC are upgraded as part of the CLM initiative.

- **Administration**:
  - ○ *LDAP configuration setup page improvements*: Validation and creation of server and web XML files for Tomcat.
  - ○ *Shared Jazz team server configuration*: Users and licenses can be shared between a set of applications and assigned and tracked centrally.

- **Planning**:
  - ○ *Traditional planning*: More support is added for more traditional planning activities and processes. This includes resource allocations, work dependencies, and risk management.
  - ○ *Roadmaps*: Added ability to see timeline and work dependencies in all plan modes.
  - ○ *Planning usability*: Plans have enhancements such as column headers, ability to resize columns, incremental loading, easier plan mode creation and filtering, and a completely new agile task board.

- **Work items**:
  - ○ *Work item customization in the Web*: Work item customization is added for the Web. This includes a web-based wysiwyg presentation editor.
  - ○ *Embedded work items*: Other products such as Rational Quality Manager can embed work items into their Web UIs even though they may be stored in another application.

- **Source control**:
    - *Distributed source control*: It's now possible to create repository workspaces, deliver, and accept across servers. Change sets can be linked to work items in other repositories and any other OSLC-CM providers.
    - *Versioned properties*: Properties can now be added to version-controlled resources that are versioned with the resources.

- **Builds**:
    - *Out of the box BuildForge integration*: The integration is now included in Team Concert and includes many improvements such as the availability of using BuildForge agents and running jbe tasks directly from BuildForge.
    - *Configurable build engine types*: Build engine types have been introduced to support having different tasks run on different environments with custom configuration options.

Packaging

Rational Team Concert 2.x has a single, monolithic WAR file that has the Jazz Platform and Rational Team Concert application. Other related products such as Rational Quality Manager (RQM) and Rational Requirements Composer (RRC) also followed the same architecture, which led to longer download times and large file sizes. With Rational Team Concert 3.0, the product functionality is decomposed into the Jazz Team Server (JTS) and Change and Configuration Management (CCM) application.

A Jazz Team Server provides basic services that enable a group of applications to work together as a single logical server. The following domain-specific applications are defined as a part of the new architecture:

- The Change and Configuration Management (CCM) application delivers capabilities for Change Management (work items), Configuration Management (SCM), planning, and automation/build.

- The Requirements Management (RM) application delivers capabilities for capturing, managing, and tracing requirements throughout the development lifecycle.

- The Quality Management (QM) application delivers capabilities for test management, including test planning, creation, and execution.

The upgrade process splits the version 2.x Rational Team Concert server into two version 3.0 applications (the Jazz Team Server and the Change and Configuration Management application). The server and application are deployed separately to an application server such as WebSphere.

The following table summarizes the deployed context roots in version 2 with that of a new installation of version 3 and an upgrade from version 2 to version 3. Note that an upgrade from version 1 is not supported. If you want to upgrade from version 1, then you need to first upgrade from version 1 to version 2, and then upgrade to version 3.

Context Root for Rational Team Concert 2.x versus Rational Team Concert 3.0

Product/application	Rational team concert/CCM
2.x	/jazz
3.0 – New Installation	/jts, /ccm
3.0 – Migration	/jts, /jazz

After Rational Team Concert 3.0 is downloaded and installed via web installer, the start menu looks like the next screenshot. Notice that the Jazz Team Server and IBM Rational Team Concert are listed as two separate menu items.

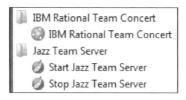

The next step is to start the Jazz Team Server and configure it. Click **Start Jazz Team Server** and wait until the server is started. Go to `https://localhost:9443/jts/setup` URL and set up the Jazz Team Server. As seen in the next screenshot, the Jazz Team Server recognizes the **ccm** application and is registered here:

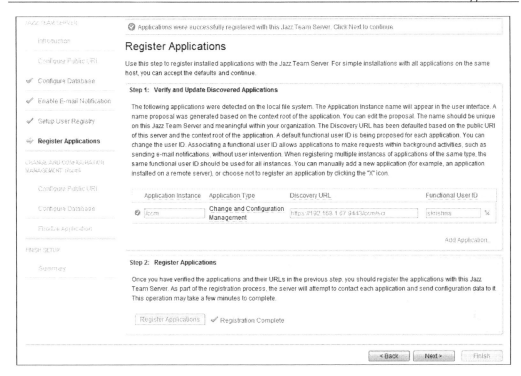

At each configuration step, you can test the configuration parameters with the help of the **Test** button. Once the setup is successful, navigate to the URL that you provided at the time of setup (for example, `https://localhost:9443/jts`). You should be able to log in with the administrative user you created during setup. The ADMIN user name may no longer be valid depending on the options you selected during the setup.

Jazz Team Server application lets you to do server administration, user management, and application administration. As you can see in the following screenshot, the Jazz Team Server recognizes the Change and Configuration Management application:

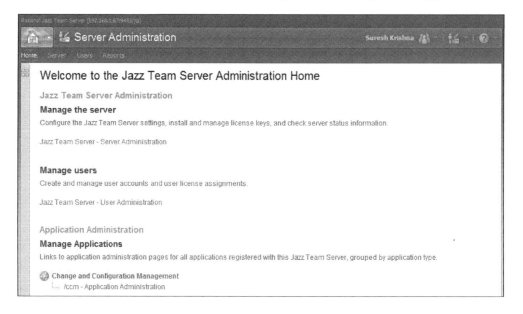

In Rational Team Concert version 3.0, the Change and Configuration Management application is installed on a separate root called *ccm*. If Rational Team Concert is migrated from 2.x, then the root will be *jazz*. Navigate to the ccm application (for example, `https://localhost:9443/ccm`) to access the project area, users, and project templates. You can do the CCM application administration right from the same UI and see the associated Jazz Team Server as in the next screenshot:

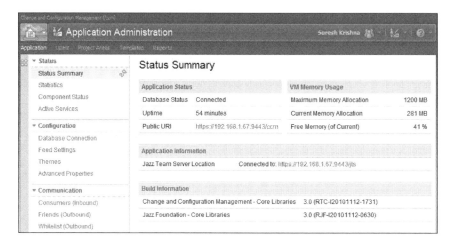

In Rational Team Concert 2.x, the Jazz Platform and Rational Team Concert modules are installed on the same application root /jazz. From the previous steps, we have seen that Rational Team Concert 3.0 has two separate applications for Jazz Team Server (with context root /jts) and Change and Configuration Management (with context root /ccm or /jazz). If you are doing a migration from 2.x to 3.0, a detailed article is available at http://jazz.net/library/article/524.

Licensing

In Rational Team Concert version 3.0, there have been some changes based on user feedback. Consider the following changes as forward-looking and for informational purposes only. Check with an IBM representative for the final licensing terms.

You can now install as many servers as you have user licenses. This means you can deploy client access licenses across as many or as few servers as you need. The most common advantages are to support disaster recovery installations, maintain separate test or training configurations, and enable teams who need many servers for physical security isolation.

A new user license called *Rational Team Concert Stakeholder* is now available as an entry-priced license for users who don't need the planning capabilities. This license instead allows a Stakeholder to collaborate with a team via work items and dashboards. An example might be a user of your software who needs to report defects and view the project's status.

Another entry-level license named Rational Team Concert Developer for Workgroups is also available now-a-days. Limited to fifty authorized users per server, it is identical to the Developer license, except it does not support the new Distributed Source Control feature. It can be combined with any other 3.x license on the same server, allowing a team to grow beyond the initial fifty, without having to trade-in their existing "Developer for Workgroup" license.

Planning

Project planning has seen new features such as the new Formal Project Template, project schedule as a Gantt chart, finer grain time tracking, and enhancements in Scrum boards.

Formal Project Template

Support for more traditional project planning capabilities has been added as the new **Formal Project Template**. This project template can be configured to tailor the needs of agile teams. In this process, you can track the project in sequential phases—*Requirements*, *Design*, *Implementation*, and *Testing*. Team members complete each phase by a certain deadline and then move on to the next phase. Phase planning is scheduled in such a way that the project is ready by the delivery date.

The Formal Project Template is ready to use and has all the necessary work items such as Defect, Task, Project Change Request, Plan Item, Risk, Risk Action, Issue, and Milestone. The **Plan View** has an additional Resources tab that allows you to allocate the resources to the plan. You can create **Risk** work items that allow you to identify the risks and mitigate them via risk action work items. You can use the **Gantt chart** in the Plan view to see a graphical representation of the plan schedule, including work item durations and dependencies. An example **Release Plan** for a project with Formal Project Template is shown in the next screenshot:

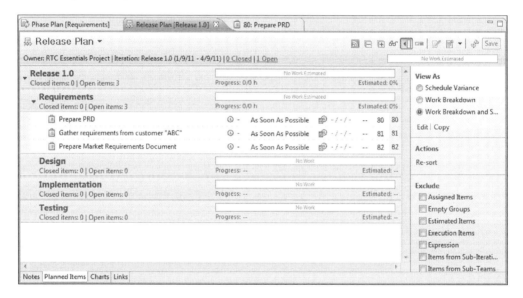

Time Tracking

When you create a work item for a project following the Formal Template Project, you will see another tab added. **Time Tracking** tab allows you to enter the time spent on specific sub-phases. For example, for the Requirements phase, you could enter the time for Coding, Review, Documentation, and Testing sub-phases as shown here:

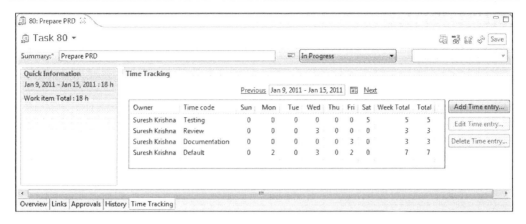

Scrum boards

Task boards have been redesigned with a couple of key usability goals in mind. First, task boards are made to look a lot closer to what you see on a Scrum whiteboard with column headings for each item, and tasks that look like sticky notes with proper drag handles. The task organization has been simplified with the layout a lot more flexible and the work item state groups can now be configured. Another cool feature is that you can now configure the kinds of overview bars to show for users by editing the view, or you can click on the bar to toggle between them.

Along with the before mentioned features, you have many more exciting features to explore in the new version of Rational Team Concert.

Work items

Many stakeholders use web UI to quickly access the project status and send feedback on certain work items. A screen capture tool is now available in the web UI for you to take quick captures of the product and annotate the current work item or create a new one. This is a handy tool that has the context of the work items as seen in the next screenshot:

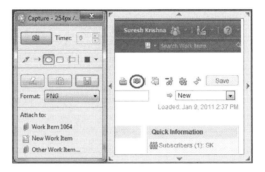

Tags have been enhanced in the Eclipse IDE to have a greater integration with work items. You can now run queries for tags directly from the Work Item editor by clicking on the tags link, and you can bulk edit tags of a query result as seen in the following screenshot:

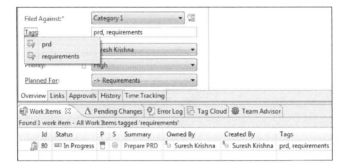

Work item customization was improved with many new capabilities. Input fields can now be validated with regular expressions or number ranges, and default values for any attribute can be provided. You can also configure enumerations whose value set depends on the value of another attribute.

Source control

Many enhancements are seen in the core Source Control engine that enables distributed source control, a native client on z/OS, context-aware search, and a source control Web UI.

Rational Team Concert 3.0 now supports distributed source control. Jean-Michel Lemieux, an architect from Rational Team Concert, describes the distributed source control as follows:

> *From a user's perspective, the easiest explanation of distributed source control is that you can now deliver and accept across repositories.*

All the concepts that worked in 2.x will continue to work, except that the Eclipse client now supports distributed source control, as seen here:

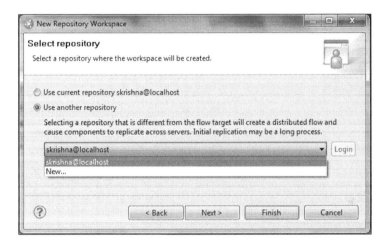

At the time of changing the flow target of a repository workspace, you can select the appropriate repository. All the changes will simply flow to the target in the selected repository. The distributed source control concept is supported across the concepts of change sets, work items, repositories, and user interface. You can link change sets to work items on other servers.

Context-aware search is added to the Eclipse client. You can now search source files by keyword, without using a work item. This is extremely useful for impact analysis, reducing code duplication, and understanding how changes you make in your source code can affect other teams.

Summary

In this appendix you saw several new features from Rational Team Concert version 3.0. We have seen a variety of enhancements in the core Jazz architecture, Planning, Work Items, and Source control modules. Source control has several other enhancements for z/OS systems to support the core MVS file system.

This appendix is a high-level overview of Rational Team Concert 3.0 features, and is not intended to be a comprehensive list of enhancements and new features. In addition, the client for Visual Studio has several new features and enhancements that are not discussed in this book, our focus being on the Web and Eclipse clients.

Index

Thank you for buying
IBM Rational Team Concert 2 Essentials

About Packt Publishing

Packt, pronounced 'packed', published its first book "Mastering phpMyAdmin for Effective MySQL Management" in April 2004 and subsequently continued to specialize in publishing highly focused books on specific technologies and solutions.

Our books and publications share the experiences of your fellow IT professionals in adapting and customizing today's systems, applications, and frameworks. Our solution based books give you the knowledge and power to customize the software and technologies you're using to get the job done. Packt books are more specific and less general than the IT books you have seen in the past. Our unique business model allows us to bring you more focused information, giving you more of what you need to know, and less of what you don't.

Packt is a modern, yet unique publishing company, which focuses on producing quality, cutting-edge books for communities of developers, administrators, and newbies alike. For more information, please visit our website: www.packtpub.com.

About Packt Enterprise

In 2010, Packt launched two new brands, Packt Enterprise and Packt Open Source, in order to continue its focus on specialization. This book is part of the Packt Enterprise brand, home to books published on enterprise software – software created by major vendors, including (but not limited to) IBM, Microsoft and Oracle, often for use in other corporations. Its titles will offer information relevant to a range of users of this software, including administrators, developers, architects, and end users.

Writing for Packt

We welcome all inquiries from people who are interested in authoring. Book proposals should be sent to author@packtpub.com. If your book idea is still at an early stage and you would like to discuss it first before writing a formal book proposal, contact us; one of our commissioning editors will get in touch with you.

We're not just looking for published authors; if you have strong technical skills but no writing experience, our experienced editors can help you develop a writing career, or simply get some additional reward for your expertise.

Application Development for IBM
WebSphere Process Server 7 and
Enterprise Service Bus 7

Build SOA-based flexible, economical, and efficient applications

Swami Chandrasekaran   Salil Ahuja

Application Development for IBM WebSphere Process Server 7 and Enterprise Service Bus 7

ISBN: 978-1-847198-28-0   Paperback: 548 pages

Build SOA-based flexible, economical, and efficient applications

1. Develop SOA applications using the WebSphere Process Server (WPS) and WebSphere Enterprise Service Bus (WESB)

2. Analyze business requirements and rationalize your thoughts to see if an SOA approach is appropriate for your project

3. Quickly build an SOA-based Order Management application by using some fundamental concepts and functions of WPS and WESB

Django JavaScript Integration:
AJAX and jQuery

Develop AJAX applications using Django and jQuery

Jonathan Hayward

IBM Cognos 8 Report Studio Cookbook

ISBN: 978-1-849680-34-9   Paperback: 252 pages

Over 80 great recipes for taking control of Cognos 8 Report Studio

1. Learn advanced techniques to produce real-life reports that meet business demands

2. Tricks and hacks for speedy and effortless report development and to overcome tool-based limitations

3. Peek into the best practices used in industry and discern ways to work like a pro

Please check **www.PacktPub.com** for information on our titles

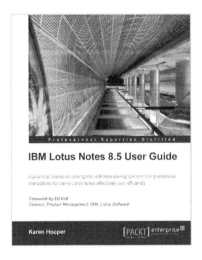

IBM Lotus Notes 8.5 User Guide

ISBN: 978-1-849680-20-2   Paperback: 296 pages

A practical hands-on user guide with time saving tips and comprehensive instructions for using Lotus Notes effectively and efficiently

1. Understand and master the features of Lotus Notes and put them to work in your business quickly

2. Contains comprehensive coverage of new Lotus Notes 8.5 features

3. Includes easy-to-follow real-world examples with plenty of screenshots to clearly demonstrate how to get the most out of Lotus Notes

IBM Cognos 8 Planning

ISBN: 978-1-847196-84-2   Paperback: 424 pages

Engineer a clear-cut strategy for achieving best-in-class results

1. Build and deploy effective planning models using Cognos 8 Planning

2. Filled with ideas and techniques for designing planning models

3. Ample screenshots and clear explanations to facilitate learning.

4. Written for first-time developers focusing on what is important to the beginner

Please check **www.PacktPub.com** for information on our titles

Getting Started with IBM FileNet P8 Content Manager

ISBN: 978-1-849680-70-7   Paperback: 367 pages

Install, customize, and administer the powerful FileNet enterprise content management platform

1. Quickly get up to speed on all significant features and the major components of IBM FileNet P8 Content Manager

2. Provides technical details that are valuable both for beginners and experienced Content Management professionals alike, without repeating product reference documentation

3. Gives a big picture description of Enterprise Content Management and related IT areas to set the context for Content Manager

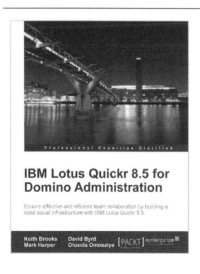

IBM Lotus Quickr 8.5 for Domino Administration

ISBN: 978-1-849680-52-3   Paperback: 250 pages

Ensure effective and efficient team collaboration by building a solid social infrastructure with IBM Lotus Quickr 8.5

1. Gain a thorough understanding of IBM Lotus Quickr 8.5 Team Collaboration, Repository, and Connectors

2. Recommended best practices to upgrade to the latest version of IBM Lotus Quickr 8.5

3. Customize logos, colors, templates, and more to your designs without much effort

Please check **www.PacktPub.com** for information on our titles

IBM Lotus Sametime 8
Essentials

A User's Guide

Mastering Online Enterprise Communication with this
collaborative software

Marie L. Scott   Thomas Duff   [PACKT] enterprise

IBM Lotus Sametime 8 Essentials:
A User's Guide

ISBN: 978-1-849680-60-8   Paperback: 284 pages

Mastering Online Enterprise Communication with
this collaborative software

1. Collaborate securely with your colleagues
   and teammates both inside and outside your
   organization by using Sametime features such as
   instant messaging and online meetings

2. Make your instant messaging communication
   more interesting with the inclusion of graphics,
   images, and emoticons to convey more
   information in fewer words

3. See how Sametime works in common, everyday, real-world situations with tips, resources,
   and detailed screenshots

IBM InfoSphere Replication
Server and Data Event Publisher

Design, implement, and monitor a successful Q replication
and Event Publishing project

Pav Kumar-Chatterjee   [PACKT] enterprise

IBM InfoSphere Replication
Server and Data Event Publisher

ISBN: 978-1-849681-54-4   Paperback: 344 pages

Design, implement, and monitor a successful Q
replication and Event Publishing project

1. Covers the toolsets needed to implement a
   successful Q replication project

2. Aimed at the Linux, Unix, and Windows
   operating systems, with many concepts
   common to z/OS as well

3. A chapter dedicated exclusively to WebSphere
   MQ for the DB2 DBA

Please check **www.PacktPub.com** for information on our titles

Made in the USA
Lexington, KY
31 August 2012